CW00919923

DEEDS NOT WORDS

DEEDS NOT WORDS

The Lives of Suffragette Teachers

Hilda Kean

PLUTO PRESS
London • Concord, Mass

First published 1990 by Pluto Press
345 Archway Road, London N6 5AA
and 141 Old Bedford Road,
Concord, MA 01742, USA

British Library Cataloguing-in-Publication Data
Kean, Hilda
    Deeds not words : the lives of suffragette
    teachers.
    1. Great Britain. Women's suffrage
    movements, 1910–1940. Biographies.
    Collections
    I. Title
    324.6'23'0922

    ISBN 0-7453-0308-0 hb
    ISBN 0-7453-0413-3

Library of Congress Cataloging-in-Publication Data
Kean, Hilda.
    Deeds not words : the lives of suffragette teachers / Hilda Kean.
        p.   cm.
    Includes bibliographical references.
    ISBN 0-7453-0308-0
    ISBN 0-7453-0413-3 (pbk.)
    1. Women teachers–Great Britain–Biography. 2. Suffragettes–
Great Britain–Biography. 3. Women Teachers Franchise Union–
History.   I. Title.
LA2375G7K43 1990
324.6'23'0922–dc20   90-31278
[B]   CIP

Typeset by Stanford Desktop Publishing, Milton Keynes
Printed in Great Britain by
Billing and Sons Ltd, Worcester

Contents

Acknowledgements

I wish to acknowledge the help I have received from many people in writing this book. Thanks to the librarians and archivists at the Greater London Record Office, West Glamorgan Record Office, Swansea Reference Library, British Library, and Public Record Office. In particular I wish to thank Michael Humby at the Institute of Education library, which houses the NUWT Archive, for unrestricted access to these materials and for permission to use archive photographs. Janet Friedlander at the NUT Library and David Dougan at the Fawcett Library deserve special mention for the enthusiasm and interest they have shown beyond the call of duty!

I want to thank those who have suggested books to read, especially Keren Abse and Sandra Jones. Special thanks to Alison Oram, Farhana Sheikh, and Paul Foley who have given their incisive comments on – if not their endorsement of – the ideas and contents of several chapters. Thanks to Claire Grey for taking the cover photograph; to Jack Jones for ferreting around in Swansea; to Nan McMillan for sharing her time and memories; to Paul Foley for use of his computer. Particular thanks are due to Ken Jones for his detailed and supportive comments on the whole book: its ideas, structure, presentation, and even typing. Without him it would never have seen the light of day: truly worthy of the order of Nelid! Needless to say, responsibility for interpretation and errors rests with the author.

For my mother and in memory of my father: Stanley Kean 1906–89.

Introduction

'Deeds not words'; 'Who would be free herself must strike the blow'; 'No question is ever settled until it's settled right'; 'The dreams of those that labour are the only ones that ever come true.' These slogans were used by women teachers, first in the National Federation of Women Teachers and the Women Teachers' Franchise Union, and then, from 1919, in the National Union of Women Teachers, the first feminist union in England and Wales. In their commitment to the cause and to the hard work, duty and dedication needed to realise it, these words were more than a summary of political beliefs. They were a guide and direction to the whole way of life led by these women. They helped create a political identity that became the mechanism by which feminist teachers explained and asserted their lives.

Women who became teachers in England and Wales in the 1890s or 1900s faced a career circumscribed by the state. They were employed by local education authorities which determined, with the Board of Education, the subjects taught and methods used. In many areas women were sacked if they married. In all education authorities women were paid less than men teachers doing the same job. Throughout England and Wales all women, irrespective of profession, age or class, were deprived even of a nominal influence on state policy because they lacked the vote.[1]

The broad suffrage movement became both a political mechanism for achieving the vote and equality between men and women, *and* a means of establishing a positive identity for its supporters. The new militant suffrage groups of the Edwardian period, especially the Women's Social and Political Union and the Women's Freedom League, were attractive to teachers. However, such women were also particular targets of the hostile novelist's pen. H. G. Wells, ostensibly sympathetic to the suffrage cause, caricatured the suffrage teacher's energy as eccentricity. In *Ann Veronica* the commitment of the activist teacher, Miss Miniver, who entices the young and naive Ann Veronica to a new world, is seen as absurd: 'I am up to the ears in it all – every moment I can spare. I throw up work – everything! I just teach in one school, one good school, three days a week. All the rest –

movements! I can live now on fourpence a day. Think how free that leaves me to follow things up!'[2]

A less benign caricature of feminist teachers is sketched in Clemence Dane's *Regiment of Women*. It tells the story of the older schoolmistress Clare Hartill who ensnares the young teacher Alwynne Durand. Alwynne initially enjoys her independent existence as a teacher. She welcomes Clare's friendship and suffragette ideas. She then meets Roger Lumsden who is appalled by Clare Hartill's behaviour: 'He was horrified at the idea of such a type of woman, in undisputed authority, moulding the mothers of the next generation ... he supposed she was but one of many ...'[3]

With the assistance of Alywnne's guardian, Roger Lumsden removes Alywnne from Clare Hartill's vampirish influence, confident she would be happy with 'marriage as a career'. Recent analyses of the book have concentrated on its explicitly anti-lesbian ideology: its anti-teacher and anti-feminist ideas have received less attention.[4]

It was, however, against a background of such negative fictional portrayals of suffrage teachers that the feminists of this narrative, Theodora Bonwick, Agnes Dawson, Ethel Froud and Emily Phipps, created their own images and identity. Frenetic activists, they nevertheless understood the importance of writing about their own achievements and those of other women. In the suffragette press feminist teachers wrote potted accounts of their own academic qualifications; in the women teachers' press they made sure their meetings and policies were publicised and their photographic images proudly displayed. The introduction to the *History of the NUWT*, written by Emily Phipps, in the 1920s, emphasises the importance of remembering such achievements as guidance for future generations of feminists:

> It is possibly true that many of these events should be forgotten; perhaps it is even better that they should be remembered in no spirit of bitterness, but in that spirit of thankfulness that recognises the courage of the pioneers and seeks to apply the same courage to the solution of the problems of its own generation. Acquiescence in injustice is not peace, it may be merely the inertia that denotes spiritual laziness. The pioneers of the NUWT have not had a peaceful time in their efforts to secure justice for all women, but they have had the joy of service in a great cause.[5]

By the time the NUWT had been wound up in the early 1960s the suffragette era had been long past. Yet it was to the politics of this past era that feminists continued to adhere during the 1920s, 1930s and 1940s. In the same way that many socialists radicalised in the late 1960s and early 1970s still imbue their beliefs and daily lives today with the ideals of those heady days, so too did the middle-aged and elderly former suffragettes not forget their past.

A study of their speeches to teacher audiences or their pamphlets or personal correspondence makes strange reading for a modern feminist. In recent years we have seen a growth in literature which has explored ideas of identity.[6] Various articles have suggested that a common and unified concept of self is inadequate for explaining the many facets of women's lives. Political activity and personal lives have been seen as separate, albeit interrelated, aspects of feminist identity. The challenge of *Beyond the Fragments* was to suggest that personal lives were subject to political analysis and activity, not that the personal and political were identical .[7]

For Theodora, Agnes, Ethel and Emily and their contemporaries, there was no division between their personal lives and their political work in the NUT, the suffrage movement and feminist teacher groups, or their professional work in the classroom. Their suffrage politics and their profession determined their whole identity: friendships, recreation, teaching methods, attitude to marriage ... For the feminist teachers there were no conflicts between their identities as teachers, political activists, or friends. Defining themselves simply as suffrage teachers sufficed as an explanation of who they were and how they led their lives.

Even in old age, when the days of the militant suffrage movement were long past, the women still referred to themselves in this way. One feminist, one of only two NUWT members in the whole of Grimsby, explained in a non-problematic way how she had dealt with the hostility of the NUT for a number of years: 'Of course it made no difference to my actions. I took my individual course as usual – (I was a suffragette).'[8]

These are the experiences and identities that are set out in the pages that follow. The first four chapters chart the feminists' attitude to teaching and to the NUT, of which they were a part until 1919, and explain how they interpreted suffrage feminism and synthesised it with their union activities. Chapters 5 to 8 deal with their lives after the franchise was (partly) won in 1918 when the days of hope soon proved illusory. These chapters describe the building of a strong autonomous feminist trade union and the development of the individual feminists' lives: working in local government; cultural and leisure activities; close friendships – and deaths. Running through the book are two strands: an account of the feminists' lives and their own perception of them. The suffrage way of life disappeared with an earlier generation of feminists; I hope their sense of purpose even in hostile times can still be an inspiration to today's reader in the bleak 1990s.

1

'A Place in the World'

Theodora Bonwick, Agnes Dawson, Ethel Froud, and Emily Phipps received their own education in schools organised under the 1870 Education Act; they went on to start their teaching careers in the 1880s and 1890s. The Act increased the state's influence on the lives of children by making elementary education compulsory. Elementary was very much the operative word. 'Education' comprised reading, writing and arithmetic. In addition girls were taught needlework and older pupils were given 'object lessons' in which they learned in mechanical fashion the parts and functions of different objects. Children spent long hours learning by rote: 'When we had been set poetry to learn at school', one disenchanted pupil recalled, 'I furtively read on and on, only anxious for more, careless of punishments earned because I refused the drudgery of repeating one passage or another till it became a mere meaningless chant.'[1]

Such pedagogy was dictated by the physical conditions of schools and the basis of payment for teachers. One teacher would be required to give instruction to some 60 to 80 children of different ages and abilities seated within one room on hard-tiered wooden benches.[2] At one time teachers' wages were related to the results obtained by children when they were tested by visiting inspectors. The schoolroom of Dickens' *Hard Times*, where Mr Gradgrind insists on facts and facts alone, may have been a fiction but the ideology it depicted lingered on in state schools as part of the legacy of the payments system.

Teaching in the late nineteenth century was no easy job. Teachers were obliged to adopt authoritarian methods simply to survive in the classroom. For men, teaching was little other than an adversarial contest:

> So large were the classes, and so unruly the boys that ... one could not educate, only subjugate ... It was a trial of strength between us. I pulling one way and they pulling another ... How I hated the whole coercive business! How I should have loved to find gentler methods equally effective.[3]

Women, too, found teaching difficult, though in different ways, as this correspondent to the *Manchester Guardian* indicates:

1

The school hours are never less than five and a half hours a day, and where there are half-timers must be six hours, and this does not include time for instructing pupil-teachers ... the keeping up of various registers, making up of the daily, weekly, and quarterly returns, not to mention the amount of statistics to be annually prepared for the use of the inspector ... when the teacher goes home her work is not finished. There are lessons to prepare for the following day, needlework to fix, and perhaps some absentees to visit. There are often advertisements for day school teachers, who are also expected to take night school and Sunday duty ...[4]

Career manuals for single women advocated elementary school teaching as a means of providing independence for women. Teaching provided an opportunity for working-class women to move, as Frances Widdowson has put it, 'up into the next class' by becoming elementary school teachers.[5] It also allowed unmarried middle-class women to have a career and independence outside the home as high school or secondary school teachers.[6] For the respectable working-class young woman unwilling to enter a factory or domestic service, teaching was an attractive alternative: '[Such women] form the majority of the shop assistants, in the West End and the richer suburbs, and more than any other class supply the elementary schools with teachers.'[7]

Even so teaching was deemed a suitable profession for only certain classes of young women: 'Until recently it was almost the only occupation open to the class above shop assistants, and even in becoming a teacher a lady was held to have lost caste.'[8]

For young working-class women, then, such as Agnes Dawson – daughter of a journeyman carpenter – teaching was a step up the social ladder. Entry into training college followed by a career outside the home was seen by many working-class women as an opportunity to raise their individual status while being of service to their own community. Agnes spent her entire teaching career in working-class schools, mainly in her childhood areas of Peckham and Camberwell. Leaving school at 14 she was obliged to apprentice herself as a pupil-teacher. This involved working as a trainee in a local school and studying in the evening. As a result she was able to pass the exams which gave her a scholarship to attend Saffron Walden training college. Agnes' family was poor but her two sisters, Mrs Tidswell and Mrs Dawson Follett, also became teachers and, in the 1920s, members of the NUWT. This was not unusual. Other feminist sisters such as the Townsends or Coombs from south London trained as teachers, shared houses and worked together in the NUWT. The frequency of this career decision for sisters may simply indicate again the lack of alternatives for bright young women.

Teaching was considered less suitable for educated middle-class women. Although Victorian careers writers felt confident in suggesting high school teaching in fee-paying academic schools as a career, they were doubtful whether such work deserved 'the respect with which it is regarded by aspirants to the teaching profession'.[9] Apart from the pay, it also was recognised as a a gruelling job: '...the work is very severe, and it is made harder than it need be by the bad methods of teachers.'[10] These bad methods included the correction of homework which took up most evenings a week. 'Such an expenditure of energy is almost pure waste', explained Amy Bulley and Margaret Whitley 'and the mistress comes to school in the morning tired and dull, incapable of exerting the magnetism which makes the lesson a living thing ...'[11]

However some women previously used to a varied social life enjoyed their evenings at home. As one middle-class teacher explained:

I think it distinctly an advantage to a teacher to have as many quiet evenings at home as possible, and I find so many occasions present themselves of attending meetings and lectures that if I were to go into society as well, I should have very little time to give to study and the quiet rest which is so refreshing after a day's work.[12]

Middle-class women were warned that although it was the highest paid of the teaching jobs, even secondary school teaching did not present a 'brilliant prospect'.[13] Nevertheless it was the career chosen by Emily Phipps, who had trained at Homerton College in Cambridge and obtained a BA degree from London University. At 29, Emily had been one of 13 candidates who had applied for the post of headmistress at the Swansea Central Higher Grade School. In theory such a school offered a more academic and extended curriculum than that of the elementary schools. The Swansea School Board, however, had described the school as an utter failure. In practice it had been no better than an elementary school in its curriculum and exam successes.[14]

However under Emily's influence the school thrived and was soon reorganised as the Municipal Secondary School for Girls. It became well known for its teaching of Latin and its excellent examination results.[15] Emily built up the school's reputation into 'one of the most efficient in the country', according to the school's inspectors.[16]

Not all graduates were attracted by secondary school teaching. Theodora Bonwick, who also had a BA from London, chose to teach in working-class elementary schools in Hackney and King's Cross rather than work in a secondary school where she would have received higher pay.

Even for the better paid high school teachers teaching was not a lucrative profession, as a 1890s survey revealed. Asked how she eked out her income one such teacher explained, 'I always made a plan of buying my winter dress [sic] at the summer sales, which in our country town came in early August, and my summer dress at their winter sale (things really were reduced). Though I did no dressmaking I made my own underclothing.' [17]

'It is the Only Brain-work Offered Them'

Teaching in the late nineteenth century and early 1900s was the profession containing the highest proportion of unmarried women.[18] Despite its many drawbacks teaching provided a means of independent living. For many women it was a form of escape from a restrictive home:

> My mother ran away from home to become a teacher because she was tired of being kept in and made to do tapestry work by her mother. We have the tapestries, and will treasure them. They will come to me and I shall present them to a museum as they are going to be a rare example of needlecraft by a little girl between the ages of 6 and 13! ... My mother was an ardent and active suffragette ... she was of course one of the first members of the NUWT ...[19]

But as feminists recognised, there were few alternatives. If women were obliged or wanted to earn a living in the 1890s or early 1900s, it was teaching which provided an income:

> It is the only brain-work offered them, and badly paid as it is, it is better paid than any other work done by women. The result is that we see girls following the stream and entering the teaching profession; after a few years growing weary and sick of it, tired of training intellects, and doubtful about the practical value of training, or altogether careless of it; discontented with a life for which they are naturally unsuited, and seeing no other career before them.[20]

According to Cicely Hamilton in *Marriage as a Trade* teaching – along with factory and office work, journalism, typing and sanitary inspection – was an alternative to forced marriage.[21] Jobs like these provided a healthy alternative, she said, to 'that form of female parasitism which gains a livelihood through the exercise of sexual attraction' – that is, to marriage. Paid employment, even low-paid employment like teaching, would make it 'unnecessary for any woman to earn her livelihood by means of her power of sexual attraction.'[22] Women's lives would change once they were recognised as 'citizens and individuals with a primary instead of a secondary existence, a place in the world as well as in the house.'[23]

Communities of Women

Because so many women became teachers it was relatively easy for them to find mutual support, friendship and opportunities for meeting socially and politically with like-minded women. Once qualified most teachers went to work in elementary schools. These were usually organised into three separate departments: boys, girls and infants, each under a different headteacher. The latter two departments were staffed *and* managed by women teachers and so provided a form of community where women classroom teachers could develop their own talents. Secondary schools were also single sex. Under Emily Phipps' headship of the Swansea Municipal Secondary School for Girls several staff went on to become headteachers of their own schools. They included NUWT members Miss Griffiths, Mary Harris and Clare Neal.

It seems likely that many women teachers chose to work in areas where there would be support networks of women outside school: London was a natural focus. Before the 1914 war there were many clubs for women in London. Some were specifically political, such as the Lewisham suffrage club in south London. This had a special teachers' section, frequented no doubt by the Townsend sisters who from their Lewisham address organised the Women Teachers' Franchise Union (WTFU) to campaign for the franchise within the NUT. North of the Thames in Hampstead were Mrs Despard's rooms, named after the socialist and feminist pioneer. Here women could come for tea, meals and female company.

Political activity also provided female companionship through an extensive network of feminist organisations. By 1913 there were 34 branches of the Women's Social and Political Union, 18 of the Women's Freedom League and 48 of the National Union of Women's Suffrage Societies in London alone.[24] The NFWT and Women Teachers' Franchise Union had London-wide branches and there were local union groups of the London Teachers' Association and the LCC Mistresses' Union.

'Communities' of independent unmarried women teachers were also created through teachers' living arrangements. Teachers frequently shared houses, and this arrangement produced close friendships that often lasted into retirement. The shared home of Emily Phipps and Clare Neal, later expanded to include Adelaide Jones, lasted 40 years. The home of Agnes Dawson and Anne Munns, a teacher at her Crawford Street school, lasted over 25 years. In these cases relationships were severed only by death. Houses independent of the family home were also established by teacher sisters. Hannah and Alice Townsend both taught, helped found the WTFU, and were active in the WSPU. They shared a house in south London with their non-teacher sister Caroline, another WSPU militant. Mary and Grace Coombs, who taught in elementary schools in Greenwich and Camberwell and were prominent in the London NFWT, also shared a home in south London throughout their lives. Such arrangements were not always a matter of choice. Many women teachers were obliged to live in lodgings and share rooms simply because they could not afford to live on their own.[25]

The Contradictions of Being a Teacher

Teaching conferred on women an independent status in the world but it did not provide a salary commensurate with that status. It thus reflected a potent new form of women's oppression in which women teachers' contradictory role was exposed. Ostensibly the job of women teachers was the same as that of males. To qualify, women had to take the same examinations and undergo the same training. They had, however, less control and influence than men upon their own lives as teachers because of their different political status within the state.

The contradictions of teaching in state schools were an important factor for Agnes Dawson, Emily Phipps, Theodora Bonwick and Ethel Froud in their political development as feminists. As one woman argued at the Class Teachers' conference of 1911, 'Women teachers were among the aristocracy of women workers.'[26] Women teachers were not, however, in a privileged relation to male colleagues. Equal pay did not exist and young male teachers earned more than experienced older women. Women were often wedded to teaching for life if they wanted an economically independent existence: a third of local education authorities operated a marriage bar.[27] The options were to marry and be sacked or to remain single and follow a career. Many women, our protagonists included, 'chose' the latter option.

In addition, women were barred from expressing any direct view on education through the electoral process. Before 1918 no woman, irrespective of her status or profession, was entitled to vote in parliamentary elections. Disenfranchisement symbolised the contradiction between on the one hand a woman teacher's professional status and public identity, and on the other her lack of political power and political identity.

Poor working conditions, inspector pressure and low wages meant that many teachers – men and women alike – organised in a union. Qualified elementary school teachers tended to join the NUT, established in 1870, specifically to promote the interests of qualified teachers employed in such newly established schools.[28] Thus it was within the NUT that the feminist teachers directed their political activities through the National Federation of Women Teachers (NFWT), a pressure group established in the NUT in 1903.[29]

Women teachers who worked in the fee-paying secondary schools usually joined the Association of Assistant Mistresses. Unless they were fortunate enough to receive scholarships working-class children were effectively excluded from these institutions. Consequently the labour movement waged campaigns for many years for such schools to be free to all children having academic ability.[30] Some of the headmistresses of these schools joined the Association of Headmistresses which also took into membership heads of public schools.

The Experience of Teaching

We know what such women taught, but we know less about how they perceived this experience. When these feminist teachers wrote to each other they focused on certain aspects of their lives such as their activity in the NUT and NFWT and their views of particular debates in feminist politics. In their letters, the job of teaching children in the classroom did not seem to occupy their attention with the same intensity as the debates surrounding their role as activists for the feminist cause. From the material available however, it is possible to gain some glimpses of these women's attitudes to their work. Emily Phipps seems to have thrown herself into her duties as head with as much gusto as that with which she used to attack the NUT executive and the state which denied her the vote. As president of the school's debating society she chaired a series of debates including those which asked: 'Is sport necessary to education?' 'Should there be higher education for girls?' 'Should the upper forms have games in school time?' 'Was the execution of Charles I justifiable?' The pupils' answer to these questions – in all cases – was yes.[31]

Any whiff of anti-monarchism amongst the girls, however, was set aside for festive occasions. For the Coronation celebrations in July 1911 tea was served to girls in their classrooms and each was presented with a box of chocolates. Then a tug of war took place in the playground between girls and teachers! Subsequently, three cheers were raised for the King – and Miss Phipps.[32] This interest in parties continued. Emily went to the Education Committee to ask for the free use of the Patti pavilion – the main Swansea theatre and concert hall – for her girls to have a Christmas social. The councillors' priorities obviously lay elsewhere and she was, more soberly, offered the use of any building – as long as it was a school.[33]

Despite festivities such as these, an air of efficiency dominated her school. Inspectors believed that her influence was indicated by the fact that 'this school is the only school in Swansea known to the Inspectors which begins at 9 a.m., and that, on the days of the inspection not a single pupil came late.'[34]

Although Miss Phipps was an enthusiastic teacher, chances to miss school were always welcomed. Writing to Ethel Froud, Emily commented on the three consecutive Fridays she was out of school: 'Who said Headmistresses were no good? Here's proof.'[35] Another 'holiday' was described thus in the school magazine: 'The pupils of both schools admired the way in which Miss Phipps cunningly wheedled an extra half day's holiday out of the mayor in order to celebrate the exceptional success [of two pupils].'[36]

In less exuberant tones Agnes Dawson noted in her logbook that holidays had arrived: 'Breaking up day!!'[37] The glimpses of disenchantment with teaching which emerge in Agnes Dawson's accounts were reserved for aspects of the job not directly concerned with children. She found administrative tasks tedious. On one occasion she had an argument with a council official over the state of a dangerous floor on which a teacher had slipped. The logbook conveys her indignation at this man who challenged her intelligence by stating that 'the corridor is *not* slippery as alleged to be by the Head teacher.'[38] Teaching children sometimes had to go by the board because of administrative duties: 'Amalgamation of the two schools together with the re-organisation and stocktaking have left no time for the Head Teacher to do much teaching.'[39]

The problems caused by children seem small by comparison. Having organised a two-week residential school journey to Loughton with children from Poplar, Agnes Dawson went to visit them at the weekend to assess the trip's success. She stayed the night and came back – with nine small children, all of whom demanded to be returned to their mothers. When the remaining 14 returned the following week she added – with relief no doubt – 'all happy and cheerful!'[40] Even in the bureaucratic language of the school accident-book Agnes managed to indicate her concern with the minutiae of children's problems:

Lily Webb at about 1.50 this afternoon lost her marble in grating in forecourt of school. She endeavoured to recover the marble and in doing so let the iron grating fall back on her big toe – the toe is considerably bruised and the flesh badly broken ...[41]

More time seemed to be spent on bureaucratic administrative tasks than on dealing face to face with children. This irritation with regulations and petty procedures was a reaction to the contradictions of the job. Headteachers were seen as upstanding authoritative members of the local community because of their important work with children. In practice they spent much time on administrative matters dealing with Local Education Authority officials who ignored their views.

Teaching 'Amid the Most Disheartening Conditions'

A further source of frustration for feminist teachers was the physical conditions in which they worked. Teaching jobs undertaken in unhealthy surroundings were very exhausting. Even the prestigious secondary school in Swansea occupied very dilapidated buildings. Despite the pleas of Miss Phipps and the Inspectorate alike, staff and girls for many years endured unhealthy conditions. Housed in temporary premises, the school lacked adequate ventilation and suffered from poor drains and dirty classrooms. There was no library, no staffroom for teachers, no assembly hall and no dining hall. If she wished to address the whole school, Emily Phipps had to take the girls into the playground. While this may have been good practice for addressing an NUT conference, the inspector commented: 'Such arrangements ... are unworthy of any secondary school.'[42]

Clare Neal, Emily's friend, contended with similar problems at Terrace Road Girls' school. As well as running the Swansea NFWT and Women's Freedom League she had to cope daily with the problems of temporary school premises, liable to subsidence and flood.[43] Classes of 42 pupils were taught in a cookery kitchen and in a narrow corridor with their backs resting against radiators. Some children were also taught in the basement of a half-derelict church and were 'much interfered with by building operations'.[44] Not surprisingly, pupils and teachers suffered frequent bouts of poor health. It was common for older women teachers to experience a total physical and nervous breakdown. Such incidents were utilised by the feminists to press their demands for increased – and equal – pay:

> We desire strongly to combat the idea that teaching in primary schools is easy work to be performed as a 'pocket money' task by an educated or partially educated person. On the contrary, it is exhausting both to mind and body, although the hours of teaching are comparatively few. It is, moreover, frequently carried on in cities, amid the most disheartening conditions of dirt, poverty, and disease and in the country in almost complete isolation from social and educational advantages.[45]

Public World: Public Scrutiny

Although teaching was an exhausting and poorly paid job it had its rewards. At the turn of the century teachers were highly regarded within their local communities. When feminists blazoned their qualifications and asserted in the feminist press the importance of their profession it should not be interpreted as eccentricity. It merely reflected the general respect accorded teachers. The teaching profession was also admired in the labour movement: for example, when the Scottish socialist John Maclean wrote his revolutionary pamphlets, he was proud to add MA after his name on the title page. His degree and profession of schoolteacher added to his standing in the socialist movement.[46]

Such status was partly derived from teachers' participation in public and civic life. The very nature of their jobs as employees of local councils meant that headteachers in particular had the 'opportunity' to engage with various committees and institutions. On one level this meant tackling the representatives of the Education Officer over the small, but important, questions of repairs and maintenance, holding one's ground against the bureaucracy.

As we've seen, the frustrations and irritations caused by such problems come across even in the stilted language of the official school logbooks. In response to Agnes Dawson's complaints that open-air classes in the nearby park were inadequately protected from rain, a workman duly appeared to place footrests on desks to prevent children getting wet feet.

'Since these would prove quite useless', Agnes wrote, 'as a protection for the children's feet the Head Teacher suggested that it was a waste of the man's time to fix them.' A stern note to the Education Office followed.[47]

More importantly, attendance – of headteachers at least – was required at care committees, governing bodies, and consultative meetings at the Education Office. Such meetings were important both to the running of the education service in schools and in giving experience to women in the ways of local government and bureaucratic structures. They often used this experience to good effect. In Swansea, Emily Phipps' attendance at the Education Committee meetings meant she could give councillors details of the school's requirements. It also meant that she could learn the workings of the Education committee. This experience was later used to good effect in her deputations to press the claims of the NUT and NFWT.[48]

Inspector Harassment

A teacher's public status entailed a public scrutiny of her job and life 'outside' the classroom. The Board of Education kept detailed records headed 'Teacher Immorality' on women teachers who had had illegitimate children and were therefore deemed no longer fit to teach.[49] The Board also sent 'spies' to teachers' meetings which were called to demand better conditions or pay. Two such lackeys attended an unemployed teachers' rally in Trafalgar Square in 1910 to report back to their superiors on the proceedings. They proved themselves unequal to this arduous task: 'It was a rather damp raw day, not very suitable for warm displays of eloquence ... [we] got our feet rather cold and so didn't stay out the whole time.'[50]

At each school the headteacher kept an official logbook to record staff absences and lateness, accidents to pupils and staff, visits of all officials, inspectors and councillors, the approved timetable and reasons for changes to it, a weekly record of what lessons she taught and for what length of time, dates of fire drills and the time taken for evacuation of the building, and details of correspondence with the Education Office. The headteacher compiled all this information herself: secretarial help was rare.

In addition, there were frequent inspections by His Majesty's Inspectors from the Board of Education, and from the local council. These were then reported to the Education Committee when the Head was 'invited' to attend to respond to comments. Schoolteachers regarded HMIs with hostility for several reasons. The majority of inspectors were recruited from Oxford and Cambridge; they had no experience of teaching in elementary classrooms. Women were barred from all inspectorships except for needlework and other domestic pursuits. Elementary teachers had little prospect of reaching such career heights and resented the class superiority of the HMIs. As one headteacher explained: 'The unpopularity of the HMI himself was chiefly the outcome of his social superiority, or of a class arrogance not always conceded ...'[51]

Even George Kekewich, secretary to the Board of Education before 1906, scorned the value of HMI inspections:

Every school is, or was before the war, visited annually or oftener both by the Inspectors of the Board and by those of the local authorities, the effect being, not to improve the efficiency of the schools, but to harass the teachers and continually disturb the work of the children.[52]

HMI reports were often shrouded in mystery. Progressive head-teachers, to whom inspectors were hostile, would not necessarily be told of adverse criticisms. The inspectors' comments, however, would be recorded for posterity in the Public Record Office. Dr O'Brien Harris, for example, the Fabian head of Clapton Secondary School for Girls, was criticised by HMIs for lacking 'brightness' and a 'sense of humour'. Her attempts to introduce a progressive educational experiment based on the Dalton Plan were criticised as unsuitable for an academic secondary school. The inspectors made these remarks to her employer, the LCC, while she was kept outside the room, unable to defend herself.[53]

Regular inspections and rigid logbook procedures meant that it was easier for local councils to intervene in the running of schools. Teachers resented this. The London Teachers Association, which represented the majority of London teachers, castigated the LCC 'for forcing the pace' and '"dragooning" just as the "hand" in the factory or the store has to obey the word of command of the departmental manager who touches a button in his desk'. The LTA argued that such pressure led to 'an increasing number of breakdowns, particularly in the case of women teachers, and the neurasthenia rates are going up'.[54]

It was not just feminist headteachers like Agnes Dawson or Theodora Bonwick who resented the bureaucratic interference of the LCC. The LTA deplored '... the multitudinous suggestions of the inspectorate, and ... the drive and grind and hustling of the administrative machine.' The solution, according to the LTA, was for 'an administrative holiday. If for twelve months the County Council would give a holiday to all but the most necessary officials, we believe it would be good for the schools, better for the teachers, and excellent for education.'[55]

'The Call' to Full-time Political Organisation

Some women teachers strongly resented the conditions in which they taught and the fact that they had so few alternatives to the job. 'Surely no-one supposed', asked one woman at a union conference, 'they went out into the world to earn their feeble wages because they liked it?'[56]

Margaret Nevinson, who quit her teaching post to become a WFL organiser, explained her frustration with the job in these words: 'The worst of all my struggles after knowledge was the fact that for young women of my day there was nothing but teaching.'[57]

It is noticeable how many women, especially women from middle-class backgrounds, willingly exchanged the public world of teaching for that of the political arena as full-time organisers of the WSPU. Gertrude Colmore, in her *Life of Emily Davison* presents Emily Davison as a martyr for the cause who relinquished teaching because of her commitment and self-sacrifice:

> She found that the carrying on of her profession and devotion to the woman's movement were incompatible ... the call had come; a call which caused her to put aside all self-interest, all personal ambition, all claims and hopes which stood in the way of its behests ...[58]

Yet Emily Davison was not a solitary example. Laura Ainsworth, one of the first WSPU members to be force-fed in Winson Green prison in Birmingham, resigned her teaching post in 1909 to become a WSPU organiser. Rachel Barrett similarly resigned to become a WSPU organiser in Wales. Dorothy Evans, a 'physical culture' teacher from Batley in Yorkshire, also became an organiser. She maintained her links with teachers and in 1916 she spoke at a NUT conference fringe meeting organised by the feminists.[59] One of the first organisers of the WSPU outside the immediate Pankhurst family was Theresa Billington Greig who had taught in Manchester, where she had helped form the Equal Pay League, the precursor of the NFWT. Edith New, a teacher in Swindon, and Greenwich and Deptford in London, became a WSPU organiser, was imprisoned several times and went on hunger strike.[60]

It is possible to read this change of 'career' in several ways. With the emphasis that feminists placed upon 'the cause' it is possible that they viewed the giving up of an independent teaching career as a necessary sacrifice for the achievement of a political goal. The personal satisfaction of a career had to be rejected in favour of an altruistic motive. This was the argument of the suffragette newspaper *Votes for Women* in its account of Dorothy Evans' arrest at Batley: 'She risked her professional position for the cause she believed in so wholeheartedly.'[61]

However, arrest for political activities in the cause of feminism did not bring an automatic end to a teaching career. Mary Thompson, a teacher at South Hampstead public school for girls was arrested (with a barrel organ) for collecting money for the WSPU in Oxford Street. Her headteacher supported her and one of the managers paid her fine. Florence Down, a West London elementary teacher, was arrested at the House of Commons in 1909 while participating for the first time in a demonstration. She continued to teach for many years after.[62] It may be, simply, that those teachers who became full-time organisers for the cause welcomed the opportunity for a different identity in the 'world' and were happy to drop a career in which they had participated with some reluctance.

'Grave, Quite Particularly Quiet and Sane Women'

Many NFWT activists were militant suffragettes who saw no conflict between their political activity and their careers; rather, they saw a clear political relationship between the two. Their status as employees of the same state which disenfranchised them, served to heighten their own consciousness. The entry into teaching of the future leaders of the NUWT was not synchronised with the growth of the twentieth-century militant suffrage movement. Many women I refer to in these pages began their teaching careers in the 1880s and 1890s some decades before the militant suffrage organisations, the WSPU and WFL, began their activities. The formation in 1903 of the first feminist pressure group inside the NUT, the Equal Pay League, pre-dated the militant organisations by several years. Founded by Miss Lane in Southwark and Theresa Billington-Greig in Manchester, its first published membership list contained only 50 names: Agnes Dawson, Theodora Bonwick, Ethel Froud and Emily Phipps, all NUT members at the time, were not among them. It was only once the militant suffrage movement *outside* teaching gained ground that they started to become involved in politics *inside* the NUT.[63]

Women like Agnes Dawson and her feminist colleagues were middle-aged teachers with many years of experience behind them when they started to campaign for the vote and equal pay. When Theodora Bonwick became involved in the suffrage movement in 1905 she was already 35. When Emily Phipps joined the WFL in Swansea in 1908 she was over 40.[64]

In fact it was their maturity of years which added to the feminists' anger against unequal pay and lack of franchise: 'Why should capable women teachers be compelled in many cases to serve under semi-capable Headmasters, to work twice as hard and receive half their pay and, almost as galling, receive less pay than assistant masters of the same grade?'[65]

Opponents of the suffrage were wont to characterise feminists as young and therefore flighty creatures whose comments counted for nothing. In 1903, for example, a letter published in the *Schoolmaster* opposing equal pay suggested the women's priorities were those of young women without responsibilities: 'Will our sisters then demand the price of their new bonnets, immaculate gloves, and a continental holiday at the expense of our children's strong boots for the winter?'[66] This common misconception about the age of the women involved was encouraged by the media. At her trial Lady Constance Lytton, then in her forties, commented upon it: '[it] was very funny, to read the newspaper account of the hysterical girls of 18! ... and then look round Bow Street – the rows of rather grave, quite particularly quiet and sane women about my age! Well, well!'[67]

It is from this political period of suffrage activity that feminist teachers marked what they regarded as the real start of their lives. One elderly woman teacher reflecting on her life wrote:

> I joined the 'Federation' in its early years, and did my best to attend the meetings and certainly the demonstrations, but never did I realise till now what they all really meant. I was only one of the crowd who followed on, but I followed to its end ...[68]

For women teachers such as Emily Phipps, Ethel Froud, Theodora Bonwick and Agnes Dawson the decision to join a suffrage organisation and to campaign inside the NUT on feminist issues was an important step in their lives. It marked a break from their previous lifestyles. To make such a break indicated a fierce commitment to the cause of women's suffrage. It showed a confidence in their own ideas and in their abilities to campaign for what they believed.

Thus, when we read of the apparent sudden conversion to the cause and of the sacrifice to the feminist movement, we are in fact reading about women who are rejecting an established way of life of many years' standing. When we hear of women saying that their lives took on meaning from their involvement in the NFWT and feminist movement, we should realise that this gaining of significance occurred with the onset of political activity, and not with their mere entry into the public world of teaching. It is at this point of the political initiation that the next chapter rejoins our protagonists.

2

'Politics Govern the Whole of [our] Professional Life ...'[1]

Many teachers in the National Federation of Women Teachers, including Ethel Froud and Agnes Dawson, were members of the Labour Party.[2] They took no part, however, in the work of the Labour Party's staid Women's Labour League, which concentrated its activities on women's role as mothers and wives. Nor did they work inside the NUT with those male members of the Teachers' Socialist Association who, between 1907 and 1911, sought to bring the NUT closer to the TUC and Labour Party. Instead, their politicisation outside teaching came from the suffrage movement, particularly from the militant Women's Social and Political Union (WSPU) and Women's Freedom League (WFL). The National Union of Women's Suffrage Societies (NUWSS), founded in 1897, was the oldest of the suffrage organisations. It organised its campaigns entirely within the law and was fiercely critical of the law-breaking activities of the militant groups. The NUWSS was the most respectable – and sedate – of the suffrage groups. Although the NUWSS numbered women teachers amongst its supporters its particular feminism held little interest for militant teachers in the NFWT.

The first feminist organisation in the NUT, the Equal Pay League, owed its origins to Theresa Billington-Greig, then a Manchester teacher and early WSPU member, who left the WSPU to help form the WFL.

The period in which the Equal Pay League grew from a loose network of 50 women in a few towns to a National Federation of Women Teachers with a central council, local groups, candidates for the NUT executive and fringe meetings at NUT conference, coincided with the growth of the militant suffrage organisations. The attraction of the militant groups to teachers was based upon their appeal to women working in the 'new' public world, and particularly to unmarried women. The suffrage movement was a campaign for the closer political incorporation of women into the state's structures. Even the most militant wings of the movement were not opposed to the state but advocated for it an extended and progressive role, as Sandra Stanley Holton has explained:

16

British feminists insisted on both the necessity of increasing state intervention in areas that had previously been part of women's domestic preserve and the concomitant need for women's participation in the work of the state. In asserting both they challenged the notion that domestic and public matters could be kept apart as the separate concerns of men and women respectively.[3]

For many women, however, and especially for those in the WFL and the small WSF (Women's Suffrage Federation), the movement was much more than that.[4] It was also an economic and ideological campaign: for equal rights for women, and for a feminist concept of women's role in society. Reflecting on her experiences in the movement, Cicely Hamilton commented:

> I have never attempted to disguise the fact that I wasn't wildly interested in votes for anyone, and that if I worked hard for women's enfranchisement ... [it was] because the agitation for women's enfranchisement must inevitably shake and weaken the tradition of the 'normal woman'.[5]

NUWSS: 'Home is the Sphere of Woman'

The constitutional NUWSS, the largest of the suffrage groups, offered a particular appeal to married women. It emphasised the importance of the home and motherhood by continuing to maintain that 'Home is the sphere of woman.'[6] It did not challenge women's traditional position, rather it believed that the vote was a way of validating this role: 'The mother half of humanity should be given its proper place ... the temperate, affectional woman nature, intent on the conservation of the home and race should have its due beside the more extreme male and appetite nature.'[7] The NUWSS made an appeal to women teachers as substitute mothers. A leaflet produced in 1913 argued that motherhood meant 'essentially the imparting of life.'[8] As married life was not available for all women, unmarried women could be of service by 'giv[ing] life' other than in a physical sense. Such women included doctors, nurses, social workers, civil servants and teachers. These new jobs for women were not seen as a break from their domestic role but as jobs which reinforced motherhood as the 'natural' sphere for women. Women in such jobs were implementing, 'in different measure the office of motherhood, in serving the larger life of the community'.[9]

The NUWSS literature for women teachers contained two main arguments. The first was that the vote was needed for women's own sakes; the second was that it was needed for the children in the teachers' care.[10] In fact leaflets encouraged women teachers to think that *children* were appealing to them to obtain the vote on their behalf: 'You need the vote for the children's sake ... how can you hope to bring up children towards an understanding of their duties and responsibilities as citizens if you have to admit that you are yourself unfit to exercise them?'[11]

The NUWSS has often been viewed as the most progressive of the suffrage organisations since it accepted that women's oppression was class-based and sought to work with the labour movement over a number of years.[12] However, it also attempted to make common cause between women of different class backgrounds by promoting an identity centred in the traditional women's sphere. Because of this latter focus and its rejection of militant action it had less appeal to 'new women' who were leading independent lives in the public sphere. Agnes Dawson was a member of the NUWSS and as such was something of a rarity in the union: 'Some of my friends of the NUWT had thought fit to twit me on occasions that I was Constitutionalist, a law-abiding suffragist. I always obeyed the law ...'[13]

WSPU: Self-activity

The WSPU had its early origins in the Manchester labour movement and initially maintained an uneasy allegiance to this progressive background. The WSPU, however, soon moved further away from the Labour Party, assisted by its analysis of the oppression of women. The Union's constitution referred entirely to political demands: women's political oppression was emphasised over and above economic oppression. The vote, rather than trade union campaigns, would secure better pay and working conditions for women.[14] By 1912 the *Votes for Women* baldly declared that 'the governing classes today are the working classes, or rather the working men.'[15]

Its appeal to NFWT supporters was far greater than that of the NUWSS. Like the NUWSS, the WPSU accepted that women had an important role in the home. However, it went beyond this position to support greater opportunities for women outside the domestic sphere and to advocate a positive role for women outside marriage. By its militant acts it challenged the traditional role of women. Individual acts of militancy provided a service to the cause and a demonstration of an individual woman's strength of feeling. By their own actions WSPU women were changing their consciousness and forging a new identity: 'Each individual woman who went through the horror of such experience [of force feeding and imprisonment] became a centre of enlightenment for all whom she might thereafter reach.'[16] This purposeful action, Elizabeth Robins suggested, had resulted in there being more free women in Britain than anywhere else in the world, even though the vote was not yet won.[17]

This was consistent with the WPSU's position on individual

sacrifice and commitment. As Christabel Pankhurst wrote:

> The beloved WSPU had winged its way through storm and stress, further and higher towards its great aim. Each woman in our army of justice had done, had given, had been her best. All had known the pure delight of self-regardless service and a self-transcending purpose.[18]

Her statement exemplifies the importance attached to the achievements of *individual* women in the academic or professional field. Individual feminist teachers' own achievements – the attainment of degrees, election to union positions, and development of speaking abilities – were also publicised as indications of what women could achieve by their autonomous efforts. The WSPU was short-lived. At the start of the First World War the group's activities for the vote were 'suspended' and instead Emmeline and Christabel Pankhurst directed their attentions to 'women's right to serve' in the patriotic cause.[19] It never resumed its activities.

Although women trade unionists in the NFWT recognised the strength of collective action, many were nevertheless attracted to the WSPU's emphasis on women's individual achievement. They also developed their own interpretations of its politics within the teachers' movement. Ethel Froud, for example, believed equal opportunities, equal status and equal pay were all 'bound up with equal franchise'.[20] Ethel was never a leading member of the WSPU, but a dedicated grassroots activist. She was a member of the WSPU's fife and drum band which paraded in purple, white and green uniforms through the streets, playing to draw the attention of passers-by to suffragette meetings.[21] She looked back on her time of membership in the WSPU with pride, describing it as, 'that wonderful suffrage organisation which called "halt" to the eighty years of shuffling by politicians and taught women how to free themselves.'[22]

Theodora Bonwick dropped her temperance work, her involvement in a church Sunday school and her singing in the Philharmonic choir to join the WSPU, seeing this as her 'life work'.[23] She became the secretary of its Hornsey branch in North London.[24] Theodora also adopted her own interpretation of the WSPU views. Unlike her former sisters in the WSPU, who dropped their campaign for the vote during the war, she maintained her commitment. She also supported the NUT affiliating to the Labour Party – a position which would have been anathema to the WSPU leaders.[25]

WFL: Complete Social and Economic Equality

The suffrage group that had the greatest influence in the NFWT was the Women's Freedom League. It challenged both the traditional concept of a woman's sphere and linked political and economic questions. Emmeline Pethick Lawrence, who worked closely with the NFWT, explained its work thus:

> The WFL developed many interesting new forms of militancy approved of in conference by all its members; it stood four square in all vicissitudes, carried on even during the years of the Great War, and is still pursuing its undeviating purpose to win not only political equality but complete social and economic equality for women.[26]

In its official objectives the WFL placed the vote in a broad context. It intended to use the power thus obtained 'to establish equality of rights and opportunities between the sexes and to promote the social and industrial well being of the community', and supported women and men organising to take trade union action.[27]

The WFL had been formed by Charlotte Despard and Theresa Billington-Greig, who had left the WSPU disillusioned with the autocracy of the Pankhursts. This negative experience caused the organisation to attach great importance to its own decision-making. WFL decisions were taken democratically by the whole organisation and, as a consequence, members had an opportunity 'of becoming conversant with the methods and procedure of representative government – an education greatly needed by a sex hitherto so shut out from public life.'[28]

In sharp contrast to the WSPU, the WFL continued its work throughout the war and many years beyond. Many of its supporters opposed the war and supported the pacifist cause. Charlotte Despard became a member of the Women's International League and subsequently joined the Women's Peace Crusade.[29] After the war it continued to campaign for full sexual equality as 'comradeship between men and women is the essential prerequisite of social progress'.[30] The WFL's interest in economic as well as political issues ensured that the feminist teachers' demands for equal pay for equal work featured prominently in its literature. Like the other suffrage organisations the League did not avoid discussion of the nature of women's oppression. Unlike the WSPU, the League believed that it was precisely because women as a group tended to be treated as an inferior class that wage differentials continued betwee n men and women.[31]

Emily Phipps, a long-standing member of the WFL, realised throughout her life that political enfranchisement alone was not an answer to women's oppression. She wrote to Ethel Froud in the 1930s:

> Don't imagine, even when we have secured equal pay, that, because we possess that and the Parliamentary vote, everything is won. It isn't! It will be necessary to fight on, not only for equal opportunities, but also to *keep What We Have Won*. (original emphases)[32]

Although the WFL was less well known for its militancy than the WSPU, it also engaged in militant and spectacular actions. The educationist Muriel Matters achieved publicity for the 'cause'. She ballooned across the Thames outside Parliament to drop leaflets to Londoners, because Parliament would not receive the women's petition for the vote. The permanent picket of Parliament from 8 July to 28 October 1909 followed as an attempt to petition Parliament for the vote. The WFL also initiated the census boycott of 1911 in which women were urged not to register because they were denied the vote.[33] Emily Phipps' friend Adelaide Jones was a long-standing member of the WFL; Clare Neal was a member of its central council.[34]

Teachers and the Suffrage Organisations

All the suffrage organisations made particular appeals to teachers to join their ranks and were successful in this. The WSPU was keen to demonstrate that its policy of individual actions was widely supported:

> If respectable wives and mothers, *girls from the Universities* and girls from the mill, stand firm behind the individuals who do the inconvenient and (for themselves) dangerous acts, it is because they understand ... good will is ineffectual until it is applied. (my emphasis added)[35]

Teachers were identified by the WSPU as a particular group who supported the militants' work:

> Anyone who wishes to know the sort of women who support the Union [WSPU] has only to look down the columns setting forth the subscribers to the funds. Such examination will show that the sinews for this moral war were provided by working wives and mothers, by doctors and nurses, by painters, musicians, teachers, domestic servants, 'great ladies' and a number of the first men in England.[36]

All groups, however, were also anxious to involve women teachers in their activities and demonstrations. The status and qualifications of women teachers were used to enhance the movement's credibility. In advertising speakers for the huge Women's Sunday demonstration in 1908 at Hyde Park, *Votes for Women* emphasised women's careers and qualifications. One such speaker, Theodora Bonwick, was described as a teacher, the holder of a BA, and a temperance advocate. Another, Nancy Lightman from Hackney, was described as a teacher, trained at Homerton College, as well as an activist in 'many by-elections during her school holidays.'[37] Speakers would have already built a reputation in the women's movement before being asked to address such an important demonstration. It seems then that the point was less to introduce speakers than to inspire other women by displaying women's broad achievements.

Teachers organised specific contingents for suffrage demonstrations. The organisers canvassed schools, sent headmistresses circulars, and contacted training college students throughout the London area. Instructions about their 'conduct' were issued to all taking part in the demonstrations: women were firmly reminded not to wear hats which might obstruct others' views![38] On suffrage demonstrations the women teachers' contingents marched alongside doctors and other professionals. At the Pageant of Women's Trades and Professions organised on 27 April 1909 teachers marched with midwives, doctors, nurses, pharmacists and sanitary inspectors – all members of respected professions.[39]

The particular circumstances of disenfranchised teachers were frequently depicted in the visual images produced by the Artists' Suffrage League or the Suffrage Atelier. The Artists' Suffrage League had been formed by professional artists to further the cause through the production of posters, postcards and illustrated leaflets. The Suffrage Atelier had similar aims but its members had been trained in the crafts and were familiar with printing processes. The Atelier's contribution included supplying advertisements, banners and decorations for the suffrage movement.[40] In their art work disenfranchised teachers, dressed in gown and mortarboard, were contrasted with criminal and lunatic men who possessed the vote. Images of educational opportunity were depicted on banners: the ladder of learning, the wise owl, and the slogan 'Learn and live'.[41] None of these images were devised by the NFWT or WTFU but were depicted by professional artists on behalf of the movement as a whole. As such they are a further indication of the importance the broad suffrage movement attached to teachers and education. In the 1920s the Union referred to this tradition. When the feminist teachers established an independent union they produced banners for equal pay and equal franchise demonstrations. What had been a feature of the broad movement would be continued as part of the women teachers' own imagery.

Teachers' Conversions

Feminist teachers saw the decision to become a constitutional suffragist or a militant suffragette as an important stage in their lives, which they remembered for years after. Emily Phipps joined the WFL in 1908 after she had witnessed the vicious treatment meted out to suffragettes at a Liberal Party meeting:

Previous to this, she had not given any serious thought to the question of Votes for Women. Of course, women ought to have votes, but why make all this fuss about it? In this frame of mind she went to the meeting ...[42]

Lloyd George, then Chancellor of the Exchequer, was in Swansea for the Liberal Convention. Along with thousands of other Swansea residents – and Miss Neal – Emily attended a public meeting he addressed in the Swansea Albert Hall. In accordance with the Liberals' endeavours to keep out feminists from their gatherings, it was a ticket-only event. However, some determined women managed to raise the 'cause' in the meeting, heckling and demanding to know why the Liberals wouldn't give the vote to women. Lloyd George, according to the *South Wales Daily Post*, retorted to the audience, 'I wonder how much she has been paid for coming here?' When the women refused to be silenced he argued that since they desired equality with men they should be dealt with as men: ' let them be flung out ruthlessly!'[43]

Because of the brutally dramatic actions of Lloyd George and the Liberal stewards, detailed accounts exist of the meeting in the local and national press. They correspond closely with Emily's own description. Twenty years after the event, Emily Phipps remembered quite clearly Lloyd George's insinuation that women were paid to disrupt his meetings and his insistence that they be violently removed. 'While this was being done, Lloyd George called out, "Fling them out ruthlessly; show them no mercy."'[44]

From that moment, Miss Phipps had become a militant suffragette. Within a few months she and Miss Neal and ten other members of the Swansea Women's Freedom League had hired the selfsame hall for a suffrage meeting:

> They had just £1 in hand, and the meeting ... would cost £16. There was no fear in those days of not obtaining an audience at a Suffrage demonstration; the people poured in bringing with them trumpets, drums, and other 'musical instruments', with pea-shooters and a large assortment of hardware, all of which they proceeded to use.
>
> Presently, however, the personality of the speaker began to make an impression on them; the cat-calls and the pantomime songs ceased, and those who had come to scoff remained to listen. The meeting was a success, and the gallant little handful of women were justified.[45]

The way in which this introduction to the suffrage movement is described, as a conversion of almost religious intensity, was itself typical of the discourse and iconography of the suffrage movement. Although Emily Phipps was describing her conversion as a personal experience it echoed similar fictional accounts in suffrage literature.

A description of a sudden conversion like that of Emily Phipps is included in Evelyn Sharp's *Rebel Women*. Here Mrs Fontenella, a middle-class socialite, hosts a drawing room meeting to 'display' two suffragettes recently released from prison: 'The audience ... was lured to Mrs Fontanella's house on Wednesday evening by a prospect of meeting two eccentric females who had been to gaol ...'[46]

Needless to say both women spoke movingly of their experiences and their political beliefs and many of the audience were visibly shaken. The main effect was upon the hostess, Mrs Fontanella, who declared to her gathered friends that another deputation would be going to Parliament:

> You know what it means – almost certain imprisonment for the women who go on that deputation, but also a chance for every one of us to do something towards winning a great reform. I am going on that deputation. Which of you will come with me?[47]

In some cases conversion to the cause meant alienation from the family and former friends. Many women underwent a change of personality because of their commitment. Constance Lytton was seen by her family as a new person: 'for the moment she has passed out of the lives of her family, except in so far as they can go with her into the new life and interest.'[48] In others the new politicisation of a woman teacher reflected a general mood in the family. Carefully preserved in the NUWT archive, for example, is a copy of the letter Adelaide Jones' father wrote to the Liberal Home Secretary in 1911. Mr Jones, a Liberal Party worker of many years standing, explained he would no longer even vote for a Liberal candidate because of the treatment of ordinary suffragist members by the courts. The text of the letter is less significant than its preservation by the writer's daughter and its deposition in a feminist archive as an example of prized ephemera which depicted the righteousness of their cause.[49]

Feminists Standing on Orange Boxes ...

Once feminist teachers had joined suffrage organisations they participated enthusiastically in their activities outside the educational arena. It provided a framework for their whole life and a means of establishing a positive identity. Various feminist teachers, writing their own potted biographies in the *Suffrage Annual*, were at pains to stress their commitment to the cause. Hannah Townsend, a founder of the Women Teachers' Franchise Union, stressed her experience speaking outdoors as well as indoors for the cause. Caroline Townsend, her sister, described her *interests* as 'speaking, paper selling and poster parading'. Ethel Llewhellin, another WSPU member, and treasurer of the WTFU, emphasised her various propaganda work: selling papers, chalking pavements, poster parading, participation in processions and action to avoid the census. Mary Gawthorpe, the former teacher and WSPU organiser, gave readers an insight into her frenetic lifestyle by describing her recreations as sleeping and not talking. What is striking to the modern reader is the juxtaposition of what are seen, by the women themselves, to be positive features of their own lives. Often accounts of illegal actions are seen on a par with academic laurels. Far from viewing such 'achievements' as somehow counterposed the feminists saw them as forming a common part of their identity.[50]

Ethel Froud, too, remembered teachers' militant acts:

> Those members [of the NFWT] who were ruthlessly flung out of Cabinet Ministers' meetings, or as ruthlessly gagged in teachers' meetings; members who have carried posters through hostile jeering or even respectful crowds, and places where there are no crowds at all; members who have stood on orange boxes at street corners or done any other outrageous thing in order to wear down opposition to our cause.[51]

Many NFWT members took part in the defiant activity the WFL organised against the 1911 census. All people occupying a dwelling on the night in question needed to be registered: only those absent from home were exempt. The penalty for refusal to register was a £5 fine or one month's imprisonment. The WFL campaign was instigated on the following basis: if women were deemed not to be citizens for voting purposes then they would not be citizens for the purpose of helping the government compile statistics. The WSPU and NUWSS soon supported the campaign.[52] In London midnight meetings were held for the same purpose of providing a venue away from home for women. This meant that women could legally claim they were not residents of their home address on census night. One such meeting, addressed by Mrs Pankhurst, was held at the skating rink in the Aldwych. Agnes Dawson's male relatives attended, she recalled. They managed to entice away disruptive male students in town for the boat race.[53] Even the non-militant Agnes participated in this action, staying with other women at a friend's house:

> [I] fondly believe[d] that it would be possible to lie on a couch or the floor, and so be fairly fit for the morrow's work, but so great was the throng of census strikers that most of us had to endure a hard wooden chair as our only resting place for the night ... We were wretchedly tired in body the next day, but still we say it was worth it.[54]

More dramatically, Emily Phipps and Clare Neal spent the night in a cave on the Gower coast near Swansea. Accompanied by two training college lecturers and a business woman they spent a sleepless night, 'Only one of their number obtained any sleep, since sitting or lying on sharp rocks was not conducive to repose. Their purpose accomplished they returned the next morning to school, college, and shop, and the secret was well kept.'[55]

... Women Teachers Making Tea

Encouraged by suffrage activities outside their profession the feminist teachers also started to bring their politics inside the NUT. This was no mean feat in the first years of this century. The NUT had been established in 1870 for English and Welsh schoolteachers. It grew slowly and had difficulty protecting the pay and conditions of its members. There were no national negotiating bodies and local bargaining was not evident on any significant scale until the introduction of the 1902 Education Act. The Union organised no 'industrial action' against this situation.[56] Although there was some trade union action in Portsmouth in 1896 and in West Ham in 1907, these were local defensive actions designed to prevent deterioration of conditions.[57] Formal links with the trade union or labour movement were non-existent.

Women NUT members took little part in mainstream NUT activities. NUT officials viewed their inactivity with complacency. A correspondent to the *Schoolmaster* felt: 'We women are not wanted by the men at Russell Square [NUT Headquarters] or in the local associations (except, of course, to prepare tea!) but our subscriptions appear to be required!'[58]

The atmosphere at local association (or branch) meetings was uninspiring. 'The meetings in those days', remembered a former NFWT president, 'consisted chiefly of bald heads and timid females who, since their limbs were swathed in twenty yards of material and other impediments, had much difficulty in mounting the platform.'[59] Women were encouraged to devote their energies to the NUT's form of charitable good work, the Benevolent and Orphans Fund. Although men and women teachers were expected to make the same, regular contribution as part of their subscriptions, differential benefits were paid out according to a teacher's sex. Miss Lane, a feminist teacher from Southwark in South London, challenged the discriminatory operation of the fund. It was in this traditional area of NUT 'women's work' that the embryonic Federation struck one of its first successful blows. Henceforth the same benefits would be available to all members from this fund. The argument was still to be won for equal benefits for women and men from the NUT's Teacher Provident Society, and, during the 1914–18 war, from the War Aid Fund. But a first step had been taken.[60]

The feminists' activities began slowly. The first resolution passed by the Equal Pay League at its inaugural meeting was to canvass candidates for the NUT executive elections for their views on equal pay. The League intended to publish the results in the *Schoolmaster*, the NUT paper. Theresa Billington-Greig and Miss Hall, the League's vice-president, moved motions for equal pay at the NUT and Class Teachers' conferences, without success. However, as a result the NUT executive declared itself in favour of equal pay for women who taught in boys' schools.[61]

From such small beginnings the Equal Pay League began to develop its policies and activities. It recognised that it was a step forward for the NUT executive to back equal pay for the minority of women who worked in boys' schools. However, it cautioned, 'if left to stand alone [it] will be dangerous, as it only improved women's salaries where they enter into direct competition with men.'[62] The Equal Pay League's new policies included opposition to the amalgamation of the junior boys and girls departments of an elementary school as such amalgamations deprived women of promotion prospects. Faced with the choice of who to appoint as headteacher of such a mixed school local education authorities would always pick the man both because of his assumed additional financial responsibilities and because it was thought unlikely that a woman could control boys. It also supported a lower retirement age. It called for the increased representation of women on the NUT executive and at NUT conference, and for the right of women NUT members to hold their own meetings for, 'many women teachers do not care for discussing their special difficulties in the local NUT association.'[63]

The first EPL secretary was Joseph Tate from Birmingham who remained the sole honorary male member of the NFWT, as the League called itself from 1906. He busied himself writing conscientiously to the *Schoolmaster* on women's issues: 'Your correspondent proceeds to declaim against the necessity of the Federation of Women Teachers. Surely the extent and depth of this apathy must demonstrate the urgent need of special effort and a special organisation ...'[64] Throughout 1907 a lively correspondence ensued in the NUT paper about the desirability of women organising autonomously within the NUT. NFWT correspondents urged women to attend their associations to oppose even the nomination of candidates for the union's vice-presidency who were opposed to women's issues.[65] Advice was given on how to deal with NUT procedures. One correspondent urged women teachers to ignore teas and dances and stick to the business:

Stick to the plan of keeping business and pleasure separate, and the interest in the association goes up by leaps and bounds. Give the

business a chance, do not drown it in tea. Women teachers who find a
man representative averse to their co-operation, vote him out.[66]

The Ladies Committee

At this time in the NUT there was a Ladies Committee (sic) of women
executive members. This was no feminist organisation. It organised
Ladies 'At Homes' and teas at NUT conference, and expressed the
wish that more women become involved in the Union. The source of
this problem, the Ladies committee argued, was women themselves:

> It is the fault of the women themselves, they do not vote for the
> women. A man smiles and he conquers; and yet women are grumbling
> that the NUT does nothing for them ... If only the women teachers
> would do their fair share in the NUT, there is no need for any further
> combination ... Women are too apathetic, too easily swayed by the
> wiles of the men.[67]

Yet the Ladies Committee refused to adopt policies sympathetic to
women's needs, which might have encouraged women's greater
involvement in the NUT. The Ladies Committee refused to support
the concept of women's self-organisation. It turned down a request
from the Women's Co-operative Guild for support for its petition on
votes for women. The committee refused to take a position in defence
of women teachers' retaining their jobs on marriage. It did not even
discuss equal pay. Nevertheless when it was suggested by NFWT
members that the NUT had done nothing for women, the Ladies
Committee was quick to rush to the union's defence: '[We cannot
accept that] the NUT had passed resolutions ... and done nothing
more. *We* know better. Neither can we advise our women teachers to
... join the NFWT ...' (original emphasis).[68]

Privately, the Ladies Committee was worried about the impact of
the NFWT on members. It recognised great dissatisfaction amongst
the women teachers throughout the country: 'it is feared that unless
some step is soon taken to show the women members that they are
being considered and their interests are our concern, we shall have
our ranks largely diminished.'[69]

Accordingly the committee decided to organise a conference for
women teachers. This was not to encourage autonomous action but
'to prevent the women teachers taking irresponsible action'.[70]
Delegates were handpicked and as a result few NFWT members could
attend.

Irrespective of the content of the conference these undemocratic
practices caused a stir. Individual NFWT members and the London
branch wrote to the Ladies Committee to complain about the

unrepresentative nature of the conference. It was closed to observers; and despite being advertised as a women's conference men executive members were allowed to attend – and vote.[71]

Nevertheless Fannie Thomas, Miss Overmark and Eleanor Mardon – all NFWT members – managed to attend and make an impact. They divided the conference with their demands for a lower retirement age as a right for women and for action to be taken against men teachers appropriating women's jobs as heads of girls and infants departments. So successful were their arguments that the Ladies Committee resorted to a reliance on the male executive members present to uphold the union's weak line.[72] Although the NFWT members did not succeed in strengthening the union's positions, a member of the Ladies Committee could still remark: 'I can quite see some future good in the Women's Federation, whereas now it is a menace.'[73]

The 'Menace' of the NFWT

The 'menace' stemmed from the feminists' acute understanding of the effect of their political and economic oppression upon their whole lives. For the feminist teachers, awareness of their political relationship to the state affected their ideas of citizenship. The NFWT believed that because women teachers were denied full citizenship as voters despite their employment as teachers of the state's future citizens, they were in a contradictory position: 'Our association together in the Federation has aroused in us not merely a keener consciousness of ourselves as a distinct body in the state, but also a keener vision of our work in relation to the state.'[74]

They attempted to transform this understanding into militant campaigns within the NUT to gain its support, especially for the vote:

> The fact is, we live, move, and have our being by Act of Parliament – *politics* – without having the only lever that will work the political machine. Our Codes are framed by Parliament – our Inspectors appointed and paid by Parliament; Parliament controls the size of our classes; it examines us, and grants or withholds our certificates; it can withdraw them too ... Finally, it provides about half the money for our salaries. (original emphasis)[75]

This understanding also made the feminists more conscious of their own role as citizens and the future role of the girls they taught. Civic consciousness highlighted the injustice of women teachers' disenfranchisement: 'Education aims at making the best possible citizens, women are denied the rights of citizenship.'[76]

To the feminist teachers the importance of the state went beyond their work within the classroom or their involvement in political life.

Their very identity as women teachers, an identity of which they were proud, was threatened by their disenfranchisement. Exclusion from the public world of parliamentary politics in turn affected their private lives. The publicity of the NFWT and WTFU consistently linked the public sphere with their private world, seeing politics as the determining factor in their whole lives. In a leaflet written against the manoeuvres of right-wing men teachers in the LTA who tried to stop debate on the suffrage and equal pay, the feminists' argued: 'We stand to lose professionally, educationally, and *as women* if we still leave the control of the LTA and the NUT in the hands of such reactionaries as those who would not "play fair"' (my emphasis).[77] The teachers' branch of the Lewisham Women's Franchise Club, to which many NFWT members belonged, produced literature which made the same point: 'Parliament interferes with the personal life of women teachers.'[78]

The conclusions the feminist teachers drew about politics, their lives and the state reflected similar ways of thinking of feminists outside teaching. Irrespective of their particular suffrage affiliation many women described the supremacy of politics in determining women's lives. The argument of Christabel Pankhurst's *The Great Scourge* was both that the oppression of women affected women in their daily lives – and that women were increasingly conscious of this. The great scourge of the book's title was venereal disease. This, Christabel Pankhurst argued, was being steadily transmitted to married women by their husbands to the extent that marriage itself almost carried with it syphilis or gonorrhea infection as 'occupational diseases'. She concluded that 'the cause of sex discrimination is the subjection of women.'[79] In other words the political oppression of women was directly responsible for disease contracted in the most intimate of circumstances.

This development of the relationship between politics and women's personal lives was also discussed by Charlotte Perkins Gilman in her *Women and Economics*. She developed her argument on the present state of marriage in relation to economic questions:

> While the sexuo-economic relation makes the family the centre of industrial activity, no higher collectivity than we have today is possible. But, as women become free, economic, social factors, so becomes possible the full social combination of individuals in collective industry. With such freedom, such independence, such wider union, becomes also possible a union between men and women such as the world has long dreamed of in vain.[80]

Such writings and Cicely Hamilton's *Marriage as a Trade*, referred to in Chapter 1, adopt different – and conflicting – feminist perspectives.

My point is not that the feminist movement was developing a *common* analysis of the political nature of women's oppression as reflected in women's daily experiences and lifestyles but that marriage, motherhood, venereal disease were all seen as personal issues governed by political considerations. The conclusion drawn by the feminist teachers and sister suffrage activists was that political activity was crucial to changing the *whole* of women's lives.

Socialists Inside the NUT

At this time the NUT was not sympathetic to the introduction of progressive ideas into its ranks. It called itself a union but cultivated and promoted a professionalist ideology which members generally accepted. The union was keen to see the status of its members raised in this way rather than to have pay and conditions improved through industrial action.[81] Moves by socialist men at the 1906 NUT conference to create a NUT sustentation (or strike) fund were heavily defeated. Most delegates agreed with A.E. Cook, a Conservative London teacher, that 'the establishment of such a fund would turn the union into an absolute trade union', and accordingly rejected the move.[82]

Some progress, however, had been made by socialist teachers keen to draw the NUT closer to the labour movement. The 1907 conference agreed to a policy of immediate reform in class size, to a maximum of 40 pupils per class. NUT Conference also agreed

> to endeavour to secure the co-operation of the Trades Congress, the Labour Representation Committee, the Independent Labour Party, the Co-operative societies, trades unions, and any other organisation interested in the educational welfare of the children, to bring about this urgent reform.[83]

A Teachers' Socialist Association (TSA) had been formed with a particular aim, 'to propagate the gospel [of socialism] amongst teachers'.[84] The TSA held fringe meetings at NUT conferences addressed by a range of labour movement speakers – Herbert Burrows of the SDF, Keir Hardie and Philip Snowden of the ILP, Dr Haden Guest of the Fabians, and Denis Hird of Ruskin College.[85] At the 1907 Class Teachers' conference a motion was moved by G.D. Bell, an ILP member from London, 'that the time has now arrived when the NUT should be re-organised as a trade union'.[86] Debate was acrimonious and wide ranging. Supporters such as William Harris from South Wales appealed to teachers' working-class backgrounds: 'We forget our parentage as soon as we leave college. We must come away from the side of the employers who exploit child labour and take the side of those who would make a real heaven here on earth.'[87]

Despite such eloquence the motion was lost, but only by a relatively small margin of 1,200 votes. It seemed perhaps at this stage that the socialists could swing the union to the left through the introduction of labourist politics. By 1908, however, the TSA's campaign for trade union allegiance had disappeared from the agenda of the Class Teachers' conference. At the height of the feminists' political campaign a few years later at NUT conference, questions of trade union organisation were nowhere to be seen.[88] The NFWT exhibited a far greater degree of tenacity and political organisation than the TSA. Many of those who opposed the introduction of feminist politics into the NUT had also opposed the politics of the labour movement gaining a similar influence. Much of the hostility to suffrage politics emanated from the belief that if the feminists had a positive impact on the NUT, socialists would have an easier time winning their positions. This was one of the main arguments used by the Anti-Suffrage teacher from Leeds, W.J. Gwillam, 'If [the conference] voted for this then the following year the socialists would come for sympathy.'[89] This sentiment was also found in Anti-Suffrage feeling outside the NUT. Mrs Humphrey Ward, a leading Anti-Suffrage League member, was of the firm view that women's votes would 'add immensely to socialist and labour strength' and thus enfranchisement should be strongly resisted.[90]

Organisation of the NFWT

Such opposition required the feminists to organise effectively inside the NUT. Taking a lead from the WFL, the NFWT (and the London-based WTFU) adopted democratic structures for their own organisations. They also campaigned vigorously for democratic decision-making procedures in the NUT and LTA. Theodora Bonwick argued against the reactionary members in the London Teachers Association who wanted to restrict the rights of the members to discuss policy and confer this right instead on the committee. She appealed to

> men and women equally, to stand by their rights of self-government, and to stand by the rights of private members ... By putting the power away from the general meeting of the Association the members were denying themselves the right of control over the policy of the Association.[91]

Because the feminists *did* understand the relationship between political and economic equality, and the way this affected their whole lives, they sought to gain the support of the NUT for the franchise as the first step in their campaign for equal rights. If Parliament acceded to their political demands, so the argument went, then other progressive measures such as equal pay could soon follow. The NUT was seen as an organisation representing professionals which could bring its influence to bear upon Parliament. After all, one of the NUT's objects was to ensure 'the effective representation of educational interests in Parliament'. To this end it sponsored the candidatures of (male) teachers of all political persuasions and provided 5 per cent of the election expenses of all endorsed candidates. All members, male and female alike, were obliged to pay a proportion of their subscriptions towards the MPs' expenses.[92]

Initially, the feminists had thought the NUT would align with other groups of professionals, such as the Association of Headmistresses, who supported the vote for women. The Association of Headmistresses had already passed a motion in 1906 calling for the parliamentary franchise for women and sent a petition to this effect to the Prime Minister.[93] The Anti-Suffrage League had also thought the NFWT might be successful in winning over the NUT: 'If suffragettes might have been expected to triumph speedily it was in the NUT', commented the *Anti-Suffrage Review*, 'But the strong sturdy and instinctive dislike for female suffrage was too strong for agitators even there.'[94]

The NFWT, however, was to change its views – and tactics – in the light of experience in the NUT and LTA, as Agnes Dawson indicated when moving a motion for equal pay at the LTA:

> She had been told rather frequently that of all bodies of workers teachers were the most conservative and that they were most fearful of any changes, and, judging from their opposition to this great reform, she was inclined to believe it was so.[95]

The feminists were calling on the NUT to take a stand in support of their rights as citizens, but the NUT did not endorse their demands. By its very practice the NUT was *de facto* aligning itself with the state in its own exclusion of women from the political process.

The significance of the NUT's position was recognised by Nancy Lightman. She was one of the first NFWT members to raise the suffrage issue at a union meeting in London: 'Miss Lightman was howled down ... Whistles were blown, feet stamped, comic songs were sung by organised opposition, and finally the meeting had to be adjourned, and broke up in disorder ...'[96]

Recalling this meeting – she described herself as 'a survivor of the 1907 meeting'– Nancy Lightman explained: 'The suffrage resolution came first and when they refused that, we told them Equal Pay would be fought for *in the* Association as they wouldn't help us to get Parliament to act' (original emphasis).[97]

At first, the feminists had little experience of the use, and misuse, of the bureaucratic procedures employed by the right wing in the union. Nevertheless, they doggedly attended meetings and organised their speakers in debates. One formerly timid feminist described the work of Ethel Froud in her local NUT branch:

> Her able generalship was apparent even in those early days, and when a fight was on, one was ordered to second Motions, move Amendments, and stay till midnight waiting for a decisive vote to be taken. In those unshingled days it was one of Miss Froud's habits to thrust a blacklead pencil through her hair, and when the stress had become so great that most of the blackleads had disappeared, to disobey was more than any meek person dared to do.[98]

NUT men used various manoeuvres to prevent the suffrage motions being discussed – or the results being forwarded to the executive. Emily Phipps recalled the efforts of the NFWT and the way these were thwarted. She kept a notebook to record these 'illegalities', as she termed them, which she later incorporated in her book, *A History of the NUWT*. She explained that, 'branches everywhere bent all their energies to [passing motions on the suffrage]. But in many places they were foiled by trickery, such as can hardly be believed by women teachers who did not experience it.'[99]

Stella Newsom, who joined the NUT in 1910 straight from college, took her first militant action within two months when the Leicester NUT refused to discuss her motion on votes for women. Over 50 years later she still remembered her feelings:

> I was so furious I dashed on to the platform and demanded my sub-scription back. And got it! I can still see the chairman – an old fellow with a beard – turning out his trousers pocket to find 7/6d while the meeting sat stupified.[100]

Nor was this the end of the matter when local branches had passed feminist policies. Lewisham NUT included in its membership Hannah Townsend, and Mrs Kate Dice, both of the WTFU. At its 1911 AGM it passed by one vote a motion supporting the suffrage for women. A subsequent meeting overturned the decision – by three votes – on the grounds that the matter was not an educational question.[101] The same acrimony continued in the following year's discussion of motions for NUT conference. First there was a tied vote on whether to support the parliamentary franchise motion, then at a special general meeting it was carried. At this point the committee tried to overturn the decision by calling a referendum of the members – which the feminists reported to NUT headquarters for being outside the rules.[102] Even when branches took clear decisions of support it did not mean a complete sea change in the way that associations conducted their business. The introduction of explicitly political ideas was still a new phenomenon which sat uneasily alongside other aspects of union life. For most members the professionalist concern for the routine 'educational' aspect of NUT business remained isolated from political consideration. For example, at the East Lambeth NUT AGM of 1912 Agnes Dawson was elected vice-president; the franchise motion was prioritised as the top motion to be discussed by the NUT conference – and then the meeting went on to hear the incoming male president address them on 'The place of handiwork in the educational system'.[103] At the Bradford NUT annual general meeting the president gave an address condemning half-time education and supporting women's franchise. This was followed by an address on spiders![104]

NUT Conference: 'Oratory on the Sands'

The NFWT also campaigned in the highest decision-making body of the union, the NUT conference. The NUT was the focus of much press attention during its weeklong Easter conferences at seaside and spa towns. The event was usually a sedate affair. Many delegates went as much for the social life as for the debates. Outside conference hours they attended training college reunions and met up with old friends. To assist them the union printed addresses of all delegates in the conference agendas and distributed them in advance. It was an important *social* event, then, in the teaching calendar. Observers from associations throughout the country attended the conference to participate in the social events, to meet friends, attend 'At Homes' and hear the debates. On Sunday members went to various church and chapel services, during which the NUT president would read from the Bible or take prayers. The waters or sea air could be enjoyed particularly by the wives of the male delegates – most of the delegates *were* male – who accompanied their husbands on what was a holiday in congenial surroundings. The conference town itself would be described in articles in the *Schoolmaster*; subsequently there were photographs of male conference delegates (and their wives) walking along the promenade of the resort in question.

When the feminists organised to become conference delegates from local associations and when suffrage groups descended on the town in force to rent public rooms and hold fringe meetings, the whole ethos and culture of the NUT conference was disrupted. Politics were injected into what was essentially a social and 'professional' occasion.

The franchise was first discussed at NUT conference in 1911. At this conference the union's first woman president, the Conservative Isabel Cleghorn, was elected thanks to votes organised by the feminists. Grassroots interest in the parliamentary franchise was emerging but as yet little organisation had taken place to get motions on the conference agenda. Consequently there was no motion as such for conference to discuss. Therefore Allen Croft, an executive member, moved a suspension of standing orders to take a motion of sympathy for women teachers barred from exercising the vote. The NUT's *Schoolmaster* recorded a 'stormy reception' for his speech. It was punctuated by cries of 'no politics' and 'this is not an educational question.' Croft tried to gain support by arguing that the feminist movement outside teaching had been 'inaugurated, fomented, organised by mischievous busy bodies to alienate women teachers from the union and seduce them from their loyalty'. Such a campaign would be stopped, he maintained, by accepting the women teachers' demand for the vote.[105] Emily Phipps described the occasion more vividly than the *Schoolmaster*: 'Hundreds of men massed at the back of the hall prevented Mr Croft from obtaining a hearing. They stamped, howled, hurled insults at the speaker and at suffragists, and utterly refused to allow Mr Croft's speech to proceed.'[106]

Croft's motion was defeated, but feminists went away from the conference in buoyant mood, dedicating themselves to the future achievement of the cause: 'Every woman will go home from this conference a missionary!'[107]

By 1912 the feminists were better organised. Seventy identical motions were submitted supporting the suffrage. They called on conference to express its 'sympathy with those members of the NUT who desire to possess and exercise the parliamentary franchise, but because they are women, and for that reason alone, are by law debarred from it.'[108] The NUT, unused to the enthusiasm and vitality of suffrage political campaigns, was shaken. Even the unsympathetic *London Teacher* could not fail to be impressed with:

... the ubiquitous suffragettes. In huge, gaunt letters an enormous hoarding outside the railway station drew attention to the condition of the voteless millions of women. Bills and placards covered the advertisement centres. Two special committee rooms, at one of which tea was provided (on payment)! Oratory on the sands! Everywhere one had evidence of their ceaseless activities, and, of course, the 'Antis' were in evidence also. Huge advertisement barrows and sandwich men assured us positively that women were content to remain voteless.[109]

The feminists were an even more visible and vocal presence at the 1914 conference in Lowestoft. The *London Teacher* counted five different suffrage organisations in attendance:

Most of these bodies had opened rooms, so that Lowestoft seemed to be in the throes of an election. The numerous 'organs' were pressed upon willing and unwilling buyers by charming newspaper vendors. Miss Nancy Lightman held forth persuasively and eloquently at the entrance to the South Pier. The most impressive and the bravest [meeting] to our mind was that arranged by the Women Teachers' Franchise League [sic] in which several London ladies took part ...[110]

At the same conference the WSPU organised its own meeting. Annie Kenney, one of its leading members, risked arrest to attend. Like other militants she was trapped by the 'Cat and Mouse Act' introduced to deal with the forced feeding of women suffragette prisoners. When the prison authorities deemed a woman too weak to endure further forced feeding she was temporarily released. When her health was partially restored she would be re-arrested and made to undergo the same treatment:

How could she get there, with detectives constantly watching the house? ... Neighbours were friendly. In a black bathing-suit, black-cap, stockings, long gloves and a mask, Annie crept at midnight from [the house], climbed a wall into the neighbour's garden and entered their house. Next morning, well disguised she drove away with members of the family. Changing from cab to cab, she broke all clues and drove by night to Lowestoft. In fresh disguise, and leading by the hand another Suffragette, dressed as a schoolgirl, she entered the Lowestoft Hippodrome, where teachers from all over the country were assembling ... Annie slipped into the speakers' room, removed her coat, changed her hat, and was ready for the platform! The great gathering of teachers was afire with enthusiasm, when they found that one of the Suffragette mice had thus foiled the Government cat ...[111]

Although her audience was 'afire with enthusiasm' the NUT conference was not won over. For the fourth year running it rejected votes for women. Even the *London Teacher*, though, was forced to praise the oratorical skills of NFWT and WTFU members at the conference: 'The Lowestoft conference brought into strong relief the rise of the woman teacher orator.' Agnes Dawson and Annie Byett were singled out for praise: *'The woman's movement'*, concluded the paper, *'is destined to affect powerfully the future of the NUT!'* (original emphasis).[112]

Unity Between Suffragists and Suffragettes

In order to achieve influence within the NUT the suffragists and the suffragettes needed to cooperate. Outside teaching, the NUWSS and the WSPU were scarcely the closest of allies – especially after the WSPU's arson attacks and extensive damage to public and private property. The war of words between the organisations was fierce: suffrage literature – in tones familiar to modern feminists – castigated opponents for extremism, or for cowardly capitulation. But, as Liz Stanley and Ann Morley have argued, the divisions of formal feminist

organisations had little relevance to everyday practical political campaigns. Women worked together in local campaigns and professional
groups. Certainly this is true for the feminist teachers.[113] Members of
the NUWSS, WFL and WSPU all shared political platforms and meetings and worked together within the NFWT and WTFU. When women
teachers in London formed a teachers' campaign to obtain the NUT's
support for the vote they made sure all shades of opinion were
included. The initial meeting of the WTFU was held in Alan's tea
rooms in Oxford Street – an establishment which let rooms free of
charge to WSPU supporters. Agnes Dawson of the NUWSS took the
chair, and Hannah Townsend of the WSPU was elected secretary. The
first meeting called on the NUT executive to reaffirm support for the
suffrage. It agreed to campaign on equal pay, opposition to separate
scales for men and women and the release of suffrage prisoners.[114] In
the WTFU's first year Ethel Froud of the WPSU was elected to the committee and WFL member Adelaide Jones was also closely involved in
its work. In 1915 Theodora Bonwick was elected President; Agnes
Dawson and Ethel Froud were committee members. All three were
regular platform speakers for the WTFU. [115]

This unity was in part achieved by the narrowness of the organisation's platform. Within London women teachers were involved in
different teacher groups such as the LCC Mistresses Union or the
Certificated Class Teachers' Association. Divisions which existed
amongst women teachers on mixed schools or on the value of
domestic science teaching were set aside to focus on specific suffrage
demands. The feminists understood that, irrespective of divisions
amongst teachers, it was important for the teaching profession to
express a united and official view on the franchise, precisely because
of the public status of teachers. The overriding importance of 'the
cause' created this unity.

The NUT's Response to the 'Supremacy of Politics'

The feminist teachers encountered great hostility inside the NUT, as
well as outside on the streets. The NUT's leaders – and many of its
local functionaries – feared that openly to introduce politics into
union life would weaken the union's standing as a professional body,
capable of influencing all parties by virtue of its 'non-political nature'.

At the LTA meeting called to discuss the franchise in July 1912
Agnes Dawson confronted the gathering with her own convictions:
'She had innate faith in herself. She wished the LTA had as much
faith in itself ... Politics ran from beginning to the end of their professional life ...'[116]

For Theodora Bonwick politics was inextricably linked to moral
questions. The inseparability of the two added force to her argument:

'There was a great misunderstanding as to what was a political subject. She urged that the moral effect of the status of the teacher is a most important factor in life.'[117]

This emphasis on the supremacy of politics was not necessarily shared by teachers outside the the NFWT, who otherwise supported the suffrage campaign in the NUT. At a fringe meeting called at the 1911 conference to discuss the franchise, tactics were discussed by over 400 women and men. James Yoxall, the NUT general secretary and a sponsored Liberal MP who supported the feminists' claim, cautioned the meeting. He believed the franchise should not be a political question but a union question. He defined the question of the franchise as 'personal politics' and argued that this concept should be rejected in favour of making the franchise a *union* question. The vote for women, he said, would give greater parliamentary weight to the NUT. Yoxall misunderstood the way in which the feminists saw the relationship between politics and personal issues. For them, there was no such thing as a separate personal issue when it came to the franchise. It was an all-embracing political question, but a political question none the less.[118]

Yoxall's argument held little sway with NFWT activists such as Annie Byett and Emily Phipps who, at the same 1911 conference, made another, unsuccessful, attempt to suspend standing orders to discuss the vote for women. Naturally, they used different arguments from those of Allen Croft, who had criticised the suffragettes as 'mischievous busybodies'. They taunted conference that teachers would be seen as afraid to discuss the question if they did not agree the suspension. Women teachers should be recruited to the NUT, they said, but this would not happen if the union was not sympathetic to the aim of citizenship for women.[119]

For the NFWT, strategies like those proposed by Yoxall, which placed union allegiance above political integrity, had little appeal. The feminists had no particular allegiance to the NUT – they had become active in the union as a means to an end: political and economic equality. The NFWT made no secret of this, so that, even in its early years, many women who supported the franchise were reluctant to align themselves with the organisation. The editorial comment in the independent *Woman Teacher* was symptomatic of this caution. Women teachers were warned against approaching the parliamentary franchise as a political question: 'There appears to be an idea gaining ground every day that the NUT has become political, and is backing the Liberal party' (sic). It distanced itself from the NFWT's position: 'Women teachers' agitation in the NUT is not a political or suffrage question but it is the just demands of the female section of the union for proportionate representation and power.'[120]

Physical and Verbal Hostility

The feminists were gaining ground in the NUT but were also attracting to themselves a good deal of verbal and sometimes physical abuse from reactionary supporters of the Anti-Suffrage League (ASL). Launched in 1908, the ASL sought to maintain the notion of separate spheres of influence for men and women. Proof of citizenship for women lay not through the vote but through women 'promoting the good of the community'.[121] The ASL organised a massive petition opposing women's franchise, which gathered more signatures than the suffrage movement had obtained in 1909. Its activities were not limited to petitioning: men were paid to parade in sandwich boards declaring that women did not want the vote and meetings of suffragettes were systematically broken up.[122]

Within the NUT ASL supporters issued leaflets designed to whip up feeling against the feminists. Their campaign was headed by Arthur Gronno in Manchester and Mrs Burgwin in Southwark, south London. The very titles of the ASL pamphlets created the impression of a union besieged by alien forces: for example 'The attempt to capture the NUT by woman-suffragists', followed by 'The fourth attempt by suffragists to capture the NUT conference'.[123] Ostensibly the main argument of the NFWT opponents was not against the vote as such, but against the politicisation of the union. However, these leaflets reveal the intense opposition to the feminists' cause:

> The Woman Suffrage movement ... is a dangerous and insidious one, for, although the rank and file of suffragists do not know it, the movement is being engineered by 'feminists', who wish for more fundamental things than the vote, only they dare not say in public what they wish for.[124]

The feminists were also criticised even for attending meetings to argue their case:

> The whole thing is skilfully planned and will be vigorously pushed by suffragists ... Suffragists ... will pack the meetings if care is not taken to rouse the usual stay-away members to come and ensure that they are not misrepresented by a noisy minority.[125]

By 1914 the ASL's tone had become more hostile still. A leaflet signed by many right-wing teachers urged teachers to rid the union of 'Woman-suffragist-obstruction-at-meetings-nuisance' (sic).[126] Particular women were obliged to bear the brunt of the reactionaries' attack. Nancy Lightman 'the finest outdoor speaker in England', according to Emily Phipps, had become adept at dealing with heckling at street corner meetings.[127] This experience proved useful when she was attacked by the Conservative A.E. Cook at the 1913 NUT conference, as this report of his speech from the *Schoolmaster* indicates :

> He happened to see the lady (who moved a suffrage motion) standing on the platform at the Hyde Park demonstration ... At the teachers' meeting she told them all the women asked for was sympathy; in Hyde Park she said: 'We do not want sympathy; sympathy was no good to us.'
>
> A woman seated in the body of the hall mounted a chair and attempted to address conference. In answer to the President's usual question she gave her name as Miss Nancy Lightman and her association as Hackney. In the noise which was going on around her, her words did not reach the platform distinctly, but it was understood that she was the woman to whom Mr Cook had referred, and that she was either contradicting or explaining his statement.[128]

Feminist teachers were vilified because of the way in which they had undermined the traditional role of women and disrupted the established practices of the NUT. The right tried to alienate them from the mass of members by depicting their behaviour as unprofessional. At NUT conference, Cook complained that officers of local associations 'had been absolutely persecuted by the suffragists'.[129] (This 'persecution' had consisted of a NFWT circular sent to its *own* branches advising them to question candidates for the executive on their record in support of equal rights within the NUT!)

Anti-suffragist teachers did not confine their hostility to argument. Like the ASL itself they also employed the tactics practised by reactionary men at street meetings and physically attacked women.[130] Several NFWT members were attacked on such occasions and some had their hair torn out by hooligans, who exhibited it in shop windows as a trophy. Speakers in Hyde Park were assaulted by opponents who rushed the platforms down to the Serpentine. Ethel Froud had to be protected by railway officials from the fury of a mob and was locked into a waiting-room – for her own safety – until a train arrived.[131]

As part of the suffrage campaign the Anglican and Non-conformist church services held in conjunction with the NUT conference were interrupted by women making public prayers for 'the cause of women'. At the Anglican service women were brutally treated. 'They were literally thrown from the church', the *Vote* reported, 'several were seized by the throat and, in one case, a girl's spine was injured.'[132] Similar ill-treatment was meted out to Miss Cutten at the 1913 conference. Heckling Lord Haldane about the education of girls, she was violently attacked by men NUT members:

... the organised stewards rushed upon Miss Cutten, seized her by the legs and dragged her from the chair on which she was standing; her weight was thus thrown on the rod which she was holding and this came down, bringing part of the ceiling with it and covering the women near by with plaster. Not content with rushing Miss Cutten from the hall, other men aimed blows at her as she was dragged along, and, in a few seconds she, with other women delegates, was ejected from the hall.[133]

Such physical violence was a further indication of the seriousness with which hostile men in the NUT regarded the threat of feminist ideas. The feminists also faced personal abuse. Mrs Burgwin, a long-time NUT member and mainstay of the Benevolent and Orphans fund, as well as a leading member of the Anti-Suffrage League, was particularly prone to launching such attacks. Deliberately misrepresenting the feminists' position, she suggested that they only wanted the vote for unmarried women.[134] She implied also that the unmarried state enjoyed by thousands of her women colleagues was one which was sadly deficient, an argument which contradicted the lived experiences of many NFWT members. Unmarried women were, by definition, 'unhappy' since they *were* unmarried and had no man to counsel them. Her views on unmarried woman were formed, she said, by her experience of canvassing them at School Board elections. According to Mrs Burgwin, such women were not able to understand political issues: 'Of course, it was not their fault, they had no man at home to instruct them.'[135] In sharp contrast to the NFWT and WTFU members' emphasis on equality Mrs Burgwin highlighted the differences between men and women. She proclaimed that 'her sex, her womanhood, and her motherhood' gave her the authority to declare that it was not the time to give women the vote.[136]

The recollection of hostile incidents became part of the collective memory of the movement. Women like Miss Cutten who had suffered at the hands of anti-feminist men became martyrs – reborn in NUWT mythology as pioneers. Miss Cutten died prematurely a few years after she was attacked at the NUT conference. In her memory the NFWT erected a school clinic for London school children. She was remembered by Emily Phipps in the NUWT's 'canon' as 'one who had paid the sacrifice, having passed away as a result of injuries sustained at suffrage meetings ... [her] death was one of the severest blows ever sustained by our union.'[137]

The feminist acts of this departed sister were commemorated in stone; the actions of the living were caught in photographs. Images of groups of feminist teachers parading with sandwich boards at NUT conference were reproduced as news items in the feminist press and became part of the official history of the feminist teachers' movement in Emily Phipps' *A History of the NUWT*. They remained a treasured part of the union's collective imagery.[138]

But the memory of the hostile treatment to which feminists were subjected became more than mere memory. It also contributed to the feminists' future decision to organise autonomously from the NUT. In the 1920s Emily Phipps looked back on this earlier experience with much strength of feeling:

> How miserably the men fought for men's privileges as against women's rights; how nauseating were their innuendos! but how easily they won every time. Women now were beginning to understand how it was the men won every time, even when they were beaten in debate: it was 'Heads we win and tails you lose' with them. Look at the election results, look at the Suffrage debates, examine the results, locally and then at Conferences, examine too the Salary debates, and those on Equal Pay; they, the men, were in possession of the machinery, and knew its cranks, every one.[139]

Feminist Assertion

In order to maintain their self-confidence in such difficult times, the feminists used different devices to affirm their identity. One such 'device' was the incorporation of particular events at NUT conference into the 'story' of the NUWT. In their passage into mythology, events were transmuted. One of the NUWT's celebrated stories concerned the behaviour of the feminists during the 1911 conference. When men 'howled and stamped' the suffragists remained calmly sitting in their seats throughout the uproar. Perhaps they did. But at the same conference, Miss Byett bated delegates. The motion on the franchise had been defeated, but she moved the motion again as a suspension of standing orders with Miss Phipps. She would have known of the outrage this would cause. During the uproar she harangued the conference about its behaviour. It had spent two days debating and condemning the Holmes-Morant circular, a document produced by the HMI which was critical of the quality of inspectors and, more importantly, of elementary schoolteachers, who were described as uncultured and badly educated. According to the *Schoolmistress*, Miss Byett reminded them of their raucous behaviour and caused a furore by asking 'How much culture did you show yesterday?' There is no record of this provocative statement in Emily's account![140] A few years later in the heated atmosphere of the 1914 conference, when security had been strengthened to prevent 'disturbances', Miss Byett again caused pandemonium by attempting to ask the president a question. She waited until the howls of 'sit down' and 'turn her out' had finished to ask – somewhat disingenuously one feels – 'would it be contrary to the regulations, Mr President, to ask if a window might be opened?'[141]

The NUWT commemorated Miss Byett's question as a product of an exemplary commitment to the cause. A closer reading of the circumstances, and Miss Byett's obituary written for NUWT members, suggests another explanation:

> She enjoyed the fight as much as she enjoyed the victory; for her as for all great souls it was an even better thing to travel hopefully than to arrive ... a long tramp in the country with friends, lunch in the open air, and *a big argument* were among her chief pleasures. (original emphasis)[142]

Confident and assertive, even argumentative, behaviour was also found in feminists' letters to the *Schoolmaster*. In her only letter to the paper Emily Wilding Davison tore to shreds the argument of Arthur Gronno – the organiser of the Anti-Suffrage League in Manchester – and noted: 'The wail of the Antis is loud in the land at the approaching nemesis of woman suffrage.'[143] Challenging men teachers' assumptions that men should be paid extra simply because they were married, Hannah Townsend of the WTFU replied in a similarly assertive manner: 'If the love, services and companionship of women are not sufficient inducement to marry without extra salary, men had better remain single.'[144]

Feminists' confidence was also reflected in their willingness to stand for positions inside the NUT. They often did this with some success. By 1912 Agnes Dawson was vice-president of the East Lambeth NUT, having served on the LTA committee and its Special Schools sub-committee. She also stood on two occasions, unsuccessfully, for the NUT executive, relishing the campaign – 'It was a good fight' – if not the disappointing outcome.[145] By 1913 Emily Phipps was president of Swansea NUT and an unsuccessful candidate for the NUT executive. She was elected at a later attempt in 1915 and took her place on the executive and the Ladies Committee.[146]

Throughout the country feminists stood for election to the local NUT committees and its national executive. In London many feminists were candidates for the London Teachers' Association committee. Irrespective of whether they were elected or not their candidatures helped to raise 'the cause' inside the union and provide a positive example of women confident in their beliefs. Certainly their intervention into such elections brought greater membership involvement in the NUT – and greater interest in the politics of the NFWT.[147] It was such actions which typified the WSPU's commitment to deeds not words. 'The need for 'operant power', as Elizabeth Robins described it, 'must be made manifest before it will move. Not active opposition – apathy is the arch-enemy of reform.'[148]

   The deeds of the feminists demanded 'courage ... not simply phys-ical courage ... but still more the moral courage to endure ridicule and misunderstandings and harsh criticism and ostracism.'[149] This courage stemmed, they argued, from their adherence to a political cause as a 'great *impersonal* object'.[150] It was this commitment to the cause and the subjugation of self to feminism which became part of the movement's ethos. As Christabel Pankhurst described it: 'There was a touch of the *impersonal* in the movement that made for its strength and dignity' (original emphasis).[151]

   Their identity as feminists was forged through an adherence to the greater political cause, of which each individual was a part. This concept of feminist identity also helped them make sense of their role as educators inside – and outside – the classroom.

3

'Men Must be Educated and Women Must Do It'*

The teaching and educational experiences of feminists gave a particular meaning to their politics outside and inside the classroom. Education was not only the feminists' trade and livelihood; it was a means by which women could change their own lives. On one level this was effected through self-education and the obtaining of qualifications. On another, education was a mechanism for creating *political* change in society through the education of public opinion, especially male opinion, about feminists' demands. Education, conducted by the right teachers, could also affect the life chances of the pupils the feminist teachers taught. The feminists, then, expected high standards of achievement from all pupils, irrespective of their class background. In London feminist teachers tended to work in working-class areas: West and East Ham, Lambeth, Lewisham, Southwark and Hackney. Agnes Dawson's teaching career was spent at schools in east and south London. After a period as headteacher of St Paul's Road school in Poplar, she went on to another working-class school, Crawford Street Infants, in Camberwell. Before she arrived at Crawford Street there was already a well-established ethos of hard work and achievement. An inspector's report of 1907 had commended the standards of the junior school as comparable to a secondary school. For their part the infants were pronounced to be 'bright and intelligent, and reach a good level of proficiency'.[1] Agnes continued these high standards.

As the head of Enfield Road Elementary girls school in working-class Hackney, Theodora Bonwick likewise urged her pupils to work hard and continue their education once they had left school. Here the inspectors noted a 'spirit of earnestness'.[2] Later Theodora moved to the Headship of York Way girls school in King's Cross, which was a major focus for the railway industry and the militant railworkers' unions. The majority of the children's mothers (as well as fathers) were employed locally. Dr Hayward, her patronising LCC inspector, commented, 'Unquestionably, the school is ... a civilising influence in the neighbourhood.'[3]

*(NUWT Banner on equal pay demonstration 1921)

The feminists promoted a rigorous but enjoyable curriculum for all their pupils. In Swansea, Clare Neal, Emily Phipps' friend, became a headteacher of the Glanmor Central school in 1922. Although this new type of school was intended to be less academic than the secondary schools, pupils were offered a range of cultural experiences. In her first year as head, outside speakers gave talks to the pupils on Shakespeare, the work of Dickens and medieval Wales. An afternoon performance of *A Midsummer Night's Dream* was presented by the third years. Throughout the 1920s pupils transferred successfully to Emily Phipps' secondary school.[4] Thanks to Clare Neal's own high standards the school was reorganised as a secondary school by 1930.[5] Emily Phipps' standards of excellence at the Swansea Municipal secondary school for girls also bore fruit. Many pupils went on to training colleges where they were 'among the most original as well as among the most hard working of the students'.[6]

Hard work and scholastic achievement would, the feminists believed, be beneficial for their pupils. Such confidence in the benign effects of education reflected similar views to those of sections of the labour movement.[7] It also blurred some of the positions the WSPU held on the nature of women's oppression as effected by men. After all, if education was able to alter people for the better, surely even the most recalcitrant male oppressor could be changed. This blurring of definitions was alluded to by the Women Teachers' Franchise Union, under Theodora Bonwick's presidency: 'Sex distinction is as invidious a thing as ... class distinction.'[8]

Feminist teachers thought education could help increase opportunities for women (and girls) as a group and as individuals. As students they had undertaken rigorous initial teacher training. This had included attending lectures for seven or eight hours a day, wearing approved plain and dark dresses, and sharing large dormitories.[9] Nevertheless, many women continued their studies, often by correspondence courses, to gain higher qualifications. Several studied for the external 'degree', open only to women, of LLA – or Lady Literate in the Arts. This attainment, the result of private study after a hard day's work, was proudly displayed after the names of teachers so qualified, among whom were Clare Neal and Annie Byett, Edith Cooper, and Misses Cutten and Hewitt. Further study enhanced an individual's status but also helped her be a better teacher. Women teachers – feminists and nonfeminists alike – prided themselves on their attendance at courses, conferences, and meetings on educational theory and pedagogy. Of the hundreds of teachers who attended classes on the work of Dr Maria Montessori at the St Bride's Institute in London, only a handful were men.[10]

The belief in self-improvement was not peculiar to feminists; it was

widely held within the mainstream of the labour movement of the
pre-war period. The founding of the Workers' Educational Association
in 1903 had grown out of the tradition of the nineteenth-century
Mechanics Institutes, with its emphasis on further or higher education for working-class people.[11] This interest in education was also
reflected in TUC and Labour Party support for a constructive education policy based on equal opportunities for all.[12] For child and adult
alike education was perceived as a means of self-improvement – and a
benefit to the nation: 'Let the children be our first care ... [there is] no
task [which] could more ennoble a nation.'[13]

The feminists suggested that education could change people's politics; again this was a view which was shared by sections of the labour
movement. Education could fashion a socialist – or feminist – future
through the creation of a new political awareness and consciousness.[14] Thus the objects of the WTFU included, specifically, 'the
education of the public on women's suffrage from the woman
teacher's point of view'.[15] The certain belief that education could
change political consciousness caused the WTFU to insist that 'more
propaganda is still necessary in the teachers' organisation if full
liberty is to be secured to those that come after us.' In turn, this
would lead to the freedom of women which 'will compass man's
perfect freedom'.[16]

On this optimistic basis, the NFWT – in the years before the First
World War – decided that they should stay inside the NUT to
'educate the men'.[17] Certainly they were happy to work with men
sympathetic to the cause: Joseph Tate, the Federation's secretary, is
the obvious example. Others such as Mark Wilks, C. Hicks Bolton or
W. Nefydd Roberts in London all worked alongside the Federation,
arguing their case in the Union or in the courts.[18]

'Really Educational Questions'

When feminists displayed their pride in educational knowledge this
was no mere identification with the usual behaviour of teacher colleagues. As Emily Phipps put it in the NUWT paper, 'In purely
educational matters we have always been in the forefront.'[19] Emily
scathingly criticised those journals aimed at women teachers which
provided columns on fashion, cookers, retirement presentations and
'how to make bedroom suites out of packing cases'.[20] Such journals
took little interest, she believed, in the political ramifications of education policy. As the short-lived *Woman Teacher* of 1911 lamented, 'Why
do the women's educational papers so-called ignore the woman teacher
herself, but give her "Tales for Infants" and "test cards" ad nauseam?'[21]

The feminist teachers wanted to go beyond these practical
classroom tasks to a broader discussion of educational ideas. Such

discussion had little place inside the NUT associations. As Helen Croxson put it, 'I have never found that I could get my local association of the NUT to discuss really educational questions.'[22] The feminist teachers developed policies and practices on the structures of educational institutions, classroom pedagogy, and curriculum content, all of which were more progressive in outlook than the policies of the NUT or the mainstream Labour Party.

On the desirability of raising the school-leaving age or extending free access to secondary schools for working-class pupils, there was little disagreement between the feminists, the NUT and the Labour Party. However, on the function and provision of nursery education there were greater divisions. The Labour Party's Advisory Committee for Education – a party think tank led by R. H. Tawney – developed a line on educational issues.[23] The best place for a young child, the committee argued, was at home with its mother. Nursery education was seen as a way of compensating for working-class deprivation by offering nurseries which would reflect the ethos of a middle-class home nursery. Such nurseries were intended to: 'send a million children on – clean, intelligent, accustomed to work in a garden ... accustomed to wear nice clothes, to eat and behave politely, well nourished and free of ailments'.[24]

This view was shared by Margaret McMillan of the Independent Labour Party, famous for her work with young children. The school health centre, she wrote, was an 'extension of the Home nursery – no more and no less'.[25] The Labour Party reinforced its view of nurseries as a middle-class institution by its staffing policies. Margaret McMillan shared with the NFWT a view that nurseries should be run by trained teachers but, according to her, the ordinary staff were to be students working without any pay. Indeed those from wealthier backgrounds would be required to pay £30 or £50 a year for the privilege of working in a nursery.[26]

The NUT supported nursery education because of the needs of children attending them. Nurseries 'liberated' children from the coarse habits of the street – and their own homes.[27] The needs of mothers, however, were ignored.

The feminists had a different starting point. The NFWT recognised the relation between the provision of children's education and the domestic burden borne by their mothers. Agnes Dawson, herself an infants teacher, wrote: 'Our first demand is that they must be opened just where they are needed.'[28]

That meant that nursery education was not seen as a form of compensatory education for children from the poorest backgrounds but as desirable for *all* children who needed it. By 1920 the feminists were demanding the compulsory establishment of nursery schools.[29] The demands of young children, Agnes knew too well, exhausted teachers, so she advocated that nurses and paid helpers should provide the necessary assistance to trained staff:

> The babies' class as women would guess, is the very hardest class to teach; the class where teacher must exercise the utmost patience, the utmost tact, the utmost skill, and exert the utmost of nervous energy, and yet she must remain for ever young.[30]

Recognising the strain such an expenditure of energy placed upon staff, the NFWT vigorously campaigned for an earlier retirement age for teachers and improved pensions. As Eleanor Mardon, an NFWT infants teacher from Reading, explained:

> ... the 65 age limit was altogether out of the question, especially for teachers in infant schools, who had to take part in children's games. She would not like to picture herself taking part in Sir Roger de Coverley at such an age.[31]

A feminist analysis was also brought to bear on the question of the amalgamation of Infants and Junior schools and the creation of mixed schools. The institutional structures affected both teachers' employment prospects and the education pupils received. In its early years the NFWT opposed mixed schools: members realised that there would be no promotion prospects for women as headteachers – the jobs would go to men. They also realised that the appointment of one headteacher to run an amalgamated school would increase the workload of that individual, which had previously been shared by two or three headteachers. The feminists also believed that women should teach girls and men should teach boys, because women understood girls' needs better than men. In mixed classes, the argument went, girls would be forced to compete with boys. Boys had educational advantages for they were free from the burden of domestic duties.[32]

However, opposition to mixed schools never became the policy of the NUT and by the 1920s the NUWT, as the NFWT then became, had also toned down its opposition. The feminists realised that such schools were usually set up for reasons of economy rather than to promote progressive practices. Mixed schools did not necessarily provide equal facilities and opportunities:

> In a mixed class the boys received the attention and the girls were not catered for. It was not a moral atmosphere to put a boy or girl into a mixed school with a mixed staff and where the women teachers were not equal to the men's status.[33]

In response, the NUWT adopted as one of its aims that such headships be open to both men and women appplicants.

Montessori and the 'Spirit of Freedom'

Particularly in the field of educational pedagogy the feminists clearly set themselves apart from the NUT at an early stage. The movement for progressive education defined itself against the rote learning of the nineteenth century. It saw education as a process of developing and freeing individual children rather than treating them as an undifferentiated mass. The progressives gained influence outside and inside the teaching profession in the years before the First World War, and they had particular organisational and ideological links with sections of the suffrage movement. The standing conference organised to discuss progressive educational ideas was chaired by the male champion of women's suffrage the Earl of Lytton, brother of Constance Lytton and president of the Men's League for Women's Suffrage.[34] The conference was established with the aim of 'freeing children of the country from useless and cramping restriction and devitalising pressure ... and ... to consider how best to "unfold the latent energy and capacity for good" in every child'.[35]

The feminists organised special education conferences on progressive education and issued pamphlets on individualised learning.[36] Muriel Matters of the WFL gave lectures on the ideas of Montessori for the East London Federation of Suffragettes/Women's Suffrage Federation. A series of explanatory articles also appeared in the WSF press. The WSF organised Montessori demonstration classes as part of its women's exhibition. Children displayed their expertise on apparatus and when the time came for tea they busied themselves 'laying and eating their meal, waiting upon each other, and sweeping up the crumbs when they had finished, without heed to the visitors crowding in to watch them'.[37] One such visitor was Agnes Dawson, who officially addressed the exhibition on behalf of the WTFU.[38] The WSF also provided Montessorian education for children attending the Mothers' Arms nursery under the guidance of Muriel Matters, who described the work in the WSF press.[39]

In addition the WFL organised discussions on Montessori's work, chaired on one occasion by Agnes Dawson. On another occasion it hosted a debate on whether Montessori preached a 'new gospel' in education.[40] The NFWT recognised in Montessori 'the leading exponent of that spirit of freedom which also inspires the activities of this organisation'.[41] The NUT was not so impressed. It derided Montessori's emphasis on learning by doing, and on the child's discovery of concepts through active engagement with practical tasks. As a foreigner and not-a-teacher[42] (a condition to which the NUT was particularly hostile if it happened to express a view on education) her opinions were deemed to count for nothing inside English classrooms. A *Schoolmaster* editorial declaimed: 'How many teachers has

Mde. Montessori seen and how many of these were not Italians?'[43]

The enthusiasm for, or antipathy to, Montessori's ideas grew especially amongst London teachers, to the extent that most teachers were described by a LCC inspector as 'suffering from Montessorimania or Montessoriphobia'.[44] Certainly many NFWT teachers enthusiastically welcomed Montessori's philosophy into their classrooms. Agnes Dawson introduced apparatus for discovery-based learning into the Crawford Street Infants classrooms and in summer organised open-air classes in the nearby John Ruskin park.[45] Conscious of the need to promote individuality in teaching, she addressed NFWT conference thus: 'While children were taught en masse they were brought up more or less like machines; they stood together and sat together, and read and wrote, and recited together, irrespective of individual ability or taste.' Such 'education', she said, might have been good for discipline, but this was only the case if military discipline was sought. The feminist alternative was a development of the individual person and preparation for civic life: 'They should aim at getting an intelligent interest amongst their boys and girls in the problems of literature, nature, and municipal citizenship.'[46]

In her working-class school in King's Cross Theodora Bonwick introduced the Dalton Plan, a version of Montessori's schemes for older pupils. This was a new scheme of individualised learning in which older children, in consultation with their teachers, chose their own areas of work across the curriculum range. Teachers who worked with Theodora Bonwick were impressed by her discouragement of the competitive spirit in lessons and in sport. Children were encouraged to work for the good of all. Her staff believed that Miss Bonwick was a pioneer in the new teaching methods who tried to give the children 'the freedom which she wished to have for herself'.[47] The LCC inspector, Dr Hayward, was decidedly unconvinced of the merits of progressive education, especially in a school catering for 'poorly kept and ill-clad girls'.[48] Even so, he could not fail to be impressed by the 'zealous staff and an enterprising and devoted head teacher'.[49]

An Equal Opportunities Curriculum

The content of the curriculum was also important for the feminists, who introduced ideas from the suffrage movement into the classroom. Emily Phipps wrote a pamphlet for the NUWT on equal opportunities in the curriculum in which she argued that girls did not need a separate curriculum. They needed one which enabled them to have access to privileges enjoyed by boys: increased numbers of scholarships, access to playing fields and swimming facilities for example.[50]

While realising that many girls would have a domestic role, Emily, Agnes and Theodora never accepted that this would be their only role. A curriculum simply based on existing expectations would lead to restrictions in education for girls. Their view was reflected in an article in the independent *Woman Teacher* criticising a Portsmouth councillor who had stated that girls should not be taught maths because they would be dock labourers' wives. The article noted ironically:

> We used to read in our younger days that the fairies did all the work provided we were very, very good. We suggest girls should be taught to be good and no doubt the modern fairies of labour-saving domestic appliances will relieve girls of requiring any education whatsoever.[51]

The NFWT, however, recognised that a broader education for girls could give them increased job opportunities. Emily Phipps, for example, lobbied the Swansea Education Committee to ensure adequate facilities for the teaching of commercial subjects – an expanding area during the war.[52]

The feminists' concept of an equal rights curriculum was epitomised by their approach to sports education. They welcomed increased sport for girls in elementary schools: 'All those women who work to obtain for girls opportunities of sports training equal to those enjoyed by boys are working to bring nearer the day when men and women shall stand together as true mates and real comrades.'[53]

Again, this curriculum initiative had strong links with the suffrage movement. Gymnastics based on anatomy and physiology had been introduced into British schools in the late nineteenth century by followers of Per Henrick Ling, a Swedish proponent. During a holiday course run by the Ling Association, a professional body formed to promote his work, the Gymnastic Teachers Suffrage Society was formed. It campaigned for the franchise, for increasing its number of supporters in the profession and for the protection of the profession from restrictive legislation.[54] Sports opportunities for girls, or rather the lack of them, also had a particular personal significance for some feminists. Agnes Dawson recalled that when she was a child she had had no opportunity to take up sport: 'As a girl she had never learnt to swim for no London bath opened its doors to women, and the most exciting game a school girl ever played was "he".'[55]

From the 1920s NUWT branches campaigned in different ways for extended sports facilities for girls. One branch set up a sports league for girls; another campaigned successfully for increased facilities for girls to learn swimming in the local council baths.[56] By encouraging young women to undertake active sports, feminists were continuing to challenge a passive role for women in society:

Women have given up vapours and megrims for athletics, running and swimming. We demand that women should be paid as workers and not as workers paid as women. We demand equal pay between men and women teachers, because we demand that women teachers should not be paid as women, but as workers.[57]

The influence of debates in the suffrage movement was seen even in the feminists' treatment of traditional 'girls' subjects' like domestic science. The state's framework for domestic science was one which saw it as a necessary skill for maintaining women's sphere in the home. The subject was regarded by the Board of Education as a bulwark against excessively feminist types of training. Only a minority of women, it argued, would work outside the home and thus a curriculum should be focused on motherhood and the home. The alternative would be to encourage 'learned spinsterhood'.[58] By 1910 the Board of Education had outlined in greater detail the curriculum to be followed by older girls in elementary school. All were to study in their later years in school personal hygiene, temperance, home nursing, housekeeping and infant care.[59]

Although the NUWSS did not officially challenge women's roles as homemakers and mothers, some of its members dissented from this view. For example Ada Neild Chew, one of the full-time organisers, bitterly opposed domestic training:

Slaves should break their chains and those who want to be free should help in the chain breaking and not try to rivet the links closer by advocating domestic training for all schools for all girls, fostering in the minds of girls that simply because of their sex they must inevitably some day be ready to cook a man's dinner and tidy up his hearth.[60]

This view was also reflected by working-class socialist women in the Rhondda mining communities of south Wales. When Mrs Snowden, member of the Women's Labour League and wife of ILP member Philip Snowden, visited the area she encouraged the teaching of domestic duties to girls. Her ideas were rejected by the *Rhondda Socialist* which called them:

... an absurd proposal ... a retrograde step ... we have to recognise the fact that the ignorant motherhood of the country arises from the class of neglected, over-worked, over-burdened girl children who have been kept at home to mind the baby and help mother when they ought to have their proper share of mental training, and to have enjoyed free hours for child play.[61]

Drawing comparisons with manual training for boys, the article continued by pointing out that if it had been suggested that boys should learn to carry firewood or coal or imitate the workings of the colliery it would have been apparent that the moves were retrograde.[62]

Debates inside the NFWT and NUT on the role of domestic science in the curriculum reflected the different views found in the suffrage movement. When NUT conference in 1909 debated the merits of mixed schools, much of the argument centred on what was taught to girls in these schools. Isabel Cleghorn, the Conservative executive member, argued that girls in mixed schools did not receive the most appropriate education. She had visited a 'slum school' and seen girls 'who would never rise very high in the social scale' undertaking scientific experiments. Turning to their male teacher she commented first on the state of the dirty floor and said, 'These girls would be better learning how to scrub floors, or how to mend their rags then learning how to make hydrogen.' Every girl, she informed NUT conference, looked forward to being a wife. It was thus far more useful for girls to learn practical subjects than algebra or chemistry.[63]

The subject was also debated at the NFWT fringe meeting at conference in the following year, when papers were given by Selina Dix and Emily Phipps. Miss Dix was a firm advocate of increasing the status of domestic science in schools. Girls should not be taught the subject too early, she argued, or they would regard it as play. Domestic science was intended to prepare girls for their roles as wives and mothers rather than to increase their expectations. Therefore she believed it absurd to teach poor children to use sophisticated equipment they could not possibly afford in later life.[64]

Speaking at the same meeting Emily Phipps set her remarks within a broader context: 'it was necessary to so train girls that they would become proficient and not amateurs at *whatever work* they took up' (my emphasis).[65] Although Emily also accepted that most girls were likely to remain in low-status work or be housewives, she believed that this should not dominate their schooling. Domestic science should not be taught until the end of their school lives. Adopting a similar position to that of the Association of Headmistresses she advocated that half the curriculum be devoted to literary subjects and the rest to practical work including domestic science. Even in her own academic school domestic science was taught.[66]

Theodora Bonwick, however, believed that domestic science training could reinforce a feeling of inferiority in girls:

The girl is taught directly and indirectly that she *is* inferior to the boy: while *he* is free to play in the open, *she* must wash the dishes, mind the baby or even mend *his* socks. In other words, she is trained to be a household drudge and to spend herself submissively attending to the needs of the men-folk, meantime the phrase 'only a girl' is frequently dinned into her ears. (original emphasis)[67]

Agnes Dawson did not oppose the teaching of domestic science but she believed it should not be compulsory. Older girls in continuation schools should be given the same freedom of choice in the subjects they could study as their brothers.[68] The view of Agnes and Emily dominated NUWT thinking on domestic science in later years. In the 1920s the NUWT strongly resisted the Board of Education view that girls should be trained to be efficient wives and mothers. Their emphasis was on preparing girls for a career outside the home. The feminists did not want their pupils wasting time acquiring a smattering of domestic knowledge which they would never need in their future life. Domestic science should be taught, the NUWT argued, to both girls and boys. Boys should study needlework and cookery and girls should study light woodwork 'as a more equal preparation for future life'. Although many pamphlets were produced by the NFWT/ NUWT on curriculum matters, one was never issued on domestic science.[69]

It was not only from the suffrage groups that the feminists drew ideas to which they added their distinctive educational dimension. The work of the feminist morality organisation – the origins of which dated back to the campaigns of Josephine Butler and the Ladies National Association, against the Contagious Diseases Acts – also held a particular significance for the NFWT.[70]

Sexual Morality: 'Our Great Hope is in Education'

There were two broad currents within the social hygiene movement. One was organised around the campaigns of the National Vigilance Association for the reform of male sexuality and the use of legal sanctions to regulate sexual behaviour. The law, according to its secretary William Coote, was 'schoolmaster to the whole community'.[71] The other current was typified by the Association for Moral and Social Hygiene (AMSH), a continuation of Josephine Butler's Ladies National Association.[72] The secretary of the AMSH was Alison Neilans, a Women's Freedom League activist who had been imprisoned for setting fire to ballot boxes as part of the suffrage campaign. The AMSH, with which the feminist teachers worked closely, opposed a legislative response to morality and instead advocated education. Theodora Bonwick was a paid supporter of the Association and of the Women's Alliance of Honour.[73] The AMSH's educational attitude towards moral behaviour was shared by the WFL and NUWSS. As the NUWSS paper *Common Cause* explained: 'Our great hope is in education.'[74]

The National Council for Public Morals (NCPM), formed in 1910, also saw education for young people as the way to promote high ideals in marriage and parenthood. Sex education was advocated as an alternative to criminal law regulation.[75] The NCPM attracted to it campaigners from the moral and medical field, eugenicists, a few feminists and Fabians.[76]

Such morality organisations existed alongside the suffrage groups which also sought to promote, in their own ways, high moral standards. The WSPU supported the NVA's attempts to strengthen the law to raise the age of consent to 18 and to enforce stronger penalties against brothel keepers. This fitted well with the campaigns against male immorality outlined with such force in Christabel Pankhurst's *Great Scourge*.[77]

The NUWSS and WFL had a more liberal attitude. Both were wary of increasing police powers, which could lead to the 'harrying' of working-class women.[78] The WFL and WSF were concerned about the effect of increased legislation against prostitutes which, as experience of the Contagious Diseases Acts had shown, would increase police harassment of women.[79] Sylvia Pankhurst noted that the latest Criminal Amendment Act which was 'passed ostensibly to protect women, is being used almost exclusively to punish women'.[80] She evoked the memory of Josephine Butler's campaigns amongst working-class people to inspire supporters to continue campaigns against similar contemporary legislation.[81]

The feminist teachers tended to support morality campaigns of an educative rather than a legislative nature. This they did outside and inside the classroom. They worked particularly closely with the WFL and WSF during the war against legislation reminiscent of the Contagious Diseases Acts, designed to curb women's sexual behaviour and freedom of movement. Early in the war legislation was enacted for the Portsmouth area ostensibly to prevent the spread of venereal disease by prostitutes. All women were banned from public houses from 7 pm and certain women were banned from being out of the house from 7 pm to 6 am.[82] This regulation was followed by section 40d of the Defence of the Realm Act. It became an offence for women who had caught venereal diseases to have, solicit, or invite sexual intercourse with members of the armed forces and carried a penalty of six months' hard labour.[83]

In her presidential address to the NFWT conference, Emily Phipps expressed her abhorrence at the insult to women embodied in the new regulations. It restricted women's entrance to public houses, she said, on the grounds that women – not men – were responsible for excessive drinking and the unruly behaviour which followed it.[84] The Federation also tried to get the support of the Ladies Committee of the NUT for the campaign for a Commission of Inquiry into legislation on prostitution and venereal disease. It did not succeed. The Ladies did, however, raise their voices against 40d. The regulations, they suggested, were inimical to the best interests of His Majesty's forces. [85]

Of particular concern to the feminists was the attempt to impose different standards of behaviour upon men and women. Like the AMSH, the NFWT supported equal standards of moral behaviour between men and women and their equal treatment by the courts. The Federation worked closely with the AMSH to support legislation aimed at curtailing the activities of men visiting prostitutes, rather than at restricting women prostitutes from their work. Such activity acknowledged that men were capable of controlling and changing their own sexual behaviour, provided the right education was given.[86]

Questions of morality permeated the NFWT's thinking both on the franchise and on an equal rights curriculum. At one fringe meeting at NUT conference, chaired by Agnes Dawson, all speakers emphasised the relation between the franchise and moral and sexual matters. Dr Barbara Tchaykovsky, a London school doctor sympathetic to the East London Federation of Suffragettes, spoke out for a raising of the age of consent as a protection against the impregnation of young women under 18. She also highlighted the peculiar relation of women teachers to the mothers of children in their classes. Mothers often consulted women teachers on many personal matters, and the teachers knew 'that a man can do worse things to his wife without punishment than he can to a woman not his wife'.[87] In the same way that male violence was a part of many women's daily life, so too was opposing it part of the lives of feminist teachers.

While writing a letter one evening to Ethel Froud, Irene Poulter was summoned from her task by the children in the upstairs flat. They were distressed because their father was beating their mother, not an unusual occurrence. She returned to her letter with a P.S.: she had given the man her candid opinion of his behaviour 'to the delight of sundry neighbours and his wife'.[88]

The Federation also opposed degrading images of women on poster hoardings or cinema screens. On the instigation of Miss Widdicombe from West Ham, the NFWT central council advised all its secretaries to approach their local authorities to protest against 'the display of pictures of an immoral, suggestive and terrifying nature'.[89] In addition they believed that children should be prevented from seeing films which were suggestive of immoral or criminal actions. Advertisements for films, described as 'the picture galleries of the poor child', should also be kept free of suggestions of vice, coarseness and brutality.[90]

Sex Education: 'True and Beautifully Worded Knowledge'

It was in the field of sex education in schools, however, that the NFWT led the field nationally. The feminists held classes for teachers, local branches organised talks and the Federation published its own pamphlet.[91] On Theodora Bonwick's instigation the NFWT went to the Board of Education to press for training in sex education to be given to trainee teachers in college so that they could 'deal ... wisely with questions of sex which arise in the course of their daily work'.[92] Training for prospective men and women teachers was not an academic question but, according to Theodora Bonwick, 'a most practical and essential method for safeguarding the health, both physical and moral, of our nation'.[93] The pamphlet produced by the NFWT on sex education reflected the ethos of the National Council for Public Morals. By educating girls their behaviour would be directed away from promiscuity.[94] Teachers, rather than parents, were seen as the appropriate educators; most parents lacked scientific training and could not explain the topic in simple and truthful language. Sex education should be taught as part of the curriculum:

> on an ordinary course, in a proper sequence of lessons with no undue prominence or exaggeration ... dealing with it in this way is in itself a reminder that right conduct is a matter of common interest and is of social importance to the race.[95]

The lessons outlined by the NFWT make strange reading to modern feminists. They were a mixture of homily, religion, science, botany and soap and water cleanliness. The teacher was expected to accept the 'Purity of the Origin of Human Life' complete with capital letters and to be 'zealous to unfold gradually and reverently the Divine Plan of Life and the Divine Laws upholding it'.[96] The emphasis throughout is on sex as reproduction; and the tone is extremely coy. Analogies with plants, birds' eggs and salmon abound. Mother salmon is accompanied on a journey by a father salmon who is obliged to fertilise her eggs:

> This he does by pouring over the eggs on the water a fluid from his body (corresponding to the pollen of the plants) containing what might be called 'half-eggs' which must unite with the 'half-eggs' from the mother's body before these can grow into baby fishes. Can you see now God's great plan for the continuance of the life of the world, and what a wonderful gift this is which God has given us – the gift of handing on life to a future generation?[97]

The pamphlet concludes by reminding girls: 'Our bodies have been likened to a casket containing precious jewels, and if the casket is injured the jewels may be destroyed or lost.' The body should be regarded as the 'Temple of the living God'. A footnote adds – for the teacher's benefit – that a warning could be given at this stage on the dangers of the street and the white slave trade.[98]

Despite its religious and moralising tones the booklet insisted that children of whatever age had a right to knowledge. Teachers were encouraged to answer the questions even of young children: 'If the teacher feels herself unable to answer the questions simply and naturally, she should promise to give the answer at a future time, and keep the promise. Under no circumstances should a child be given an untruth for an answer.'[99]

Theodora Bonwick was a leader of the NFWT's sex education work. She drew up a syllabus which she used in her own school. It emphasised self-awareness and a pupil's right to knowledge. She believed both that sex education should be given in schools and that it should be taught to older pupils as a 'natural and gradual development of [pupils'] ordinary work'.[100] Aligning herself with the anti-regulation faction of the social hygiene movement, she argued that self protection was more effective than 'external protection'. Theodora wrote articles in the *Woman's Dreadnought* and gave talks for the WSF. She stressed that young women adopted unhealthy attitudes to sex because of lack of knowledge. As a result, children were led to view 'the most delicate organs of their bodies as something shameful'.[101] If young people were offered 'true and beautifully worded knowledge' it would protect them from being 'poisoned by ignorance or impurely-minded persons'.[102] Theodora's work was welcomed by ELFS member Mrs Charlotte Drake, who described her own experience of lack of sex knowledge:

> ... I have realised how wrong it is that children should obtain garbled information as I did, and how difficult it is for mothers to teach their children ... nearly all mothers are afraid of this subject. They do not know either how to teach or what to teach their children.[103]

In Miss Bonwick's school the subject only appeared in the curriculum after an explanation was given to and support obtained from parents. Theodora's concern for involving parents in the curriculum reflected the general support the feminists gave to working with parents. As part of her activities on the Care Committee for St Paul's Road school Agnes Dawson had organised meetings for parents to explain its work.[104] In due course such activities with parents led to the establishment of the Parents' National Education Union, in which NUWT members played a leading role in the 1920s. Theodora Bonwick organised meetings for parents at which she explained her intentions regarding sex education. Mothers were presented with alternatives.They could be given information which they themselves could transmit to their children, or they could consent to this being done directly by teachers. The women overwhelmingly asked Miss Bonwick to give such lessons in school. At one such meeting attended

by 120 parents only one raised any objections to the lessons.[105] On
the contrary, many women thanked her for her actions and expressed
the view that it should have been done years before.[106]

Frank Mort has interpreted Theodora Bonwick's attitude to parents
as elitist and one which saw 'local parents [as] morally and intellectually bankrupt'.[107] This misconstrues the *educational* philosophy of
Theodora and her feminist colleagues by simply situating sex education within the discourse of the social purity movement. Parental
involvement was to be invited in sex hygiene as in other aspects of
the school's life, but teachers as trained professionals were more
skilled in this work. There is no evidence that Theodora thought
working-class parents were less moral than their wealthier counter-
parts. The Enfield Road School's catchment area, as defined by the
LCC, was 'a fairly good one [with] little extreme poverty'.[108] Although
Theodora Bonwick believed that the majority of parents – not specifically those of her school pupils – were 'incapable, sometimes morally,
sometimes intellectually, of teaching their own children' it is clear
that she saw parents as essential participants in a sex education programme, in the same way as Agnes Dawson saw parents as essential
participants in nursery education.[109] This stance was echoed more
generally by the feminists in the 1920s. By 1922 parent-teacher guilds
had been formed under their aegis throughout London to bring about
'a closer co-operation between parents and teachers' to 'safeguard'
children's education.[110] Their activities included discussion on education cuts, the use of public libraries, 'things parents should tell their
children', birth control, and the Montessori method. There were also
campaigning successes, including the opening of the children's
reading room of Battersea library all day on Saturday and during the
school holidays, and campaigning for grants for children to continue
their education.[111]

Unfortunately, Theodora Bonwick was very atypical in her beliefs
and practices. When the LCC set up its own commission of inquiry
into the teaching of sex education it found only one school, Miss
Bonwick's, where sex education was taught as an ordinary class
subject.[112] The LCC interviewed many headteachers on their attitudes
to sex education in schools, amongst them Anti-Suffrage Leaguer Mrs
Burgwin who found the subject very difficult to discuss.[113] Some
heads advised talking to pupils individually to 'set them right', or
placing older girls under a 'sensible married woman'.[114] Others
argued that London girls were not ignorant: 'It was not what a girl
said or did in front of her teacher, it was what she did when the
teacher was not there.'[115] The LCC concluded that sex education
should not be taught as a class subject and the LTA concurred with
this view. It believed that

... most teachers are averse from the subject being introduced into the schools ... Important as may be the question of sex hygiene, it sinks into insignificance, in our opinion, beside the need for personal right-eousness and the stiffening of moral character in a materialistic and pleasure-loving age.[116]

Undeterred Theodora Bonwick maintained her proselytising role, writing to the *Schoolmaster* outlining her views.[117] Her attempts to arouse teachers' interest through the NUT paper came to little. A subsequent issue of the *Schoolmaster* contained only one letter in response, from a pessimistic male teacher. 'The number of women who are able to give this instruction "with tact" is infinitesimal', wrote a Mr Lewis, 'while the man who can do it has yet to be born.'[118]

It was such pessimistic adherence to the status quo that epitomised the obstacles which the feminist teachers faced throughout their work. Their activities inside the social hygiene movement had sug-gested to them that it was possible to change people's behaviour – women and men alike – through education. Their work inside the suf-frage movement had shown that it was possible to win support by informing opinion through leaflets, papers and militant activities. Their work inside classrooms had shown them that given the right curriculum girls could achieve. Their experiences of raising support for a progressive curriculum with NUT colleagues, however, mirrored much of the feminists' experience of educating the NUT on the rela-tion between politics and education. Although articulate cases could be made it was difficult to win any significant support for positions from most male colleagues. In the same way that suffrage organisa-tions continued to discuss for several years their attitude to men's role in women's oppression and the nature of women's sisterhood, so too did the NFWT ponder on its work inside the NUT. No decision to work entirely autonomously was taken until feminists were confident in their own ability to campaign and educate public opinion for the good of the cause – irrespective of the NUT's policies.

4

'A Monstrous Injustice to Women'

I find myself utterly at variance with the entire policy of the Executive in its attitude towards women teachers ... in [its] apparently joyful acquiescence, through the pages of the *Schoolmaster*, in local scales of salaries which increase rather than diminish the already existing differences ... I cannot silently consent to what appears to me to be a monstrous injustice to women.

Thus wrote Emily Phipps to the *Schoolmaster* in March 1917. She asked members not to vote for her in the forthcoming NUT elections and pledged that she would use her energies more usefully for women in the future – outside the NUT executive.[1] So vehement are Emily's words, that the anger and disgust they express is easily felt and understood. They provide answers to the question 'why did the suffragettes leave the NUT?' but they do not explain why they remained in the NUT for so long – until 1919 when the NUWT was founded. To understand this we need to look at events outside the NUT.

By the end of the First World War the state had finally acceded to the feminists' demand for the vote – before the NUT had even passed a paltry motion of support for its disenfranchised members. The irony of this was not lost on Emily Phipps when she wrote to Ethel Froud: 'Cheer up. We have got the vote without the "expression of sympathy" from the NUT. That was what I wanted.'[2]

Teachers' living standards meanwhile had dropped drastically, while the war had seen jobs opening up for women outside teaching. During the war there was an influx of women into factory work. Here they received regular employment, relatively good wages and thus an improved standard of living.[3] In contrast, although the ratio of women to men teachers increased, women teachers' wages did not improve. Instead their wages were undercut by unqualified 'guinea girls', classroom assistants taking over the jobs of male teachers at even lower wages that those of qualified women teachers. These were untrained women, barred from entry to the NUT (or NFWT), who worked for small wages in the tradition of supplementary teachers of the nineteenth century. Such women had been employed simply on

63

the production of a smallpox certificate and the approval of a school inspector.[4]

The end of the war weakened women's overall position in the labour market. Many women were sacked from their relatively good factory jobs, with union backing. By March 1918 40,000 women were dismissed from government employment. Yet in some areas women still retained jobs at higher wage levels than before the war. In retailing, catering, finance, commerce and clerical work there was an overall growth in women's employment.[5]

Teaching now had to compete with these alternative jobs for women. Such opportunities undoubtedly attracted many women teachers. By the end of the war Emily Phipps was arguing that women teachers needed equal pay to prevent them leaving teaching altogether.[6] Unlike the NUT, the NFWT and WTFU had maintained their support for better wages for teachers and working conditions *throughout* the war. It was the feminist teachers who held meetings in opposition to war economies and who opposed the introduction of low-paid unqualified teachers by the LCC.

'Laying the Foundation of Social Peace'

The feminists had long realised that it would be a hard fight to win acceptance of their views inside the NUT because of its bureaucratic manoeuvres and opposition to political discussion:

> There is little doubt judging from the tone of the Aberystwyth meetings [NUT conference 1911] that the men of the local associations will fight the [suffrage] motion, and it will take all the enthusiasm and energies of the friends of the feminist movement to carry it through. [7]

What *had* changed were the politics *outside* the NUT. The feminists perceived the granting of the parliamentary franchise at the end of the war as a concession by the state to their political demands. Alongside this political gain the state had also deeply affected the lives of women teachers by giving increased importance to the ideological role of education in ameliorating class conflict within its reconstruction strategy. In the Commission of Inquiry into Industrial Unrest and in the weekly reports to the Cabinet on subversive organisations, the extension of state education as well as its perceived shortcomings were seen as factors in creating a greater political consciousness in areas such as industrial south Wales.[8] Education, in the form of the 1918 Education Act, was to play an important part in the state's strategy of raising 'the social condition of the people' through diffusing class conflict and promoting individual equality of opportunity. As Herbert Fisher, President of the Board of Education, explained to a Cabinet meeting: 'Ignorance is now the enemy: it is only by education of the democracy that we can hope to lay the foundation of social peace.'[9]

Consensus was also to be created by binding teachers closely to the state ideologically. Fisher's view was that the state that valued harmony should begin by making its teachers happy.[10] In order to foster an ideological identification between teachers and the state new structures were created to determine teachers' pay nationally. The Burnham pay agreement comprised local education authorities, the Board of Education, and the NUT.

This state strategy foundered to some extent in that the growth in educational expenditure which national wage rates implied was not endorsed by the Treasury. Proposals for educational expansion and a state/teacher alliance were not backed up by state finance. The 1918 Education Act had envisaged the doubling in real terms of the average wage of teachers.[11] But neither women nor men teachers were to benefit from such proposals against a background of rises in the cost of living by 81 per cent between 1914 and 1924.[12]

'Sex Differentiation in Salary'

In the war years more than ever, the issue of equal pay for women teachers and higher pay dominated NFWT campaigns. The first major pamphlet by the Federation was entitled 'Sex Differentiation in Salary'.[13] It was printed in 1914 – during the same year in which the feminists seemed to have reached an impasse in the NUT on the franchise question. The author of the pamphlet, Helena Normanton, came from outside the Federation's ranks. Miss Normanton was a WFL member and well known in the feminist movement as one of the first women KCs. She was chosen not just because she was a barrister – and therefore an eminent woman in a respected profession – but because the question of equal pay for teachers was not an isolated case but one which affected all women workers irrespective of job or professional status.

The pamphlet outlined economic and ideological reasons why women teachers should receive equal pay and sought to dispel several myths about women teachers. The allegation that women took more sick leave was statistically disproved; the allegation that women had no dependents was refuted by reference to the findings of the Fabian Women's Group. Economic theories were criticised. Ricardo's 'iron law of wages' was exposed as india rubber: when bodies of workers such as miners took strike action and organised, then economic 'iron laws' were bent.[14] Teachers, she argued, should be undeterred by the 'melancholy fallacies of misled philosophers' and should claim their just rewards. Men and women teachers were carrying out valuable work for the state and as such needed financial rewards: 'Now is the golden moment to demand it.'[15]

This argument for equal pay, which focused on the broader role of women's work within the state, was taken up by NFWT members within the NUT. Arguing for the LTA to support equal pay, Agnes Dawson contended that a great deal of the suffering of the masses was brought about by the miserable pittance women generally received for their labours.[16] At the same conferences when the franchise was hotly debated so too was equal pay. At the 1914 NUT conference, Agnes Dawson agreed with reactionary men who hyperbolically suggested male teachers were going the way of the dodo. She added that this process was likely to continue so long as the employer was encouraged by the NUT to exploit women's labour at men's expense. The economic position of women as much as the political one was in need of change.[17]

'Equal Pay Is Not a Good Programme'

By the end of the war the NFWT had decided not even to mount a campaign for a 'yes' vote to equal pay on a referendum run by the NUT executive.[18] This was determined, as Ethel Froud later explained, not because they thought that the vote would be lost but precisely because they thought that even if it were won the NUT would still do nothing: 'We were convinced that *whatever the result*, the NUT would do nothing to make equal pay practical politics, and that, on this question, as on all others, women must work out their own salvation' (my emphasis).[19]

Although political questions had dominated teacher suffrage campaigns they had been closely linked to those of social and economic policy. This perception of the link between political and economic issues was not commonly held within the NUT. Many men, including those who had supported the women's campaign for parliamentary suffrage, sought to separate the two issues. Political questions were different from those on which one negotiated with local education authorities. William Hurden, a suffrage supporter in the LTA, took this view. LTA president for 1892–3, he was an 'old timer' – as he was wont to proclaim in his letters. With a view typical of the middle ground of NUT opinion, he attempted to get the feminists to drop their position on equal pay. He believed both that equal pay was not a good programme for teachers and that women were taking advantage of the absence of male teachers in the war to argue their case:

Equal pay is not a good programme. It might be granted by our enemies in such a way as to do good to no one, and do great injury to large numbers of teachers ... The power of the men is not as great as it was before the war. All the strong and active members have been taken and only the old and comparably feeble left to carry on the work of the Association ... The women teachers of London have great ability, plenty of very good speakers, and a very great majority of votes. They can whenever they like take control of the LTA ...[20]

But the very fact that such views *were* widely held within the teaching profession meant that despite great efforts the feminists never succeeded in converting the LTA to this policy or 'taking it over'. For much of the debate on equal pay there was no difference between the feminists and anti-feminists on the substance of the argument. Women crowded into one profession, William Hurden and his colleagues complained, forced down salaries. The feminists did not disagree – they also were conscious of the way in which women could be used as cheap labour, undercutting the wages and employment of men teachers. Speaking as president at the 1916 NFWT conference, Emily Phipps recognised that an influx of women into jobs traditionally carried out by men represented a great danger to male workers. Cheap labour would inevitably oust dear labour – unless equal pay was won.[21]

The NFWT arguments for equal pay linked economic demands with educational questions and appeals to natural justice. In a leaflet introducing a deputation to the LCC the London NFWT made these points eloquently: 'The hours of work are equally long and arduous and the difficulties and responsibilites are as great ... The education of girls and younger children are as important as that of boys and of equal value to the community.'[22] Time and time again they based their arguments on the job done rather than on the sex of the teacher doing it. Rejecting the idea of women's separate sphere, the NFWT in turn rejected the view that women should get particular and different consideration based on their sex. They found support for this view outside the teaching unions from trade unionists such as Herbert Elvin of the Clerks Union, and from the Vehicle Workers Union.[23]

There was also support from some men inside the NUT who understood that equal pay would put an end to low wages for all teachers and who accepted the argument of the 'rate for the job'. Nefydd Roberts, for example, the leader of the unemployed teachers in the London pre-war campaigns urged colleagues to support equal pay to stop low wages for *all* teachers and the consequent elimination of men from schools.[24]

Much of the hostility to the idea of equal pay was rooted in ideological opposition to an independent career for women. The ideas which had been promoted by the Anti-Suffrage League on the political role of women continued to be expressed and were to find new expression in the NUT in the work of the National Association of

Men Teachers. By the 1920s the most reactionary of these men teachers had broken off to form the NAS precisely over the NUT's 'support' for equal pay. According to these men, the *NUT* was a feminist union and as such the NUT (as well as the feminists) should be bitterly opposed. Using the Anti-Suffrage League arguments for a separate sphere for women, these men emphasised the domestic role of women and suggested that women's role was entirely subordinate to that of men. When the men started to organise their own grouping in the NUT, prior to quitting the union altogether, the Women's Freedom League produced literature specifically to counter their arguments. To the men's lament that 'the cry of equal pay' was growing rapidly and that it was in men's interests 'to fight it tooth and nail', the feminists countered: 'It is as much a man's interest as a woman's to fight for it tooth and nail.' To the men's view that equal pay would mean more for women teachers, less for men, and men working for women's wages, the feminists retorted: 'It would mean more for women teachers, no undercutting of men: Are women prepared to work for less wages than men?'[25]

Feminist Democracy: Bureaucratic Obstruction

Although it proved easy to maintain a united public opposition to such tirades, it was less easy for the feminists to uphold an agreed strategy about how to campaign against such hostility. The alliance of women from different suffrage organisations – Agnes Dawson in the NUWSS, Theodora Bonwick and Ethel Froud in the WSPU, Emily Phipps in the WFL – could comfortably agree on the necessity for propaganda and agitation on the suffrage position inside the NUT, even though their respective organisations had fierce disputes. More difficult to sustain was agreement on the continuing involvement of the women inside a union whose obduracy confronted them at every turn.

Matters came to a head, in London at least, over the way the London Teachers Association conducted its business. As the establishment had reacted to the suffrage question, so too did it respond to equal pay: the matter should not be discussed. A motion in favour of equal pay was ruled out of order. Led by Agnes Dawson, Theodora Bonwick and Nancy Lightman the NFWT and WTFU conducted a campaign to get the LTA to support equal pay. This campaign developed alongside that on suffrage; it had gained momentum in the Autumn of 1912 at the LTA annual general meeting.[26] At the 1916 national NUT conference Clare Neal was also ruled out of order for trying to propose a motion from the Swansea Association supporting equal pay.[27]

The feminists, however, started to become skilled in the bureaucratic practices of the NUT. Subsequently the women called, according to the rules, special meetings of the whole London membership to discuss making equal pay an official part of the LTA's constitution. Hundreds of women – and men – from all over London packed such meetings to discuss feminist politics in heated fashion. Attendance was so great that even the big meeting halls of the day – the Memorial Hall in Farringdon Street and the Essex Hall – were packed with teachers keen to debate radical policies. Evening meetings ran on to after 11 pm and were then adjourned only to be reconvened another day. All-day Saturday meetings were also called and were well attended.

It is often difficult to conjure up moods of meetings from verbatim reports in union journals. However the *London Teacher*, with its conscientious reporting of hecklers' comments, helps convey an atmosphere both of excitement and sharply divided opinion. Charles Hicks Bolton – with the backing of the NFWT/WTFU – moved the equal pay motion at one such meeting at 10 o'clock at night. He received cheers and applause; his chief opponents – William Hurden, he of union longevity, and G.D. Bell, a fellow member of the ILP – were greeted with cries of 'shame'.[28]

The atmosphere at meetings was fiercely acrimonious and often became litigious. It was clear that the feminists were just as tenacious as their reactionary male opponents. At first sight their tenacity seems to have paid off. The vote supporting equal pay was won – after four adjourned annual general meetings had debated it – by 377 votes to 209.[29] But the feminists were less experienced in the manoeuvres of union politics than the men. Within a *week* of the vote the LTA committee conducted a referendum designed expressly to overturn the democratically decided position on equal pay. Wording the referendum question carefully to characterise the feminists as upstarts reversing long-considered salary policy, they achieved success. The policy, so hard fought for over many months, was overturned by a 2 to 1 majority.[30]

This war of attrition reached another climax when the LTA establishment was unable to cope any longer with late-night meetings and the constant politicisation of what they considered to be simply educational debate. The rulebook, by which the feminists had gauchely operated, was torn up and rewritten by an unconstitutional body. Henceforth the mass meetings at which the feminists had received so much support would be scrapped. No longer would there be quarterly meetings open to all the thousands of London members. Policy would be decided exclusively by the LTA committee – on which Agnes Dawson (but not Theodora Bonwick or Nancy Lightman) sat – and which was controlled by men and women teachers opposed to the 'cause'.

The involvement of the union membership in democratic decision-making was an important element in the feminists' campaigns; mass meetings provided both an arena for their policies and an opportunity for women to engage in politics. To mass meetings, the LTA officers counterposed plebiscites (or referenda) – the tactic they had used to quash resolutions supporting the franchise or equal pay. Agnes Dawson argued in opposition that 'when the time arrived that they could not get the whole of their members into the Albert Hall ... she would go for a plebiscite'.[31] The women were astounded at the officers' flouting of the rules – curtailing the mass meetings without any constitutional backing – and the feminists took their case to court. The case was in the name of Charles Hicks Bolton, the original mover of the successful and overturned equal pay motion. He had been chosen, according to Agnes Dawson, because of the prejudice against the suffragists in the courts. The feminist teachers' own public prominence would probably ensure unsympathetic treatment despite the merits of their case.[32] Their tactic seemed to work. Judgement was given and costs were awarded against the LTA officers. They were forced by the courts to do what the feminists had wanted, namely to call a mass meeting at least to discuss their rule changes.

The meeting was advertised for a Saturday, in London's largest concert hall, the Royal Albert Hall, starting at 11 am. Three thousand members of the union turned up, some as early as 9 am, to discuss the rule changes until the late afternoon. According to the *Schoolmaster* Theodora Bonwick made 'what was undoubtedly the speech of the day'.[33] She argued that the general meetings held quarterly should determine policy rather than referenda. This would ensure the 'right control over policy'. Nancy Lightman reiterated the point made by Agnes Dawson at a previous meeting – that when the Albert Hall could no longer contain members, then would be the time to hold referenda. Members could easily find seats and 'direct self government was better and more democratic than government by proxy'.[34]

The feminists – and democracy – again won the day. Indeed this was one of their achievements that lived on in union practice, for it was not until 1979 that the successor to the LTA, the Inner London Teachers Association, finally prevented the membership from attending and voting at the decision-making annual general meetings.[35]

The women also paid a price for incensing the establishment and winning. The election for the 1913 LTA committee was fiercely contested and many leading London teachers were defeated: Theodora Bonwick in Finsbury; Miss G.E. Johnson, former NFWT national president, in Deptford; Nancy Lightman in Hackney; Mrs Elizabeth Tidswell (Agnes' sister) in Hammersmith; Mrs H. Samuel in Lambeth and Agnes Dawson and Miss L.E. Lane in Southwark. Two years before, just prior to the first discussion of suffrage politics in the national union, Agnes Dawson had topped the local poll. Now she was not even on the committee. Nearly two-thirds of the London membership had voted: an increase on previous years. But in the whole of London only 26 women had been elected compared to 91 men. Of these women, only a handful could be relied upon to uphold the 'cause'.[36]

The LTA establishment was still unable to defeat the feminists' spirit. Although the women were temporarily removed from the LTA committee in 1913 they stood again in the following year. In 1914 Agnes Dawson contested the important position of vice-president and, although she lost, polled over 3,000 votes. When an executive by-election was called they fielded a candidate and lost to G.D. Bell, who had opposed equal pay. Undeterred, the same candidate, Miss A.K. Williams, stood again in the next full round of executive elections and was elected. Agnes Dawson also stood for the executive in London in 1916 and 1917 but was not successful.[37] At this stage Agnes Dawson, Theodora Bonwick and other leading London members were not arguing for an autonomous union; they had not yet proved to themselves that they could succeed in such a project. Instead they continued to work in the union, putting forward motions and standing for office. In 1915 Emily Phipps was returned unopposed, on her third attempt, as one of the members for the executive area of Wales. She kept her position for only one year. By 1915 nine of the 37 executive seats were held by women. These were not all NFWT active members but certainly it was the caucusing and political climate created by the feminists which led to their election. Such numbers of executive members did not, of course, reflect the number of women in union membership at the time. Women then – as now – were in the majority. However, such was the influence and organisation of the suffragettes (and the sexism of the NUT) that no higher proportion of women has been elected since.[38]

But discontent and exasperation was growing inside the Federation. Nationally the cumulative effect of a number of issues over a period of several years led to discussions about the feminists' relationship with the NUT. Progressive motions passed by local associations did not reach conference agendas. Delegates urged to vote for the women's cause ignored their mandate. A series of small and undemocratic manoeuvres undermined the feminists' campaigns. Increasingly aware of these bureaucratic games the Federation denounced them with force and a certain exaggeration. To Emily Phipps the manoeuvres were not the routine antics of trade union bureaucrats opposing grassroots campaigns but 'illegalities' specifically directed against the feminists.[39] It is surely a measure of the feminists' strength and perceived threat that these measures had to be used against their message. It had not been necessary for officers to call special meetings to overturn democratic decisions or to 'lose' voting papers or fail to send in nominations when the Federation was first founded.[40]

Agnes Dawson and Emily Phipps, viewed such tactics with intense anger. Emily kept a notebook in which she noted down the 'illegalities' she found inside the NUT. Both expressed their views forcefully in *The History of the NUWT*. They remembered with intensity the details of their actions and their feelings at the time. It was the feminists' political *and* professional integrity that was being undermined.

The Effects of the War

The economic effects of the First World War played a more significant part in severing the NFWT from the NUT than any ideological distancing of the women from the NUT's patriotic stance. It is significant, though, that while some feminist organisations 'shut up shop' for the duration of the war the NFWT continued to campaign for general adult franchise, equal pay and equal opportunities. In contrast, the WSPU suspended all its activities to support the war.[41] Like the WSPU, the NUWSS also suspended all political activity in August 1914 and members were urged to help the victims of 'economic and industrial dislocation caused by the war'.[42] The WFL continued its campaigns.

Ethel Froud, Theodora Bonwick and other WSPU teachers continued their political activity throughout the war. Theodora worked on sex education with the East London Federation of Suffragettes/ Women's Suffrage Federation which vigorously opposed the war. She also organised campaigns against war economies and their effects on education in schools and opposed the employment of the unqualified 'guinea girls'.[43] Agnes Dawson successfully moved a motion at the 1916 LTA conference that new supplementary teachers would only be tolerated during the war after all available qualified teachers had been employed. Theodora Bonwick strengthened this motion by adding that such workers should not be given the title of teacher but of 'helper'.[44] On first consideration this seems to be merely an act of professionalism. However, the feminists supported unqualified teachers who wanted to obtain certificates. In Swansea the Federation supported a teacher's campaign for backdated pay for her classroom experience after she had obtained her certificate.[45] The issue here was that the feminists had often worked hard to achieve a position which in itself was poorly paid. They did not want this threatened further by wage-cutting untrained workers.[46]

Agnes Dawson deplored the economic and ideological effects of the war, which she blamed for a reactionary climate:

Reaction runs riot anywhere, everywhere, and the excuse is the war ... There is another war, one that is being fought always ... a war against power, power to keep low the already lowly; power to throw dust in the eyes of a gullible public ...[47]

She advocated a 'revolution writ large without blood' which would be achieved through educational and housing reforms to benefit the new generation.[48] She opposed militarism and objected that heroes of war were glorified while the heroes and heroines of peace were forgotten.[49] Her views on the war put her in a minority on the NFWT central council. When members were asked to protest at a teacher forced to resign because of her political activity outside teaching, she was one of only three members to propose sending a letter defending teachers' liberty of thought and action.[50] Similarly, when the NFWT was asked to sign a general petition protesting against teachers being penalised for their views on the war, the council took no action.[51]

The Women's International Congress was held in the Hague in 1915. It called for international disputes to be settled by means other than war. It was supported by several WFL members, Helena Normanton among them. The sole NFWT supporter named was Mrs Stanbury, a future London president of the NUWT.[52] However, there is no evidence that as a Federation the women adopted a jingoistic position. Motions at London NUT meetings that saluted the contribution of teachers to the armed forces were not moved by the feminists.

Emily Phipps, like Theodora Bonwick, opposed the effects of war on women. In her presidential address to the 1915 NFWT conference she criticised the DORA regulations as an insult to women and opposed the class effects of war on children.[53] Children in elementary schools were obliged to work to bring in the harvest: those at Eton and Harrow were not. With her WFL colleagues Emily insisted that campaigns for equal pay and political rights should continue during the war.[54] On internationalism, however, Emily was less progressive. She uttered anti-Kaiser rhetoric – and a distinctive feminist line. On Empire Day she described to her pupils the horror of Britain under German rule. She catalogued German attitudes to women and the Kaiser's view that women should confine their attention to children, church and kitchen: 'He forgets that there are women who though paying attention to these very important things in our lives have room for other interests as well.' Her call for self-sacrifice to beat the Germans had the desired effect on the assembled young women who concluded the proceeedings with 'a fervent rendering of the National Anthem'.[55]

If the *Daily Mail* reportage is to be believed she continued to utter anti-German diatribes after the war, in her campaign for a parliamentary seat. She met women who

blaze when they talk about the Huns ... As for the Kaiser, they invent
punishments for him, but confess that they cannot think of anything
bad enough. I entirely agree, for I have read many German books about
the war and am convinced that Germany deliberately planned it.[56]

It must have been evident to the feminist teachers that to attempt to
agree upon an NFWT position on the war – the same issue which had
split the suffrage movement – would be unproductive, if not
impossible.

The War Aid Fund

It was one small public difference with the NUT on a war-related issue
that proved decisive in breaking feminists from the NUT. The NUT
had set up a War Aid Fund at the start of the war to provide sums of
money for teachers or their dependants affected by the war. This was
primarily for the families of teachers killed or injured in action. All
union members were urged to contribute equally to the fund. Women
applying to the Fund for assistance, however, were denied equal payments with men. In essence this was a rerun of the issue raised over a
decade before by Miss Lane when she successfully challenged discriminatory payments to men and women through the union's
benevolent fund.[57]

Although local NUT associations had been sharply divided before
on the franchise and on equal pay, attitudes to the War Aid Fund
were the final straw for some. In Tottenham opinion was polarised.
The association included Charles Crook, the Conservative NUT
national president in 1916, and several feminist teachers. Mary Sims,
the NFWT local secretary, described the situation to Ethel Froud: 'We
have got our men's backs really up very high (the first time in
Tottenham) over the refusal of our women to contribute.'[58]

Many women were seriously discussing refusing to pay a NUT levy
for the first time in their membership.[59] At the same time the local
Tottenham NUT committee had passed a motion supporting equal
pay. Pressure was on Crook, the executive member: 'On Tuesday ...
Mr Crook comes to his home Association and I think he will get a
warm reception. The women will not vote for him on the executive –
that I feel sure about.'[60]

It is the tone of such correspondence as much as its factual content
which best illustrates the mood of the times. This is not the letter of
the tired activist bemoaning the number of tedious meetings she
must attend. It is a letter to a friend, full of enthusiasm and energy
written about something that the author feels affects her life deeply.
Such strength of feeling led the feminists to establish their own charitable fund, the Mutual Aid Fund, as a counter to the NUT's venture.

'I Want You to Bring in Secession'

By 1917 the NFWT had clashed with the NUT on a number of questions: the franchise and equal pay, combined departments, progressive education, democratic discussions and decision-making, and the War Aid Fund. With this record of conflict it was not surprising that there were public and private debates on whether the feminists should stay inside the NUT. Debates also took place about the relationship between the Federation and women members on the NUT executive. The NFWT set its central council meetings to clash with NUT executive meetings, thereby ensuring that feminists had to choose to whom they gave their allegiance.[61]

No longer were women NUT executive members given pride of place at Federation meetings: that honour had to be earned. Those women executive members who were only nominal supporters of the Federation at election time were dealt with sharply. They were respected for their record, not their status. True to the WSPU maxim of 'deeds not words' Ethel Froud explained to members that the fact that women were on the NUT executive was not enough:

> It is also our policy to require more than promises, we also desire to know what a candidate has done or tried to do to further our interests ... Most of the women on the executive have done little or nothing to establish the principle of equal pay – according to our point of view. [62]

Emily Phipps, with her first-hand experience of the executive Ladies Committee, was even more scathing. She had heard that in Manchester Miss Woods, facing re-election, was suggesting that support for equal pay, as national NUT policy, was gaining ground because of her own role. Castigating her as an opportunist, Emily raged: '[she] never spoke for equal pay at a single conference, but now, when it is in the air, comes out and "leads", *again* to get votes. But the Manchester women are hoodwinked. It is a ruse against the Federation.'[63]

Signs of disengagement were evident on small but cumulatively significant issues. In February 1915, with no dissent, the NFWT central council declined to produce leaflets recruiting teachers to the NUT, although one of its constitutional objects, known as object E, was to encourage such recruitment.[64] Some members carried out grassroots organisation in earnest to alter this object. Emily Phipps was in the forefront of this campaign. Part of her plan involved persuading Ethel Froud to come to Swansea to meet other members and win them over to the correctness of this position:

> I want you to bring in *secession from the NUT* not *calling* it that, necessarily. Reason – two of our *best* Federationists, headmistresses,

with influence, still believe in working through the NUT. I want to get them here to tea when you come, for you to talk to them. I have done all I can and so has Miss Neal (She has come round to our views during this year). Now, don't forget all this, there's a dear creature. (originally triple underlinings)[65]

The methods of persuasion – the invitation to tea, the select group, the important 'outside' luminary – indicate her political tactics. They also show that even the winning over of a couple of individual members was important in the internal debates of the organisation. It is also clearly suggested that these women had influence because of their professional standing, rather than because of holding Federation or union office. The status they had acquired in their career was an integral part of their political importance. It was, no doubt, due to the effect of such 'teas' nationally that the 1918 NFWT conference went on to drop the object and to institute further measures of autonomy.

' A New Heaven and a New Earth'

The achievement of the vote did show, so the NFWT thought, that the state was willing to accede to feminist demands provided there was a campaign. Many feminist teachers now thought that equal pay for equal work was only a step away. Change was possible, they believed, in their relationship to the state. This may seem naive when we read with the benefit of hindsight. However, such a mood was neither unique nor confined to teachers. Education was seen by the mainstream of the trade union and labour movement as a way of transforming society and of increasing individuals' opportunities within that society. Commenting on the popular response to the 1918 Education Act, Fisher, President of the Board of Education, said: 'For the first time in our national history education was a popular subject ... large audiences were attracted to educational meetings.'
He recalled a particular Sunday meeting of Bristol dockers called to discuss the legislation.

I have never encountered such enthusiasm ... the prospect of wider opportunities which the new plan might open to the disinherited filled them with enthusiasm. Alas! for these good folk they expected from an education bill what no bill on education or anything else can give, a new Heaven and a new earth.[66]

The sense of a dynamic of change present within the NFWT at this time was a reflection of the broader political mood. Although the politics are not the same, the mood of change mirrors that present in the industrial struggles of Red Clydeside and the support for the Russian Revolution in sections of the labour movement. It was a view that change was possible and that the oppressed, whether they were women teachers, leaders of the shop stewards movement or delegates to the founding conference of the Communist Party, were the people who could take action for themselves to achieve it. This was a new situation for revolutionaries, reformists and feminists. It was *this* mood which made the NFWT and WTFU join forces, take militant union action against the LCC, and – in due course – leave the NUT. It was a confidence in their own strength that led to this decision, it was not simply a defeatist gesture which accepted that the NUT would never listen to the feminists' demands.

'Wifehood and Motherhood'

The 1918 NUT conference did pass a motion on equal pay, but not on feminist terms. An amendment was passed which linked equal pay directly to adequate provision for 'wifehood and motherhood'. Equal pay was not related to the job of teaching but to the sex of the teacher. Even this weakened policy was not passed intact. The conference agreed on the recommendation of 'left' delegates W.G. Cove and J. Corlett to refer the whole issue to a membership referendum. The procedure the women had met in the LTA was now being used nationally to undermine even this weak policy.[67] The same procedure had been used to deal with attempts of the left-wing Teachers Labour Group in 1917 when it had tried to win the NUT to TUC and Labour Party affiliation. Although the group generated much grassroots support, even from former Conservative teachers, the proposal was defeated by a 2 to 1 vote in a referendum of the whole membership.[68]

In April 1918 the NFWT debated whether to organise a campaign inside the NUT for a yes vote in the referendum on equal pay. With only two votes in favour the central council voted to have nothing to do with such a campaign. By the time this decision was taken, many leading members had already resigned from the NUT. In Swansea Emily Phipps had herself resigned and urged other NUT members to withold their current subscriptions until salaries improved and resign in the meantime. In retaliation the NUT was threatening legal action.[69] Agnes Dawson did not stand for NUT conference in 1918 and never again attended. Whatever the outcome of the equal pay policy voted there, the NUT would do nothing, she was convinced, to implement the policy. Agnes and the NFWT were again proved right.

The absence of NFWT members from the 1918 NUT conference was noticed and welcomed by the NUT bureaucracy. No reference to women's business meetings or fringe NFWT meetings appears in the *Schoolmaster*. With glee Isabel Cleghorn wrote in the NUT paper that the passing of the equal pay motion would give an answer to those women mistaken enough to say 'we will not play in your yard any longer.'[70] The NUT leadership did not hide its relief that it no longer had to answer the feminists' political and economic arguments. The women who had been at the conference were of a different political persuasion and could be easily won over by the NUT leadership. An editorial on the conference noted the attitudes of women members:

> The burning question of equal pay, no matter how strongly they felt upon it, did not set fire to the links between them and the union ... We trust that with the Cambridge conference begins a new period of general and non-sectional effort by members of the union, those who favour joining a particular political party co-operating with those who do not, and women in favour of 'equal pay' adhering to the union line none the less while labouring towards better pay for all. We hope that the period of denunciation and recrimination is over ...[71]

At the 1918 conference equal pay was passed but not on feminist lines; the results of the referendum on TUC/LP affiliation were announced and the socialist Teachers Labour Group defeated. Two progressive strands had lost ground in different ways inside the NUT.

Breaking from the London Teachers' Association

Irrespective of national NUT conference decisions equal pay policy counted for little in local negotiations. By the end of the war the LTA had endorsed equal pay both through general meetings and even through a referendum of the membership.[72] The LCC had offered a differential pay award: the LTA had accepted it. The NFWT did not endorse this. The outcome was explained by the press thus: 'Men class teachers ... obtained practically all that they asked, while the 12,000 women teachers received little or nothing.' [73]

The LTA had agreed to a £1 a week 'war bonus' from the LCC which did nothing to prepare the way for a new structure of teachers' pay based on equal pay. The LTA officers argued that independent action – which the NFWT was to undertake – would undermine possibilities of improving pay and conditions in the future. It is evident that the LTA's idea of a 'permanent improvement of the position and status of the teacher' took precedence over the realisation of equal pay for equal work. To the LTA conditions, status and pay were separate issues. To the feminists status, pay and justice were inextricably linked in their strategies.[74] In the same editorial in the *London Teacher* the officers made a concerted attempt to divide the NFWT/WTFU from 'ordinary' women teachers. Castigating the NFWT as extremists it argued: 'We believe [sic] that the majority of women teachers will not sacrifice the men.'[75] The tirade was the first of many over months and years to come. Divisions were growing, with many women not renewing NUT membership. The LTA uttered appeals to unity in increasingly hostile tones. Such hostility stemmed, in part at least, from the type of action being organised by the NFWT.

A petition of 10,000 signatures seeking equal pay was collected from London teachers within four days.[76] It called for the LCC to go to arbitration on the starting salary for women teachers and for an immediate improvement in women's wages. It reminded councillors that many women teachers would be unable to take any summer holiday unless there was some salary improvement. Appended to the petition was a 'typical balance sheet' indicating expenditure for a typical young teacher. It gives insight both into their poor wages and their lifestyle:

Salary £94 and £20 16s War Bonus

	£	s	d
Board and Lodging	68	8	0
Train fares for school in East End	5	7	8
Train fare to Scotland in August	4	10	0
Incidental train & bus fares & country excursions	3	8	0
Clothes (1 costume, materials for hats, part-payment for rainproof coat, shoes, repairs, gloves, hosiery, handkerchiefs etc) (All underwear & other necessities supplied by parents)	14	3	0
Toilet necessities (soap, tooth powder etc)	1	1	0
Medical attendance	1	0	0
Superannuation	2	8	0
Subscriptions (Aspirants' club, Tennis club, LTA, NFWT, War Subscriptions & other charities)	4	15	6
Stationery and stamps	2	7	3
Literature & newspapers (several given up now)	2	3	0
	109	11	1

Balance: £5.4.7 or 2/- a week to be spent on holidays, lectures, concerts, hobbies etc. No reserve fund for sickness.[77]

The leaflet further suggested that a boarding house of a good type could only be afforded if four women teachers shared a room, sent all their laundry home and received food parcels. Discounting the excesses of propaganda this shows how women teachers' demands were rooted as much in their economic circumstances as in their political convictions. Assuming the petition of 10,000 signatures was signed by teachers alone, it represented about 80 per cent of London women teachers and a majority of the whole workforce. It also indicates the strength of grassroots organisation which must have existed in schools. Subsequently Ethel Froud busied herself organising a demonstration of thousands of women teachers in Trafalgar Square against the LCC's pay offer and against the employers' refusal to go to arbitration. Appalled by the pay offer Ethel Froud argued: 'Women who have passed a severe educational test get less than omnibus girls, munition workers, or clerks in Government offices. They get less than many domestic servants.'[78]

Creating the 'Strike Spirit'

The feminists held a mass meeting in Trafalagar Square and voted to take strike action if the pay issue was not resolved satisfactorily. Then Agnes Dawson got backing from the central council of the NFWT. The council agreed to set up immediately a sustentation fund to be used in conjunction with a 'strike policy'. They agreed to prepare themselves 'at any time direct action becomes necessary'.[79] Outside inner London some members were also anxious to take industrial action to bring home the argument. In Leyton the Labour councillors ignored the women's demands. Miss Grinter, the local secretary, wanted to organise strike action. Ethel Froud wrote to her explaining the problems:

> We must have more funds, but this sort of thing [unsympathetic stance of councillors] will help to create the strike spirit in the women for the 'next time'. My idea is a big concerted action in the London and Extra-Metropolitan district. I wish we could do it today: if we could, we could win, but the women are so timid and constitutional ... I do trust the women will leave the NUT. If they don't see how what their membership of that body does for them then there is no hope for them at all.[80]

I think it would be wrong to describe the central council's decision or Ethel Froud's response simply as the rhetoric of a union bureaucracy. If there had been a strike, it would have been organised by an under-funded union not yet out of its fledgling stage. There was no history of industrial action in the teachers' unions. It is true that the Teachers' Socialist Association and then the Teachers' Labour Group had tried to organise interest in the ideas of trade union organisation and LP affiliation but such campaigns were seen as separate from industrial action by teachers. The actions that had taken place were geographically disparate, since teachers were employed on different wages, contracts and conditions, depending on whichever local education authority employed them.[81] In several localities links were made with other trade unions and class teachers' associations affiliated to local trades councils. On occasion expressions of solidarity were given to workers in the struggle. Funds were raised, for example, for the children of the Dublin transport workers in 1913.[82] When such issues were discussed at the NUT executive, though, or in the pages of the *Schoolmaster* there was no suggestion from any quarter that teachers take sympathetic industrial action. Their support was of a philanthropic kind, centred on the children.

That the NFWT and women teachers considered the strike tactic at all in this period is significant. Even without strike action the *Times Educational Supplement* felt it appropriate to state that the LCC should refuse 'to be bullied by the women teachers.'[83] The women continued to lobby the LCC education committee meetings and this too was unusual for teacher unions. On one occasion the NFWT organised 2,000 women for such a lobby after school.[84]

The NFWT did have some success without having to resort to strike action. The LCC – much to the annoyance of the LTA officers – did withdraw its discriminatory salary scales, for the time being.[85] But the LCC also refused to go to arbitration on a future scale. The LTA denounced them, using the fact that arbitration – which the women wanted – did not happen *and* that the NFWT did not organise industrial action: 'We have no desire to push our advantage further. We will not taunt the women with their change of policy, nor comment on the amazing record of misleading statements and declarations which their leaders have made ...'[86]

The excitement and exhaustion of those days must have reminded the feminists of their earlier suffrage campaigns. Indeed the mass meetings in Trafalgar Square, the petitioning and the lobbying were exactly the same sorts of action the suffrage groups had organised and the teachers had supported.

As the only full-time organiser/secretary Ethel Froud was worn out. Writing to express her concern Emily Phipps asked: 'Are you nearly dead? I know you are. I think the next thing we must do is appoint an organiser ...'[87] Nationally the feminists established an office fund. They hired a suite of rooms and staff. A part-time typist was employed. Adelaide Jones left her teaching post in West Ham to become treasurer. The yearly subscriptions were raised to 2/- and branches organised events to raise funds.[88]

'A Distinct Severance'

By the autumn of 1919 the NUT had also endorsed a new structure for determining elementary teachers' salary scales *nationally* (the Burnham scale). Within this, no woman teacher whatever her qualifications or experience would ever receive more than four-fifths of a male teacher's salary on the same grade. The Federation was excluded from Burnham. Only the NUT was recognised by the Board of Education and the four women NUT representatives on the committee all voted for differential payments. The Burnham Inquiry had established that, although teachers should be paid on the same national salary scale wherever they taught, they should continue to be employed by local authorities. An 'alliance' would be formed of the Board of Education, local education authorities and the NUT, meeting in a body to negotiate pay rises. To this arrangement the NUT willingly acceded: it would offer them recognition of their professionalism and help teachers in rural areas where union organisation was weak and wages low. All this was agreed just months after the referendum on equal pay had been endorsed by the NUT membership. The LTA had also accepted a differential pay scale despite the national policy. As the NFWT had predicted the policy on equal pay had been won but nationally, as well as locally in London, the NUT would not lift a finger to see it implemented.

The situation was just as severe outside London. In Swansea Emily Phipps, as local NFWT secretary, organised a petition to the local education authority to urge the Board of Education to allow LEAs to pay higher salaries for teachers in their own areas.[89] It was signed by 350 women teachers. The NUT had organised no protest. Emily wrote to Ethel explaining:

> We are bound to make a splash over this, as the NUT is straining every nerve; they have called a meeting for Friday – their secretary is in London fighting for them; I hope to call a meeting for Thursday ...[90]

The straining of the nerve came to nothing. The following week Emily briefed Ethel:

> That shows what our NUT is (not) doing. They won't divulge what they decided last Friday, and have refused information to the Press; as there is no action possible other than Parliament, that means they are hiding *nothing* in a cloud of mystery. (original emphasis)[91]

Parliamentary action is mentioned here as the only possibility because it was Parliament, rather than the local authority, which had established Burnham and agreed pay rates throughout England and

Wales. In many other areas too, differential payments and wage cuts were agreed by the NUT and then proclaimed by the local NUT leaderships as a victory.[92] By the end of the same year an editorial in the *Schoolmaster* was castigating NFWT members as 'wildest Amazons' and 'fierce Hippolytas' because of their advocacy of equal pay, supposedly the *NUT's* own policy![93]

It was inevitable in such circumstances that the NFWT would draw further away from the NUT. The feminist teachers had seen the enactment of the Representation of the People Act and the Sex Disqualification (Removal) Act for which they had campaigned during so many years. They had proved to themselves, to other teachers and to local education authorities that they were quite capable of organising lobbies, leafleting, mass meetings and petitions. These were forms of militant action which had been adopted by the trade union and suffrage movement alike. By continuing to advocate such tactics the feminists were not only organising as a union but were carrying through the politics and organisational methods of the suffrage movement. A joint meeting of the London NFWT and the WTFU agreed to join forces as the London Unit of the Federation and 'to concentrate their energies upon their own organisation'.[94]

In September 1919 the Federation issued its own paper, the *Woman Teacher* with Emily Phipps as editor, with the call to establish 'a freedom and equality of opportunity amongst women workers which has been denied them hitherto.'[95] It was against this background that Agnes Dawson moved decisive policy at the NFWT central council meeting in November 1919. Her leadership in London had proved that autonomous action *could* be organised. The winning of the vote had also proved, so they believed, that with sufficient commitment and organisation feminist positions could be won. The NUT's inaction, of course, also proved again that they could not be trusted to implement progressive policy. Accordingly Agnes moved that the central council recommend to the membership there be a 'distinct severance' from the NUT.[96] The decision was so uncontroversial in the central council that no named vote or voting figures needed to be recorded.

'Extraordinary Rumours'

Without any formal decision many women had already dropped their NUT or LTA membership. There was some dissent about the way in which the split from the LTA had been carried out: members left before a formal decision was taken. Theodora Bonwick was not one of the first to leave the LTA. This was remembered bitterly in an otherwise flattering biographical piece written some 20 years afterwards in the *Woman Teacher*.[97] Animosity towards her and Irene Poulter was intense. Irene Poulter felt obliged to write to Emily Phipps explaining her absence from a mass meeting at the Royal Albert Hall. For some reason, Emily also felt the need to pass this on to Ethel Froud. There were, Irene Poulter said, 'extraordinary rumours' that she and Theodora Bonwick had been thrown out of the Federation over their views about continuing to work for the time being in the LTA. Setting the record straight she explained that they had merely resigned from the committee. Those quick to spread rumours and argue for separation from the LTA had not even yet left the union themselves![98]

Having agreed to a distinct severance, the feminists organised enthusiastically: for representation on Burnham, for equal pay and for women members to join the NUWT, as the Federation would now be known. This they did, initially, in a buoyant frame of mind. Despite setbacks the mood remained militant. Initiating a motion against the policy of the Board of Education Grace Coombs, London president, argued that: 'We must make Fisher [president of the Board of Education] know that he cannot deal with the teachers as the Government has dealt with others.'[99]

Although feminists recognised that the miners and railwaymen had been defeated they were still determined to push their case. Lobbying of MPs was vital, said Ethel Froud, as 'ignorance ... was stupendous'.[100] Internal differences such as those raised by Theodora Bonwick and Irene Poulter were to exist in the NUWT in future years, but little indication of this acrimony appeared in public. The NUWT developed a public image of a union united against the state and NUT alike. Its image as a national authoritative body would be further enhanced by the actions of individual members, in particular Emily Phipps and Agnes Dawson, standing for public elected positions.

5
Life in the Enfranchised World

When the Representation of the People Act was passed, Millicent Fawcett of the NUWSS declared it was the greatest moment of her life, 'We had won fairly and squarely after a fight lasting fifty years. Henceforth, women would be free citizens.'[1] Her optimism was shared by the Women's Freedom League which hoped for full equality between men and women in every respect.[2] Such days of hope mirrored those in the trade union and labour movement. Trade union membership had grown to $8^1/_4$ million by 1920, of which $6^1/_2$ million were affiliated to the TUC.[3] In 1919 the number of days lost in strike action more than doubled the pre-war figures. Miners, cotton workers, railworkers, Clydeside engineers had all taken militant strike action during 1919. Such action was often of a proactive kind to achieve better hours, pay and conditions of employment, including working-class control.[4]

Within the Labour party too there were signs of radicalisation. The Labour Party, which had defined itself as socialist for the first time at its 1918 conference and called for common ownership of the means of production, had supported the Russian Revolution at its 1919 June conference. The call for an immediate end to intervention against the Soviet Union was supported by a 2 to 1 majority. The 'Hands off Russia' campaign numbered amongst its leaders luminaries of the TUC. It achieved significant support for its aims among grassroots trade unionists. Within the socialist movement the founding conference of the Communist Party was held in 1920.[5]

A similar confidence in self-activity was reflected in the deeds of the feminist teachers, although they drew back from aligning themselves too closely with the structures of the trade union and labour movement. The question of allegiance and support for particular political parties had split the pre-war suffrage movement in its election-time campaigns. The feminist teachers had been unwilling to risk such divisions within the Federation. When the NUT had debated whether it should affiliate to the Labour Party and TUC, the feminists had called a special meeting of the Women Teachers' Franchise Union to form their own view. Theodora Bonwick had argued the case for Labour Party affiliation and Agnes Dawson had argued against it. Although no vote was taken there was an apparent consensus that, as far as enfranchisement went, '[there was] no special guarantee of help from Labour any more than from the other political parties.'[6]

However, when the feminist teachers decided to make a 'distinct severance' from the NUT they also resolved to organise themselves as a *union*, with all the implications the term suggested. In due course this was endorsed by NUWT conference, as moved by the Swansea branch and Emily Phipps.[7] The women were reluctant to take the further step of affiliation to the TUC. Registration as a trade union, they were legally advised, would entail disclosure of assets, liabilities and membership figures. Moreover, the central council believed that TUC affiliation implied political endorsement of the Labour Party. Some members – notably Mrs Muir Stanbury and Helen Croxson and Miss M. Conway, who were all Labour Party members – supported affiliation. Others did not. Again it was Agnes Dawson who led the opposition: women could not expect any particular support from the Labour Party or TUC. Speaking on behalf of the officers she contended that 'women in the Labour Party and in the TUC were, and would be, swamped.'[8] The vote was close. She won her motion by only two votes at the central council.[9]

Her position does not necessarily reflect a bureaucratic conservatism but perhaps simply her personal experiences in the party. Other suffrage socialist feminists had the same view. Hannah Mitchell, for example, refused to join the Labour Party because she did not wish to become an 'official cake-maker'.[10]

Ethel Froud, also a Labour Party member, was less than enthusiastic about the party's support for feminist policies. When Labour councillors in Leyton ditched Labour Party national policy on equal pay she wrote a strong letter of protest to the national secretary demanding disciplinary action:

> Time and again we have been assured that equal pay is an integral part of the Labour Party's policy. Time and again we have found Labour men parting from this policy when voting at Education committees ... the Labour members voted with the men and against the women.[11]

The *Woman Teacher* 'Takes All My Out-of-school Time'

One of the most important steps the feminists took to create an independent public political identity was the establishment of their own weekly paper, the *Woman Teacher*, in September 1919. As Agnes Dawson wrote in the first issue, 'What the women's suffrage movement has begun is left for women workers generally to continue.'[12] No longer were their public written statements confined to leaflets or letters in the unsympathetic *Schoolmaster* or condensed reports in the more sympathetic *Schoolmistress*. The *Woman Teacher* was printed in London. However its editor and – if her private correspondence is not exaggerated – the mainstay of the venture was Emily Phipps, who still lived and worked in Swansea. Renowned for her writing as well as oratorical skills, she seemed likely to make a good editor. Yet she was discouraged by the paper's early reception. Reporting to the central council on the first issue of the *Woman Teacher* Emily Phipps thought the response had been poor. Distribution had been muddled because of the railway strike and because the press date for London was too early. Moreover in London the 'rival' *London Teacher* was distributed free to teachers. In response the London Unit resolved to buy 5,000 copies a week and then circulate them free of charge.[13]

There were other problems caused by lack of membership contributions to the paper. Only five months after the paper's launch she complained in martyred tones to Ethel Froud that she had to continue unwillingly to be editor as no one else was willing to do the job.[14] Emily carried out her duties as editor and continued her job as headteacher of the Municipal Secondary school for girls in Swansea while also pursuing intensive private study to become a barrister. The Sex Disqualification (Removal) Act had for the first time permitted women to be accepted at the Bar.[15] In the early 1920s when she was more than 50 years old she led a hectic life: working, studying, editing the paper, speaking at public meetings and attending central council meetings. Not surprisingly she became exhausted and wrote to Ethel Froud asking to be relieved, at least temporarily, of her post as editor until her studying was complete: 'There are some days in which I cannot do any private work [i.e. study] at all, as reading for "The Woman Teacher" and writing for it takes all my out-of-school time.'[16]

Parliamentary Action: Emily Phipps

Once they had decided to form their independent union, the feminist teachers worked hard to publicise it. Agnes Dawson, president in 1919, went round the country 'preaching', as she put it, 'the gospel of independence'.[17] In London women such as Theodora Bonwick busied themselves demonstrating against Lord Fisher, President of the Board of Education, for his refusal to grant equal pay or to allow the NUWT onto the Burnham committee. The women's behaviour, at one meeting at least, sent *The Times* and *Schoolmaster* alike into paroxysms of fury. For unlike many of their erstwhile sisters, the NUWT had not forgotten what they had learned in the suffrage movement about militant campaigns. Lord Fisher had been heckled in what his audience, the press, and public knew to be the manner of the pre-war suffragettes. Now, however, it was 1920 – and yet this group of feminists was acting as if they still needed equality. The *Schoolmaster* was unsympathetic:

> Last Saturday some fifty or sixty teachers so demeaned themselves as to smirch the repute of every teacher in the land. To have to explain that the National Union of Teachers knew nothing beforehand, is in nowise responsible, and does not approve, is in itself degrading ... We cannot apologise to Mr Fisher for them because we do not represent them; but here, in public, and formally, as well as most earnestly and sincerely, we express the disclaimer and the regret of the whole profession.[18]

The NUWT took action such as this to press their demand for union places on Burnham from which they were excluded. They also acted to obtain direct representation within the structures of the central and local state. Emily Phipps stood in the first general parliamentary election in which women could vote in December 1918. Agnes Dawson stood for the LCC, and Ethel Froud for St Pancras council in the Euston area, where she worked at NUWT headquarters.

The 1918 general election was disappointing for feminists and socialists. Despite the years of campaigning only 17 women candidates stood in the whole of Britain and Ireland: eight Independent, four Labour, four Liberal and one Conservative. Only one was elected: Countess Markievicz, the Sinn Fein candidate for St Patrick's, Dublin.[19] The election had borne out what Emily Phipps had previously said, that women as a group were not automatically progressive or feminist and that they would not spontaneously support a woman candidate.

Emily Phipps stood as a NFWT candidate in the unwinnable seat of Chelsea against the Conservative Sir Samuel Hoare. Her platform proclaimed the feminist cause, but in the mildest of terms.[20] She directed the reader's attention to the role of women in 'settling the affairs of the nation' at the end of the war:

> You, who are looking forward to coming back to your home and country, do you not want to see progress and reform in the matter of housing, greater attention to education, improved laws to secure better health and pure food? Do you not want your children to be better educated, and so more prepared to meet a national crisis than we were?[21]

The feminist teachers had prepared carefully for Emily's campaign. The Federation formed a parliamentary committee in May 1918 on the initiative of the London Unit and of Agnes Dawson, who subsequently persuaded the National Federation to support the idea and establish a parliamentary fund.[22] The committee produced leaflets that encouraged women to enrol themselves on the electoral register. When the general election of Autumn 1918 was called the NFWT took the decision to stand (only) one candidate, in a London constituency. It also decided to send a questionnaire to all parliamentary candidates, questioning them on their attitude to equal pay and the steps they would take to promote the issue.[23] No women other than Miss Phipps were discussed as candidates. Whether this was because no others were willing to stand or because her 'independent' views, as she defined them, made her a better NFWT candidate than Agnes Dawson, for example, is unclear. Some women questioned the tactic. Ray Strachey of the NUWSS, for example, wrote to Ethel Froud explaining why she had privately opposed Emily's candidature. She had not wanted women to stand in 'hopeless' seats unless there was strong local political organisation. Nevertheless, she had been encouraged by reports of the effect of Emily's candidature.[24] Emily received 20.9 per cent of the vote (2,419), in a two-way contest with the Conservative candidate.[25] She seems to have gone about the business of organising votes in the same hectic fashion in which she organised everything else:

> Miss Phipps sweeps through artistic and industrial Chelsea like a whirlwind. She speaks incessantly. She holds meetings for men only, meetings for women only, and meetings for both. Her supporters patrol the streets with sandwich boards, after the manner of suffragette days.[26]

The campaign set up creches where women could leave their children when they went to vote. NFWT members in London raised £300 and helped Emily in the campaign, perhaps unaware of her past hostility towards the London Unit – a hostility which she had freely expressed to Ethel Froud: 'Did the London meeting have any real effects, as distinguished from emotional flag-waving? Are we going to get a Branch (beg pardon 'unit') there worth calling one?'[27]

In future years the NUWT participated in general elections as vigorously as they had in the suffrage days. Ethel Froud issued circulars which stressed to the 'politically-minded' membership that they should not allow 'a reactionary government ... to come back to power'. But the union was not party political; rather it sought to return to parliament: 'men and women of honest purpose and high ideals, whose chief desire is to serve the best interests of the whole community, no matter to what party they belong'.[28]

The NUWT did not support women candidates irrespective of their politics. Women, like men, needed to prove their support of the 'cause'. In the 1923 general election, for example, the London Unit urged members to work for eight candidates in the London area: six Labour and two Liberal candidates. The only woman on the list was Susan Lawrence, Labour Party and LCC member, who defeated Charles Crook, the Tory NUT president, in East Ham. In Agnes Dawson's area of Camberwell, the London Unit supported Charles Ammon, a Labour candidate, against a woman Conservative candidate, Dame Helen Gwynne Vaughan.[29] As they canvassed, worked in committee rooms and held outdoor meetings, NUWT teachers hoped to demonstrate that women teachers were 'women of public spirit'.[30] The election campaigns were important both in influencing electors to vote for candidates with pro-feminist views *and* in demonstrating that an integral feature of feminism was to perform such public duties.

Every branch was encouraged to elect parliamentary secretaries so that the union could continue its pressure on MPs outside election periods. The parliamentary secretaries were responsible for informing MPs of the union's views and for organising petitions. In November 1922, for example, they organised a petition to the prime minister containing 100,000 signatures. It demanded that the government 'bring into full and immediate operation the Education Act, 1918, this being the very minimum of educational facilities to which the children of our land are entitled'.[31] Ethel Froud sent letters to the branches urging support for parliamentary activities which echoed the sentiments expressed by the suffragette teachers before the war:

> It is necessary to reiterate the fact that the union is not *party* political – but it must be politically minded. The whole of a teacher's life, the conditions under which she works, her salary, her pension, her status, the code etc. etc. depend upon action by the Government and Parliament. It behoves us, therefore, as teachers, as voters, and as women, to exert every ounce of influence we have to see that MPs are fully informed on matters we have at heart and thus to try and secure action on right lines. (original emphasis)[32]

But the NUWT never again stood a parliamentary candidate. Emily herself declined to stand: 'Holding the views I do, I should never secure election, as I should antagonise every party; and we have proved already that it is useless to count on the women's vote, under the present franchise.'[33]

The union discussed possible candidates in the 1920s. Few members were willing or able to stand. Miss Conway, a Labour Party member, could not get the party to support her; Kate Palmer, from Birmingham, was reluctant to stand because she felt that the union would lose and would waste its valuable resources. Instead she agreed to stand for Birmingham council.[34] The union then looked outside its ranks for a suitable candidate. A Miss Bathurst, an inspector with the Board of Education, agreed to stand and pay her own expenses. Her candidature seems to have been supported by Agnes Dawson, who described to the central council her work on behalf of the Federation.[35] But there was dissent. Miss Conway did not agree with Miss Bathurst's politics on national issues, nor on Ireland. Other Labour members did not support her. Miss Hewitt argued that the union could not be expected to find a candidate with whom they agreed on everything; rather, they should concentrate on agreeing upon a candidate who would put forward the 'woman's point of view'.[36] Although the central council had agreed to accept Miss Bathurst's offer to stand, Ethel Froud nevertheless pointed out to her that there was opposition to her candidature and that the decision regarding support for a candidate resided ultimately with the London Unit which actually would be undertaking the campaign. Possibly because of this lukewarm support Miss Bathurst finally declined to put herself forward.[37]

Municipal Feminism: Agnes Dawson

Like Emily, Agnes Dawson took the decision late in life to enter a new career. For Emily this career had been the law, undertaken for the cause in general and the union in particular. For Agnes the career choice was local politics, which she entered specifically to obtain a platform for the union's demands on equality. In the council elections of 1919 the feminist teachers had supported several candidates. In London Mrs Lamartine Yates stood successfully as a Labour candidate in North Lambeth in the LCC elections with the support of the feminist teachers and the Women's Freedom League. Her platform included: support for equal pay; increased numbers of nursery schools; more teachers and hence smaller classes; increased income tax to be distributed in the form of grants to local authorities to build municipal housing; and grants of cheap milk and coal. Most of her election workers were NFWT members.[38]

In south Wales, Fannie Thomas, a former NFWT president, stood for the Ogmore and Garw Urban District council and topped the poll. The interest she had expressed as president in improving the home conditions of pupils was reflected in her platform which combined feminism with municipal socialism: 'In the past men have built houses, but now the opportunity is given by an Act of Parliament, for women to have a voice in their construction, position and aspect.'[39] She advocated municipal housing with proper kitchens, larders and space for a coal cwtch; improved refuse collection with rubbish burnt at a council amenity site and 'converted into a useful and profitable asset'.[40] Although other NUWT members were later elected to local councils,[41] it was Agnes Dawson who had the greatest impact. In 1925 at the age of 52 she resigned from her secure and now pensionable post as head of Crawford Street Infants school to stand for the London County Council as a Labour member in the safe seat of Camberwell, her local area. The London unit viewed her as their candidate and agreed to finance the venture and pay her a weekly wage.

Agnes took this decision at the time of life when many people are simply looking forward to the leisure of retirement. That she did so reveals two different aspects of her attitude to politics. The first is her commitment to the political cause, which was a firm part of her life, even though she faced a financially uncertain future. The second is her belief that the campaign for equal rights was one which could be achieved in the *short* term. To say this is not to detract from her commitment but to try and explain why the feminists would see it as politically expedient to stand one of their most famous leaders for a council which was a conservative one and which would remain so until 1934. Nan McMillan, who started to work in London in the late 1920s, believes that:

> They felt if women could get a position anywhere, anywhere on a local committee, they would make the point for the women's case ... To them if they could have got equal pay, equal opportunities ... achieved that, to them society would have put itself right almost ... They thought they could achieve this in their lives.[42]

Agnes' manifesto was a middle-of-the-road Labour Party programme. She wanted more council houses, increased educational provision, a restructuring of the rating system and a supply of cheaper food through wholesale markets. It was a very conventional programme with little overtly feminist content. The lack of dynamism in the written word seems to have been compensated by the energetic canvassing of the London unit members. Ethel Froud ensured that they turned up at the committee rooms warmly clad and equipped with their own torches. Members with 'motor cars' were particularly welcome! As a result, Agnes was returned with over 4,000 votes, marginally less than her male colleague, Cecil Manning.[43]

On her election Agnes wrote to members thanking them for their support and kind wishes:

> I am prouder than ever to-day of the NUWT and of its loyal members. I hope so much I shall have opportunities and courage to serve the Cause inside the LCC. The knowledge that I have so many real friends will ever be a joy and strength to me. Believe me.[44]

Once elected, Agnes found it difficult to deal with the anti-feminist attitudes surrounding her. In particular as a member of the Education

Committee she had to spend a great deal of time in meetings with the very leaders of the LTA whom she had opposed for so many years. Ethel Froud observed:

> At present the 'party' is depending on her tremendously for informa-tion etc on Education and she is really doing a good deal behind the scenes and in the 'party' on educational matters connected with the LCC. She says she receives little or no support from men who are sup-posed to represent education, even on academic questions.[45]

Agnes was hard working but not, in political career terms, suc-cessful. Outside the LCC she had been the president of the National Federation, the leader of the London feminist teachers and a leading activist in the Women Teachers' Franchise Union. Once on the LCC, she remained for many years a backbencher. The leading member of the Labour opposition group on the Education Committee was Mrs Eveline Lowe, a friend of the Salter family in Bermondsey, who, while deeply interested in education, had never been a teacher – nor mili-tant in the suffrage cause. Although Agnes was, even according to her opponents, a fine orator she was rarely called upon to move or second motions in Education Committee or council. Certainly a reading of the dry minutes of the LCC education committee gives little indica-tion that she had, or could have had, any great impact on the proceedings. She served on the Special Services Sub-committee (which she chaired from 1934 to 1937) and on the management committees of several nursery and special schools and of Peckham children's home.[46] Her influence seems to have been minimal, even on nursery education. In 1928, for example, the London Unit wrote to the Special Services Sub-committee on which she served to demand that nursery age children be entrusted to highly qualified women, and to set out its views on pupil–teacher ratios and the type of training teachers needed. There is no indication Agnes Dawson even moved a motion of support. Later the same committee agreed that nursery assistants be employed as unqualified teachers – using the model of the Rachel McMillan school, on whose management committee Agnes sat.[47]

This is not to suggest that Agnes Dawson necessarily agreed with the decisions taken by the Conservative-dominated committees. Indeed – given her views on nursery education as discussed in Chapter 3 – she undoubtedly disagreed with them. But sitting for nine years as an opposition member, and a feminist at that, she was given little oppor-tunity to develop her views into practical politics. In 1932 she was given the largely ceremonial position of 'deputy chairman'. But it was not until the election of the first Labour council under Herbert Morrison in 1934 that she held any significant office, that of chair of the General Purposes Committee. Even then she was not elected to represent the Authority on the national Burnham committee, the body which still determined teachers' pay – and which continued to exclude the NUWT.

'Too Deadly for Words'

Agnes seems to have taken little interest in the structures and hierarchy of the Labour Party and did not stand for positions, even for a place on the the Advisory Committee on Education (ACE).[48] This committee was given the responsibility of developing Labour Party policy on education and of co-opting individuals to carry out this task – the NUT and NUWT took up co-opted places. Agnes expressed no interest in representing the union on this body.[49] Those members who did found it a dispiriting occasion. Dominated by men hostile to feminism, the ACE included the very NUT members who the NUWT had campaigned against. The men brought their opposition to equal pay and equal opportunity for women and girls to committee meetings. 'It is like attending a meeting of the NUT now', commented Miss Savage, an NUWT member on ACE.[50] Florence Key expressed a similar view: 'I find this job the hardest I have ever undertaken for the union because of the NUT atmosphere and the House of Commons (ditto) is too deadly for words' (sic).[51]

When opportunities did arise for developing feminist policies, men on the committee derisively spurned the chance. In 1929 Charles Trevelyan, then Labour President of the Board of Education, was invited to address the ACE. The committee drew up a list of items of the utmost importance to discuss with him. Equal pay was omitted. This did not stop Miss Savage and Mrs Key tackling him. Rather than leave him exposed, the NUT men at the meeting joked that a Labour government would give women twice as much pay as men. Chuter Ede, W.G. Cove and other NUT men joined in the laughter. The women did not.[52] Small wonder then that the NUWT saw little point in working in the ACE and described its activities with scorn: 'I think our committee [ACE] now numbers thirty, of whom I am surely the most useless member as I never serve on the sub-committees, or write learned essays on various branches of education which are quickly out-of-date.'[53]

The Teachers' Labour League: No View on 'Propaganda in Matters of Salary'

The NUWT had a more positive experience of working with the left-wing group within the Labour Party, the Teachers' Labour League. Until the secession of right-wing members in 1926 the TLL functioned as a broad group of teachers and socialists interested in education. It aimed to organise teachers in the socialist or labour cause and to develop positions on curriculum questions. Motions that it submitted to Labour Party conference attempted to win the party to a class perspective on curriculum content and the control of education.[54] The pages of the TLL's paper, *Educational Worker*, were full of debate about working-class educational needs and what the TLL called class-conscious against 'neutral' education. The majority of the League favoured an approach to education which related schooling to a social context. This was defined by H. Stanley Redgrove, the TLL president in 1925, as:

> opening up to the child ... every channel of happiness and enjoyment ... It should equip the child in such a way that he [sic] might prove a useful member of the community ... citizenship, seeing as it served both aims ... should come first in a list of school subjects. The child when he left school should realise his true place in society, he should thoroughly understand his rights and privileges and ... what the community exacted from him. This meant, of course, that he must understand the principles of socialism.[55]

Although the NUWT members did not necessarily share these conclusions, they did share an emphasis on the social context of education and a keen interest in curriculum development. The NUWT supported a TLL visit to the Soviet Union to study the new forms of Bolshevik education. It was the only teachers' union to support the venture. The delegation included Ethel Froud, who had been an individual member of the TLL in the early 1920s. She valued highly her time in the USSR, she said, and spoke at many NUWT meetings on the topic after her return. She declined, however, to write any introduction to the TLL book that described the visit for fear of alienating NUWT members intent on maintaining their independence from any specific political organisation. Her name on such a piece, she said, 'would be sufficient [for many NUWT branches] to sever connection with the NUWT. This would serve you no useful purpose and do much harm.'[56]

After the right wing had left the TLL, the Labour Party took the opportunity to disaffiliate the League from the party. Its membership was reduced to CP members and other left-wing educationists. Despite reminders from the secretary, David Capper, Ethel did not renew her membership.[57] The relationship between the NUWT and TLL weakened not because of the Labour Party decision but because of the League's position on pay. The TLL was not a 'ginger group' for any particular union; rather it sought to draw together socialist teachers from the NUT, NUWT and NAS – no mean feat in the 1920s! Of necessity this meant a wary approach to the major issue which divided the three unions: equal pay. Many NUWT branches naturally distrusted the TLL's aim of forming one teachers' union. To them it seemed that the League was simply trying to urge them back into the NUT. [58]

When Ethel Froud sought clarification from the TLL on its position on equal pay she was told: 'the League, as a political organisation, cannot and does not assume to itself the function of undertaking propaganda in matters of salary.'[59]

At this time the League was still affiliated to the Labour Party. David Capper offered the 'argument' that the Labour Party already had equal pay in its programme.[60] This was hardly reassuring, particularly since the League had already campaigned for higher wages and better conditions for teachers without promoting equal pay. Such a response was unacceptable to Ethel and several other NUWT members in the TLL. Several left the TLL and organised within the new, right-wing, National Association of Labour Teachers. But when some NUWT members protested to Ethel about TLL literature which implied the NUWT had given official backing to a League fringe meeting at the union's annual conference, she attempted to pacify them. She argued that it was up to the TLL to hold meetings where it wished, 'regardless of the feelings or wishes of the other people. We did the same ourselves in suffrage days, so perhaps I have a sympathetic understanding of the peculiar methods of the propagandist.'[61]

'An Aggressive Champion for the Cause'

Agnes Dawson, no supporter of the TLL, continued to spend her time lobbying the right winger Herbert Morrison within the LCC Labour Group to win his support for the feminists' demands. Under Morrison's leadership in 1934 Labour for the first time captured the LCC. Agnes too had a personal victory, doubling her vote from the 1931 election. Yet it was still an uphill struggle to get any feminist issues discussed.[62]

In the 1920s the NUWT had campaigned in different ways against the marriage bar of many local education authorities, including the LCC. It used the courts and petitioned and lobbied MPs and the Board of Education. The Sex Disqualification (Removal) Act of 1919 should have protected married women teachers from dismissal. But during the 1920s the terms of the Act were widely disregarded in a number of court cases, the most prominent of which took place in the Rhondda in 1922. Here the LEA won the right to dismiss married women on the grounds of 'efficiency' of education in the area.[63] W.G. Cove, who had been one of the leaders of the 1919 Rhondda strike for higher wages, had projected himself as a great socialist trailblazer in the NUT. Despite this, he became NUT president in 1922 and did nothing to support the sacked Rhondda women teachers. The NUT general secretary sent a circular to all branches bitterly criticising the NUWT for taking the matter to court – but the NUT took no action on the women's behalf.[64]

By August 1922 at least 2,500 married women teachers had been sacked in England and Wales. By 1926 about three quarters of all LEAs operated some form of marriage bar, requiring teachers to resign or be sacked on marriage.[65] In London through the 1920s and early 1930s women teachers and school cleaners were sacked on marriage. Married women cleaners were to be employed only if 'eligible women' were unavailable.[66] Every month the LCC Education Committee discussed which married women should be sacked. Occasionally schools employed a married woman teacher for one or two weeks on a casual supply basis. Such transgressions were reported to the Education Committee, which often condoned the breach of policy with the stern proviso that it should not happen again.[67]

One of the first things Agnes did when she was elected was to move a motion to relax the regulations which forbade married women teachers to be supply (or casual) teachers even if unmarried women teachers were not available. This modest proposal was defeated.[68] This policy, as the NUWT realised, was both discriminatory and a direct interference by the state in the personal lives of teachers. Women had a 'choice': to keep a job and stay unmarried or to marry and lose a livelihood. In such circumstances, as Annie Byett wrote in a NUWT pamphlet, marriage was perceived by bright young women as 'so great a drawback that many, not the least intelligent, deliberately choose a single life'.[69] It is not surprising then that Agnes Dawson focused her energy, once Labour was elected, on the ending of the marriage bar. Nor is it surprising that Nan McMillan was insistent that this particular campaign should be successful. As a socialist feminist she ardently opposed the marriage bar; as a single woman living with a man outside marriage because of the LCC regulations she also had a personal interest in its abolition:

It was a very awkward position for her [Agnes Dawson]. For even if she didn't report anything I'd bring it up ... at the end. I was dying to get married so we could make ourselves respectable. I think she dreaded my question, 'Any advance on the abolition of the bar?' 'No, no, no.' This was 1934 and the year was going on and it got round to 1935. She came up with the suggestion that she would go to Herbert Morrison and if he would do nothing – his attitude was there's so many more important things – if he would do nothing, she would resign. She'd call a press conference and say why and we would back her on that. I think she knew at the back of her mind that such a threat he dare not let happen. I always remember when she reported back ... Oh good God, Agnes, you can't do that, we'll set up a committee ... to look into it.[70]

Over a year after Labour won the elections, the July 1935 council meeting finally voted to end the marriage bar. At the conclusion of the debate Herbert Morrison congratulated Agnes Dawson on her tenacity as 'an aggressive champion of the cause'.[71] But the vote was not a foretaste of things to come. While Agnes remained a councillor the LCC still took no steps towards equal pay. When the NUWT presented the teaching sub-committee with a memorandum on equal pay, it remained 'on the table'.[72] Certainly Agnes's work against the marriage bar was the achievement by which she was remembered on the LCC. An article in the *Daily Herald* that described Agnes's work on the general purposes committee in 1936 was headed 'She made wives into teachers.'[73]

Inside the NUWT Agnes Dawson's election inspired other women to emulate her. Dr Esther Rickards, a feminist supporter of the NUWT though not a teacher, stood in Mile End in east London. NUWT members canvassed for her in an attempt to elect an ally for Agnes: 'Miss Dawson wants her support on the Council in the fight that she and the opposition party are putting up against the many cuts in education.'[74] They were not successful.

Ethel Froud, too, stood for election in London, to St Pancras council in the ward in which the NUWT's Gordon Square offices were situated. Her decision – and endorsement of the Labour platform – was less than enthusiastic. 'I do not stand as an NUWT representative, but merely as an individual', she informed possibly hostile members.[75] Duty to the cause had made up her mind. She had written frequently to the parliamentary secretaries urging them to do more in the way of electioneering; now she had the opportunity to put her own words into practice. Women should, she said, 'undertake more interest in public affairs and try to get elected to committees concerning themselves with the professional, social, and economic problems of the time'.[76]

Despite NUWT canvassing, Ethel Froud was not elected, but her candidature at least had an effect on the Labour Party campaign. The local Labour Party secretary urged comrades to support 'an all red St Pancras'. However, the slogan which the party adopted for the election was the old WSPU motto: Deeds not words.[77]

6

New Feminism and Old Reaction

The NUWT continued to uphold the suffrage feminist claim to political and economic equality, but within a climate increasingly hostile to such feminist ideas. No longer were Agnes, Emily, Ethel and Theodora part of a thriving feminist movement outside teaching. Women had been incorporated more effectively into the structures of the state, without achieving the economic reforms for which they had hoped. The Women's Freedom League soon recognised the problems which still beset women's equality:

> The old generalisations about the disabilities of women and their proper 'sphere' are revived. The magnificent creatures who had saved the country were now denounced as irresponsible flappers, as giggling girls clinging like limpets to office chairs which should be occupied by demobilised soldiers ... The iniquitous differentiation in the salaries of men and women teachers, the refusal of common human rights to a body of women obviously of the highest importance to the state, show the tenacity and blindness of sex prejudice.[1]

Before the imposition of the Burnham pay scales the feminists had had some successes in local education authorities where the NUWT was strong, but these had now been eroded.[2] It was no longer possible for local education authorities themselves – even with councillors with the politics of Agnes Dawson in 'control' – to concede equal pay claims. They too were bound by the national agreements of Burnham.[3] But even the higher wage levels gained through Burnham were under attack in the 1920s. In 1922 the Geddes committee proposed cuts in teachers' salaries. The NUT voted to accept the 5 per cent wage cut it recommended, thinking thereby to gain public support and to defend the national Burnham pay scales.[4] In 1925 further cuts in conditions were proposed. Again, the NUT conceded. Women teachers were badly affected by this measure. Although the NUT recognised that there was increasing unemployment and a poor economic situation it believed that acceptance of wages cuts would 'show and obtain goodwill'.[5] Realising that women teachers would be disproportionately affected the London Teachers' Association implored its female members to 'take a broad and reasonable view of the award'.[6] The NUWT never 'accepted' cuts in educational expenditure or wages, but with no representation on negotiating bodies members were forced to suffer cuts agreed to by the larger NUT.

The imposition of the Geddes cuts was symptomatic of the state's growing severity towards the trade union and labour movement. The energy and optimism of the immediate post-war period was subdued by political reaction. The break up of the Triple Alliance in 1921, the so-called 'Black Friday', when railway and transport workers refused to come to the aid of the embattled miners in their campaigns against wage cuts and deregulation heralded the new times of the coming decade. Defensive actions against lock-outs or wage cuts became the norm replacing positive industrial action to win higher wages or better conditions of employment.[7] In the 1920s the concerns of the wider women's movement were not those related directly to the issues which had preoccupied the teacher suffragettes for so many years. The ideology of the movement in which the teachers had achieved their first political education was set aside. Equality between men and women in the political and economic field was no longer fashionable as a political aim. Instead, the 'special' attributes of women were emphasised. These were not defined according to social attributes (or conditioning) but rather to biologically based assumptions of women's role as mothers.

'Woman, Home, Family'

There had never been a period in which the media had not been hostile to women's self-organisation. But the hostility expressed towards the politics of the women of the NUWT was not confined to the reactionary press. Time and again women's politics were equated with their sexuality. The state of being unmarried in itself came to be seen by the feminists' detractors as a political statement. *Shall Flappers Rule?*, a diatribe against the extension of the franchise to women under 30, epitomised the new ideology. Flappers were no longer the tomboyish young women, the 'good bricks', the 'daring old things' of a few years before. Flappers were now a threat to the established order and a danger to men.[8] The author of the piece blamed continued feminist agitation on elderly women who had failed to realise their hopes and sought to avenge themselves on men. Assuming that all such women lacked was a man, the writer believed that their single state was the source of their alleged unhappiness: 'Soured and disappointed they blame the men for their woes, oblivious to the fact that life is what we make it ... Instead of looking within themselves for the cause of their unhappiness they search without, and fasten on man.'[9] Such feminists, he argued, were not only emotionally inadequate, but were acting against nature itself by refusing to submit to motherhood:

> The truth is that man is the positive, woman the negative pole of the battery of life; each is necessary to the other – they are complementary ... Man has the intellect, the driving force, the constructive ability etc ... Woman, on the other hand, is specially organised, first, last, and all the time, for the purpose of motherhood.[10]

This appropriation of the term 'flappers' by ideologically reactionary currents was mirrored in the different interpretation given to the term 'spinster'. This was an expression used confidently and positively by single women teachers. But, as Sheila Jeffreys has documented, it was also used in the 1920s by those seeking to define unmarried feminists as outdated, unfashionable and possessing a warped sexuality:

> [Spinsters'] fanaticism and crankiness have caused them to take up freak science, freak religions, and freak philanthropy. They are the chief supporters of movements, such as anti-vivisection, which does its best to retard the advance of experimental science in this country; of dogs' homes and cats' homes; of missionary societies, and a 'kill-joy' propaganda.[11]

Women teachers who did not marry were seen as a threat to the married state and to the girls they taught. Some male medics argued that spinsters possessed an energy which was the result of sexual frustration; others that spinster teachers would make girls critical of men. In either case women teachers' independence and careers were undermined.[12]

The changing mood of the times can be illustrated by reference to Emily Phipps' local paper, the *South Wales Daily Post*. When she resigned her headmistress' post in 1925, the Swansea education committee held a special meeting to express their thanks to Miss Phipps for her hard work in developing the Municipal Secondary School for Girls. The *Post* did not cover the event. Her achievements which had been so loudly trumpeted when she had stood for Parliament seven years before were now ignored.[13] In the week in which she left her teaching post the *Post* included an article entitled: 'Popular women: contrast of victorian and modern, a Swansea girl's view': 'They [feminists] will not realise they are to blame for the casual treatment they at present receive from the other sex ... I would wish a return of the days when women were at least women and were decent wives, and mothers.'[14]

Unmarried feminists were seen as a threat to 'the family' by press, Parliament and the NAS. In 1921 Parliament discussed introducing clauses against 'gross indecency', which applied to lesbian women. These were attached to a bill introduced primarily to raise the age of consent to 16. On the bill's second reading the dangers of lesbianism were discussed by MPs: 'In the first place it stops child-birth, because it is a well-known fact that any woman who indulges in this vice will have nothing to do with the other sex. It debauches young girls and it produces neurasthenia and insanity.'[15]

'Perversion' – for this was how homosexuality was defined by parliamentarians – had been encountered in times past. On such occasions perpetrators had been treated as lunatics or as meriting the death penalty.[16] The unspecified 'evil' practised by lesbians was not disputed by any MP. The issue was how to eradicate it from British life. Many MPs argued that if legislation was introduced against lesbian practices this would simply invite special attention and assist in its spread. As Col. Wedgwood, who opposed the clause, expounded: 'It is better advertised by the moving of this clause than in any other way. I do not suppose that there are any members of the Labour Party who know in the least what is intended by the clause.'[17]

The proposed legislation was eventually defeated, but the suspicion with which unmarried feminists were regarded, irrespective of how they saw themselves, still remained.

The NAS and the Threat of 'Tremendous Virility'

The link made by the reactionary press between feminism, lesbianism and the unmarried state was also reflected in the statements of the newly organised NAS. This breakaway from the NUT was formed specifically 'to safeguard and promote the interests of men teachers'. Further objects were added which sought separate consideration of men teachers because of their 'greater responsibilities'.[18] It started to recruit on such a platform, especially in London. Within its first few months membership had reached 3,000: according to the NAS press, 'behind it there [was] tremendous virility.'[19] By 1929 membership had reached 7,000. It claimed to represent the majority of male teachers in Liverpool and Leeds, the latter being the former base of the Anti-Suffrage League campaigner Arthur Gronno.[20]

The NAS advocated state endowment of motherhood to encourage women teachers to remain in the home – and not to have the temerity to *want* a career after marriage. Motherhood was, the NAS believed, the noblest of professions aspired to by the 'best women' who found in motherhood their chief work and 'most absorbing interest'.[21] Members of the NAS not only argued on ideological grounds for separate spheres for men and women; they also contended that women's biological capabilities and functions were innately different. In human reproduction women were the passive element and men the active: man was an expender of energy and woman a conserver.[22] The brains of men and women were also reputed to be different. This explained why men were needed to teach boys to be men as their own brains 'were habituated by man's function'.[23] Those women arguing for equal pay were going against natural law by supporting this 'evil doctrine'. Women's place was in the home as wives and mothers, not in the schools as teacher colleagues. Accordingly, the home was praised by the NAS: '[There are] three words which transcend all others in their import and comprehensiveness – "Woman", "Home", "Family". Nothing can add force and tenderness to these names.'[24] Women teachers campaigning for equal pay were undermining the very concept of motherhood; they deserved to be treated with contempt:

> In the eyes of the state the mother is more important than the spinster. Any doctrine which attacks the mother is bound to fail. Indeed it is surprising that *women* teachers, above all people, should have espoused such a pernicious doctrine. (original emphasis) [25]

Ironically, the NAS belief in promoting the 'sacred claims of Home and Family' necessitated their spending much time away from home at meetings. The men's journal therefore included special articles explaining the rationale for this to members' wives who asked 'is it worth it?' when 'brooding in silence during their lonesome vigils'. [26]

Motherhood and marriage were inextricably linked: 'It cannot be too closely recognised that a marriage unconsecrated by children is hardly a marriage at all ... in nearly every childless marriage the difficulty lies with the woman.'[27] Women teachers who rejected motherhood were decried for not wanting to give up 'a lucrative profession', lose their looks, or give up their 'liberty and pleasure'.[28] The very idea that women should want to be independent was challenged. Women who chose to stay in teaching and build a career were dismissed as fakes: 'It is probably quite true to say that every woman in the silence of her own soul thinks and hopes she will escape from the classroom through the door of marriage ...'[29]

Women who went beyond modest career aspirations and desired equality between men and women in all aspects of society were dismissed as 'faddists': 'There is a tendency on the part of some faddists to convince the public that the rearing of an efficient womanhood was as important as rearing an efficient manhood; that, in fact, the two are identical.'[30]

The NUT's attitude towards the feminists complemented the hostility of the NAS. The NUT used the epithet of suffragette – which the NUWT still proudly embraced – as a term of abuse, synonymous with 'sex hatred'. A *Schoolmaster* editorial of 1921 castigated the NAS and

← *of 'sex hatred', women tend* [handwritten annotation]

NUWT alike as organisations consisting of unreasonable people. The NUWT was referred to as the NFWT – they did not merit the title of 'union' in the eyes of the NUT:

> It was a child of the WSPU as an effect of the refusal of conference to approve of women's suffrage. [Behind the façade of equal pay] there is
X an effort motivated by something very much resembling sex hatred, and the leading members of the Federation are probably no more anxious to exalt the interests of women than to depress the cause of men.[31]

'Ad feminam' attacks by the NAS were the norm. The *New Schoolmaster* frequently contained cartoons mocking feminists. In one case a stereotypical schoolmarm is depicted standing over a hutch containing LTA and NUT rabbits. Outside – and hidden from her view – is an alert NAS rabbit. The NUWT schoolmarm explains 'My pets are dreadfully worried by a nasty creature I can neither capture not kill.'[32] In another issue, Agnes Dawson was erroneously stated to have defined marriage as legalised prostitution. The NAS was forced to withdraw its allegation when Agnes threatened to go to court.[33]

Theodora Bonwick's local LCC inspector, Dr Hayward, a prominent NAS supporter, criticised her professional judgement as a teacher implementing progressive education. He had appended his name and comments to the pamphlet against equal pay which the London NAS members had produced. In particular he had claimed that 'most men now know that women, when acting collectively, are of even baser clay than themselves.'[34] Realising that their members risked possible victimisation at his hands, the NUWT campaigned vigorously for his removal as an inspector. Thousands signed a petition demanding that Dr Hayward withdraw his comments. After much correspondence he finally made an apology and agreed to ensure that 'future editions' of the pamphlet would omit such remarks.

As general secretary, Ethel Froud too became an object of vilification, derisorily described by the NAS as 'The high priestess of the women's movement'. Her charm, conviction and oratorical skills were not positive attributes in the eyes of the NAS but targets of abuse:

> It certainly was a pleasure to listen to her. She looked so serene and smiling, and was evidently so much at home. She hurled herself into the discussion with a resounding thump on the desk, and was evidently master of all the oratorical wiles and the best ways of appealing to the gallery of women. She made up for her deficiency in logic by the vigour of her attack upon the NUT, whose failure to do anything for women she loudly denounced.[35]

The NAS also resented the NUWT's organisational skill and its ability to fund new offices. In 1921, just two years after the feminists left the NUT, they opened new headquarters in Gordon Square. Women teachers celebrated the move to Gordon Square with various toasts of the edible variety.[36] At the opening ceremony Emily Phipps proudly stated that women teachers were to lead the whole of the women's movement, not only for the betterment of women but for the general betterment of all. At this the NAS raged:

> We presume this means men teachers as well, even the effeminate ones. We now know where we are and what we need. Evidently we are a few notches below the women teachers and need their moral support ... How long will it be, before the men teachers have *their* 'commodious and well equipped offices?' And have they nothing to say about their own 'betterment'?[37]

In 1935 the Union moved again to better offices in South Kensington. To commemorate this move Winifred Holtby presented Ethel Froud with a speaker's bell for her office in the shape of a tortoise 'to symbolise the NUT'.[38]

The Home-maker and Unmarried Feminist in Fiction

The hostility to independent unmarried women teachers and to women who rejected an existence entirely constrained by the framework of home and family was also depicted in contemporary fiction. Ruth Adam's *I'm Not Complaining* is an account of a year in the life of a school teacher at a Nottinghamshire elementary school. The narrative is developed through the depressed and depressing voice of Madge Brigson, 'A woman, now mature, fixed in my ways, trained from my childhood in the school house for this one job.'

Adam portrays the only feminist, and significantly the only socialist on the staff, Freda Simpson, in a very critical light. She treats Miss Simpson's views and commitment to principles scornfully:

> She was extremely earnest. She was given to causes. It seems as if she could not accept the general wickedness and cruelty of the world, but had always to be putting her little bit of weight against its irresistable force. Of course, she never made any real headway.[39]

The likely explanation of her dedication was her confirmed spinster status, not her commitment to a better society. A teacher colleague explained that she was dedicted 'because she was repressed, and that she would throw all her societies over if she could only get married'.[40]

A more lurid example of fiction that extolled the joys of wifehood and motherhood was Nalbro Bartley's *A Woman's Woman*. The main character, Densie, changes under the influence of feminist ideas from the home-loving wife her husband married – 'some stupidly sweet little thing who can make flaky pie crust and wear ruffled white-muslin dresses'[41] – into a neglectful wife. As a result her husband becomes increasingly distraught, her daughter becomes a drug addict and her son is shot while 'lured' from his military barracks by a loose woman. By the end of the narrative the established order is reaffirmed: woman's service and subjection to man. Though tempted by the 'home-destroying spirit' Densie finally realises her 'sacred duty' to her home and comes to appreciate the lofty status of homemaker: '... the only art which has been denied the laurel wreath is the art of the homemaker. Was it for the homemaker that this verse was written: "They also serve who only stand and wait".'[42]

There was no shortage of books that offered advice to women who had failed in the marriage stakes. They were urged not to feel miserable and were cheered up by inspiring stories of happy spinsters. The happy schoolteacher of one such book applies a mixture of feminism and resilience in dealing with apparently unwanted circumstances: 'She had been a pioneer in everything pertaining to the equality of the sexes ... and she's had a marvellous time ... not bewailing her loneliness, but congratulating herself on her independence ...' An important contributory factor, however, to her happy mode of existence was a friendship with a man.[43]

Even novelist Winifred Holtby, who was a longstanding supporter of the work of the NUWT, did not hesitate in ridiculing the work of some of the 'old feminists' in her *Poor Caroline*. The humorous novel plots the life and exploits of the elderly Caroline Denton-Smyth who busies herself raising funds from businessmen of dubious morality for the production of wholesome films by the 'Christian Cinema Company'. Caroline's crusade in the film industry is a complete failure. Winifred Holtby mocks her views and her idiosyncratic ways by depicting her as distinctly odd. There are accounts of male hostility to Caroline's campaigns for social uplift, a hostility which is best depicted in the statements espoused by Clifton Johnson, an unscrupulous script writer who exploits Caroline's gullibility:

> Don't you see what's wrong with 'em all? Sex-starved. Sex-starved. Must use their energy somehow. Good works. Purity and social welfare. Nosing around to find nice juicy stories about child assault an' prostitutes. Rescue work. Excuse for bishops to talk sanctimonious smut to a lot of sex-starved spinsters. Anti-slavery. Feminism. Peace. Pshaw! Relax their complexes a bit. Get on a box an' spout at Marble Arch. [44]

While Clifton Johnson is certainly not seen as the hero of the piece, Caroline herself is portrayed as a woman out of time whose commitments and enthusiasms are mere eccentricity. The novel is not intended to develop an alternative feminist position on questions of morality but to amuse. That such a topic was chosen for a humorous novel, and by a feminist too, is in itself indicative of the changing political and ideological climate within which the feminist teachers were living. A feminist concerned with questions of morality was quite a legitimate target of fun, even for a sister feminist!

'New Feminism': Equal Pay 'a Vain Hope'

At first it had seemed that the suffrage feminists could work within the new organisations of the 1920s, especially the National Union of Societies for Equal Citizenship (NUSEC), formed out of the old NUWSS. But this was to change, especially under Eleanor Rathbone, NUSEC's president. Her political outloook assumed both that there was a separate sphere for women and that women and motherhood were synonymous:

> We can demand what we want for women, not because it is what men have got but because it is what women need to fulfil the potentialities of their own natures and to adjust themselves to the circumstances of their own lives.[45]

As early as spring 1918 she had published a pamphlet entitled 'Equal Pay in the Family. A Proposal for the National Endowment of Motherhood'. Perhaps significantly this pamphlet was published at the same time as the NUT's Easter conference was endorsing equal pay with the caveat that it went alongside state endowment of motherhood![46] Rathbone's argument was that men's wages were designed to support a family and that state payments to mothers and equal pay for women were two versions of the same issue. She neglected the position of unmarried women, stressing the specific needs of women as mothers and homemakers rather than as individual, independent workers with the same economic role as men. Thus the sex of the worker was the determining factor in wage rates rather than the job in hand.

Eleanor Rathbone's 'new feminism' was a conscious break with suffragette politics. The adherence to equal pay as the rate for the job was a 'vain hope' especially since, she argued, women workers did *not* have the same output as men.[47] Rathbone criticised feminists, such as the NUWT, who linked demands for equal pay with equal opportunities. She believed the measures of equal opportunities which did exist for women had been secured by women accepting unequal pay.[48] Like the NAS, Eleanor Rathbone saw the typical woman teacher as an individual woman without dependents and contrasted her with the

typical male teacher with his dependent children: 'It would be pecu-
liarly unfortunate if any group of women, especially one whose
profession is concerned with the welfare of children, should seem
indifferent to the welfare of their colleagues' own families.'[49]

In *The Disinherited Family*, in which she argued that equal pay was
an unwinnable strategy, Eleanor Rathbone went further by writing
out the NUWT from teacher politics. The NUT – and NAS – were discussed but the existence of the NUWT was ignored, making it easier
then to argue that 'It is neither justifiable nor politic for women
teachers to press for "equal pay" without making it clear that it must
be accompanied by some form of family allowances.'[50]

The NUT, not surprisingly, took up her ideas. When it belatedly
appointed a woman's officer in 1924, one of her chief tasks was to
promote state endowment of motherhood amongst the membership.
The union did not campaign for equal pay. They preferred instead to
press for payments to women based on their sex and child-bearing
functions rather than on their job in the classroom. Leading women
NUT members voiced this line in the union's press:

> The demand for equal pay will, as I have repeatedly stated, be substan-
> tiated only when we have some system of family endowment involving
> the recognition of responsibilities of both men and women. I beg of
> the women teachers to remain loyal to the union.[51]

From the 1920s onwards, NUWT 'suffrage feminists' were attacked
on all fronts: by the media, by colleagues in the teaching unions and
by erstwhile sisters in the women's movement. Their politics, professionalism and sense of identity as feminist teachers were all
threatened. The NUWT responded in various ways, reasserting their
sense of identity and maintaining their political views.

The NUWT Response

The NUWT feminists did not avoid arguing their own position on
support for women with childcare responsibilities. Their views on
family allowances, however, were very different to those of Eleanor
Rathbone. Emily Phipps favoured mothers getting help with their
work in the home so that their leisure time would be increased.[52] She
argued that single women as well as married women should receive a
form of state endowment, albeit of a different kind:

> Single women objected to being in lodgings at the beck and call of
> other people, and a single woman with a house of her own was as
> much entitled to extra salary from the state to maintain her house-
> keeper as a man was to maintain a wife.[53]

Her idea of a state allowance was counterposed to maintenance by a man: 'The term "being maintained" by a husband seemed ... dreadful; so lowering of one's dignity.'[54]

Emily opposed men's salaries being increased on marriage to support a wife. This too would imply that men obtained emoluments because of their sex and not because of the job they did in the classroom. In order to confirm its position on family allowances, the NUWT set up an inquiry into forms of family allowances. Analysing the different possible schemes, the central council report concluded that where forms of family endowment were established in no case did they bring about equal pay. None of its advocates had suggested establishing equal pay first, although this was the logical procedure. None of the schemes recognised dependants other than 'a married man's children'. Further, family endowment deflected from the concept of the rate for the job. Instead, 'the scheme implies that salaries are not a reward for work done, but that teachers "give" their labour to an employer who proceeds to "keep" them and those of his dependants whom he chooses to recognise.'[55] In other words the employer would be placed in the traditional position of a husband!

Opposition to Protective Legislation

Throughout the 1920s the NUWT had opposed NUSEC's position on family allowances. This was reiterated at the 1929 Buxton Conference. Members supported special allowances in principle for children, with the proviso that this should not be a substitute for equal pay for equal work.[56] Keen to see themselves as women, as teachers and as autonomous individuals, the NUWT rejected the implicit assumption of NUSEC that all women were mothers. Instead they continued to argue for equal pay separate from any family allowance. In similar vein the NUWT rejected the NUSEC support for protective legislation. NUSEC had urged the introduction of legislation to protect women workers, solely on the basis of their sex, from some of the poor working conditions endured by men. This again smacked of policies based on a person's sex, not on their job. Instead the NUWT feminists argued that conditions should be improved for all workers. If nightwork, for instance, was bad then it should be cut for all. If working hours were too long then they should be reduced for women *and* men workers.[57]

The NUWT was not alone in its opposition to protective legislation. Other feminist organisations, notably the *Time and Tide* journal and the Six Point Group, which demanded equal political and equal occupational rights, held similar views. The Six Point Group reflected the pre-war equal rights feminism in its demands for equal political rights, equal pay and opportunities, equal occupational rights. It echoed the WFL in its campaigns for better legislation against child assault and for support for the unmarried mother and her child. Intent on upholding its belief in true equality between men and women, the NUWT seceded from NUSEC and went on to form the Open Door Council to promote equality in employment and to oppose protective legislation: 'Women's societies organised to secure the equal status of men and women [need] to put first things first, to refuse to divert time, energy or money on subsidiary questions until the great equality reforms have first been won.'[58]

The Open Door Council had a clear appeal to suffrage feminism focused on equal rights. Cicely Hamilton wrote approvingly of its work:

> Since its aim was to correct the tendency of our legislators to be over-kind to women who earn their livelihood; to treat them from youth to age as if they were permanently pregnant, and forbid them all manner of trades and callings in case they might injure their health – forgetting that the first need of women, like the first need of men, is bread to put in their mouths.[59]

Equal Standards of Morality

It was not only on its position on protective legislation that the NUWT continued to uphold the pre-war position of the militant suffrage movement. It remained committed to equality between men and women in all respects. Individuals such as Theodora Bonwick worked with the Association for Moral and Social Hygiene (AMSH), another feminist organisation of the pre-war period, campaigning still for equal standards of morality between men and women. Theodora Bonwick seemed to have been attracted to this type of campaigning even before she converted to feminism. Theodora was from a Protestant non-conformist family. She had been a social worker in the temperance movement and had visited slums and brothels 'against the wish of the clergy'.[60] She had also taught for some years in a religious Sunday school before she dropped such activities for the 'cause'. Other NUWT leaders had different religious beliefs which also gave them a keen interest in the feminist morality movement. Agnes Dawson had worked with the Church League for Women's Suffrage, an Anglican organisation.[61]

The NUWT also worked with the Catholic St Joan's Social and Political Alliance, which continued the campaigning traditions of Josephine Butler. It opposed legislation which criminalised prostitutes but which paid no attention to their clients.[62] Some of the Alliance's leading members were prominent in the NUWT. They included Florence Key, London LP member and friend of Ethel Froud, and

Nancy Parnell, NUWT president in 1936 and grand-daughter of Charles Stewart Parnell. However, the NUWT was decidedly ecumenical in its approach. Nancy Lightman, who was a practising Jew, attended a parliamentary deputation to Sir Douglas Hogg organised by the St Joan's Alliance to lobby him about extending the franchise to women under 30.[63] Ethel Froud addressed a St Joan's Alliance public meeting on the educational equalities still to be won.[64]

Unsurprisingly, the interest feminist teachers displayed in groups campaigning for equal moral standards between men and women was not shared by the NUSEC. Eleanor Rathbone was sceptical:

> An equal moral standard is something intangible. It cannot be brought about by one or a dozen parliamentary Bills, only by a change of heart, of neutral outlook, on the part of society and its members ... the existence of a strong ad hoc society [i.e. the AMSH] entirely devoted to these questions and affiliated to our union restricts the part which a wholly women's organisation like ours can play.[65]

Although the NUWT gave attention to moral standards such campaigns did not have the support of the earlier campaigns such as those against the Contagious Diseases Act or section 40d. When a European conference on educational cinema was held in the Hague in 1928 no governmental or film industry representatives attended. Theodora Bonwick, on behalf of the NUWT, was the only British delegate.[66] Theodora also led the London Unit cinema group. She organised and introduced a deputation to the Cinematograph Exhibitors' Association to establish cooperation between the trade and those keen to 'further the healthy all round development of young people'. She wanted to ensure regular film performances for London children which were 'wholesome, instructive, and amusing'.[67]

The Women's Freedom League continued its work on equal standards of behaviour between men and women. The NUWT and the League worked together especially against discriminatory sentences given to women by the courts. A particularly important case for the Women's Freedom League was that of Elsie Kathleen Smith, who attempted, unsuccessfully, to suffocate her illegitimate child. She was imprisoned for four months in Holloway prison and the WFL campaigned for her release. In court the identity of the child's father was withheld to protect his position as a member of the Canadian Air Force. The mother's 'status' counted for nothing and her name was published in the press. The WFL demanded that men and women be treated equally by the courts and be held equally responsible for the care of children.[68]

'Equality First'

It became increasingly difficult for feminists outside teaching to work together on similar campaigns. The WFL, AMSH, Open Door Council, *Time and Tide* and the NUWT reflected the 'old' feminism of the pre-war militant suffrage days, which emphasised equality and equal rights. The 'new feminists' typified by the NUSEC focused on women's responsibilities as wives and mothers and referred back to the separate spheres argument of the Anti-Suffrage League. Writing in *Time and Tide* Winifred Holtby summed up the 'old feminists' in this way:

> The Old Feminists believe that [sex differentiation] and the attempt to preserve it by political and economic laws and social traditions not only checks the development of the woman's personality, but prevents her from making that contribution to the common good which is the privilege and the obligation of every human being ... But while the inequality exists, while injustice is done and opportunities denied to the great majority of women, I shall have to be a feminist, and an Old Feminist, with the motto Equality First. And I shan't be happy till I get it.[69]

Such strength of feeling and conviction persisted too in many members of the NUWT despite several setbacks. The feminist teachers had not received recognition on Burnham. The state had not gone on from the 1918 Representation of the People Act to pass legislation giving economic reforms. Feminists had had to campaign hard even for the extension of the vote to women who were 21. Yet the arguments which split the feminist movement so drastically also emerged in less destructive form inside the NUWT. Young women entering teaching and the NUWT did not have a suffrage background nor the political understanding that represented. In the 1930s the union even had to hold a conference to 'give the younger members some knowledge of the significance of the women's movement'.[70] Exasperation inevitably filtered into their internal discussions.

A particular source of argument was the character of the *Woman Teacher* under the editorship of Emily Phipps. In 1927 she expressed the wish to resign as editor because of opposition to her views: 'I have known for some time that my policy is out of harmony with the ideas of a considerable section of the union.'[71] Agnes Dawson believed that the young teachers now working in schools were uninterested in the old feminist struggle which Emily Phipps' editorship represented.[72] According to Emily the disgreement was between the London Unit and the rest of the membership. She particularly resented their view that the character of the journal was responsible for the drop in the London Unit membership. A paper written by Mrs Ada Ferrari on behalf of the London Unit had argued that the content of the journal was too controversial and its tone too propagandist. Articles were, the London Unit said, too long and of insufficiently broad educational interest.[73] In response Emily scribbled down her thoughts in a hurried note, complete with her usual underlinings: 'You cannot *state* a case in a short paragraph, let alone *answer* it.'[74] Exasperated by the London Unit she complained to Ethel Froud that the London members neither sent in articles nor provided information she could use, even though she had 'personally entreated prominent London members'.[75] Emily became very despondent and even thought of relinquishing her post as secretary of the Law and Tenure Committee: 'I do not feel like going on with it, as the continual dissatisfaction expressed over the *Woman Teacher* has taken some of my nerve and much of my courage.'[76]

Such despair was inevitable. By the late 1920s many of the leaders of the fight for the franchise inside the NUT were reaching retirement age. The views which they had held through the difficult days of the First World War had not been realised in the post-war reconstruction. Instead the feminist forces which had organised so strongly had been dissipated. Those advocates of 'equal rights' were no longer part of a mass movement. Even amongst so-called feminist organisations the ideas of Emily Phipps, Theodora Bonwick, Ethel Froud and Agnes Dawson had little currency. Although the NUWT was becoming increasingly politically isolated, members did not consider dropping their convictions. Instead they looked to new ways to keep alive a feminist movement and their sense of political identity through an extensive range of cultural activities organised by, within, and for NUWT members. The suffrage movement had evolved powerful images of women to promote the 'cause'. The feminist teachers continued this tradition with the purpose too of reaffirming their *own* commitment to the cause of equality, as the next chapter will elaborate.

7
The Community of the NUWT

Banners of Optimism

In the hectic pre-war days women teachers had experienced many forms of 'women's communities' outside the school staffroom. A plethora of women's political organisations and clubs had thrived. Here both married and unmarried women could meet like-minded friends. The situation had changed by the 1920s. Not only was that form of organised culture a thing of the past but unmarried women were no longer seen as making a positive contribution to society. It was against this background that the NUWT organised autonomously its own images of feminism and leisure and recreational activities referring back to the traditions of the pre-war suffrage movement. In the hard times of the 1920s the images created by the NUWT had the function of making the feminists' existence known to the public world and of reaffirming, to themselves, their own value. The political demonstrations which the NUWT organised continued the tradition of suffrage 'spectacles'. They shared the same intention – of creating positive alternative models of feminism, counterposed to the haridan, the harpy or the spinster which were the staple figures of media imagery. An important visual component of such events was the banners made by NUWT branches. The suffrage banners had been professionally designed and executed and they had often presented an idealised image of women as individual heroines. In contrast the NUWT banners were designed and produced by the women themselves and carried slogans which emphasised the union's collective commitment to sexual equality.[1]

The national NUWT banner encapsulated the feminists' emphasis on self-activity, freedom, and militancy in the former suffrage motto: 'Who would be free herself must strike the blow.'[2] The slogan was embroidered on a scrolling riband surmounted by crossed quills, with an image of the rising sun framed by a circular riband with the words 'National Union of Women Teachers'. The banner was made in the union's colours of green and gold with cream.[3]

The banners of individual branches reflected suffrage, literary, religious and labour movement themes. 'Laborare est orare' proclaimed the Willesden banner; 'Liberty, justice and freedom', stated West Ham; 'Woman's cause is man's – they rise or sink together', announced the Woolwich banner drawing on the Tennyson epithet well used in the suffrage movement.[4] At an equal rights demonstration in 1920 a private competition was held for the best banner. All but four of the 27 London NUWT branches made banners and the competition was won by the St Pancras branch with its optimistic 'Women arise, the dawn is here' – a slogan embroidered against a rising sun accompanied by the assertive motto: 'Men must be educated and women must do it.' In true suffrage style, on the march the banners were paraded to the strains of the Marseillaise.[5]

Today, the usual props of a demonstration are simple, mass-produced placards with no visual content beyond a bare slogan. It was different for these women. Banners were seen as an almost permanent synthesis of a branch's views rather than as a one-off measure for a particular event. Women teachers raised money to make elaborate banners: demonstration drill classes to illustrate the latest Board of Education syllabus, 'American sales', or 1/6d per head levies.[6] The slogans of the NUWT were a constant feature of their political activities and lives. In Ethel Froud's room at the Union's offices there was mounted in stained glass on the window the motto which she believed guided her own life: 'The dreams of those that labour are the only ones that ever come true.'[7] Members proudly displayed their allegiance to the NUWT by wearing green and yellow badges 'as a sign of comradeship'. These became treasured items: in her will Miss Annie Byett bequeathed her badge to another Birmingham colleague.[8]

... And Demonstrations of Hope

While banners and badges served to indicate the general strength of feminist feeling of the NUWT, demonstrations provided a means of showing publicly the Union's view on particular questions. During the 1920s the Union organised several demonstrations, often with other groups such as the Women's Freedom League, Six Point Group or Association of Women Clerks and Secretaries, to demand equal pay, equal political rights or extension of the franchise to women under 30. Agnes Dawson and Ethel Froud frequently spoke at such demonstrations, but the meetings also communicated feminism, sometimes spectacularly like the great suffrage marches of the past, by nonverbal means. On Women's Sunday 1908 the WSPU had organised 30,000 women dressed in white to symbolise women's purity.[9]

The 1926 demonstration to extend the franchise included a similar idea. The disenfranchised under-30s were asked to wear green, one of the union's colours. For the occasion bulk purchases of green silk were made from John Lewis's store so young teachers could make their own dresses. The march was divided into various contingents: university graduates, Irish pipers, NUWT central council, and a lorry carrying a Montessori class. Bicycle riders stewarding the demonstration sported green and yellow ribbons.[10]

Women's sections of the Labour Party, the Women's Cooperative Guild, and the Parents' Guild sent contingents. Feminists distributed leaflets widely. They 'bombarded' tennis clubs and urged participants to forgo their sport for the day. In East Ham leaflets were given out at the schools' sports day and children were told to post leaflets in letter boxes on their way home. In central London the women left leaflets in restaurants and Lyon's cafes, aimed at customers and the low-waged, young – and thus voteless – women who worked there as waitresses. The suffrage movement might have died, but its methods of meticulous organisation still existed in the NUWT.[11]

Demonstrations, banners, feminist spectacle all performed the dual function of keeping alive the cause within society at large and of reaffirming to individual members of the NUWT their collective identity as feminists in a world increasingly out of step with such ideas. The feminists were becoming isolated from the dominant ideas of the teaching profession and of the women's movement of the so-called new feminists. Agnes, Theodora, Ethel, Emily and their colleagues never faltered in their commitment to the cause, but their strategies for creating their lives around this ideal changed. In particular the NUWT, rather than the teaching profession or the 'new' women's movement, formed the framework of their social existence and the source of their friendships. In the politically depressing times of the 1920s and 1930s the feminists' personal friendships were increasingly important in sustaining their political beliefs.

Personal Friendship: Emily Phipps, Adelaide Jones, Clare Neal – A Separatist Community

Emily Phipps, Agnes Dawson, Theodora Bonwick and Ethel Froud approached their relationships with women in different ways, reflecting their individual attitudes, choices and temperaments and also mirroring their specific feminist interests and their past allegiance to the ideas of different suffrage organisations.

Throughout her adult life Emily Phipps enjoyed close friendships with Clare Neal and with Adelaide Jones, friendships which affected her professional life. Emily began her friendship with Clare Neal in her 20s when they were both teachers in Devonport, the naval dock-yard which was Emily's hometown. When she was only 29 Emily decided to apply for the job as headmistress of Swansea Higher Grade School. She must have impressed the school board because they decided to appoint her and were most anxious to secure her services when she at first declined the post. The School Board invited her to discuss the matter with the Education Committee, reassured her about the school's premises and paid her generous expenses.[12] Within a week Emily changed her mind. She would accept the post with the proviso that Clare Neal be offered an assistant teacher's post in the same school. Although the school board had not previously adver-tised such a vacancy, it agreed to secure Miss Neal's services. The couple uprooted themselves to another coastal town. In Swansea they lived far away from the docks and the metalworks, in Sketty, over-looking the Swansea bay which afforded easy access to the bays of the Gower.

For 30 years they shared their Swansea home, until Emily was obliged to move to London. Her new legal career as a barrister necessi-tated her gaining admittance to the Bar in London. On this occasion Clare Neal stayed behind in Sketty for another five years. Unlike Emily she had no new career, nor an income from the NUWT to look forward to. Clare stayed in Swansea continuing as headteacher of the Glanmor Central School until her retirement in 1930.

Meanwhile Emily moved to Brondesbury, then a respectable suburb in north west London. Here she set up home with her WFL friend of many years, Adelaide Jones, the NUWT financial secretary. They spent much time in each other's company – at home and at NUWT head-quarters where Emily organised her Law and Tenure work and her writing for the Woman Teacher. They seem to have been polar oppo-sites. As their photographs show, Miss Phipps was a tiny woman; Miss Jones was unusually tall. Their characters too seem very different, but perhaps complementary. Emily was a born speaker with 'a quick brain, untiring energy' and an acerbic tongue.[13] Adelaide was a backroom organiser, a poor speaker but a doer. As Ethel Froud said of her, 'She will tell you she is not a speaker ... though speakers certainly have their place in union propaganda, yet the welfare of any organisation is tremendously dependent upon faithful, day to day, routine and drudgery ...'[14]

Adelaide did not supplant Clare in Emily's affections. In 1930 when Clare retired, she too moved to London to Emily and Adelaide's Brondesbury home.[15] Such ties of friendship were as strong as those shared with the women's families. In illness Emily was nursed by her brother and sister – and by Clare and Adelaide.[16] When Clare died in 1938, her funeral was organised by both her sister and Emily.[17] In retirement from their respective jobs with the union, Emily and

Adelaide shared a new home. In hectic fashion they first retired back to Emily's native county, Devon, to the seaside resort of Babbacombe, near Torquay.[18] Shortly afterwards they moved again to yet another coastal town, Eastbourne. Any hopes of a peaceful time were shattered by the bombardment of the town, and the two women retreated inland to the cottage belonging to Edgar, Emily's brother. Here Emily spent her last years at Cremyll Cottage, named after the Devonport district, not far from Newbury, the site of future feminist activity at Greenham Common.[19]

Throughout her life Emily held the friendship and expertise of women professionals in high esteem. Characteristically, when she became ill at the end of her life it was a woman doctor who attended her.[20] Her political 'origins' in the militant wing of the suffrage movement were replicated in her lifestyle. Her entire political work was undertaken in the women's movement – either the WFL or NUWT; her life as a teacher for 30 years was conducted as head of a separate girls' school; her home life was shared with feminist colleagues. The quasi-separatist nature of her life was very different from Agnes Dawson's life and Agnes's portrayal of it.

Agnes Dawson: Daughter, Aunt and Friend of Munnsie

Like Emily, Agnes Dawson had close friendships with women in the NUWT. For Agnes, however, the relationship to her parents and the experiences she drew from her working-class background were also very important. She once wrote to Ethel Froud requesting her to write up 'a little summary of me'.[21] Information which Agnes thought was relevant included her knowledge of working-class poverty, drawn from her direct experience:

> Of working parents – father a journeyman carpenter often out of work. Attended elementary schools in Peckham from 4 until age of 14 ... In capacity of H[ead] T[eacher] sat frequently at Care Com[mittee] meetings and was made aware of the hardship of the casual labourer and his children. Always endeavoured to get relief given irrespective of the earnings of older members of the family – maintained that these young people should not be kept in state of perpetual destitution because of misfortune of parents.[22]

This interest in 'class' issues, which was also reflected in her Labour Party and former NUWSS membership, seemed to affect her attitude to friendships and relationships. Her own working-class family played an important part in her life. Until 1925 she lived at home, acting as housekeeper for her father, Isaac, after the death of her mother, Sarah, in 1917.[23] She formed a close attachment to her niece, Mary. In an interview with *Time and Tide* she included an account of days out with her niece at the seaside, taking her for donkey rides. In adult life too Mary described how 'very very fond' she was of her aunt.[24] Agnes stressed her role in 'traditional' family life as a daughter and an aunt. When interviewed as a member of the LCC she was quick to emphasise her attachment to children:

> If I ever regretted leaving school teaching after 30 years in the London service I would only have to take one look at the children I meet as I do this job to realise that this is real work for a woman.[25]

Although a single woman, in her campaign for jobs for married women teachers, she criticised a school atmosphere dominated by 'celibate' teachers, that is unmarried women like herself:

> To debar married teachers the opportunity to serve was to do a disservice to education. Men would not send their boys to schools where all the male teachers were celibates. They would consider it an unhealthy atmosphere. She claimed the same for girls.[26]

Such pronouncements might suggest at first that Agnes did not have close friendships with other feminists to the same extent as Emily. In fact she did, but was less open about it even within the NUWT. In 1925 when she was a full-time LCC councillor she set up home with Anne Munns, who three years earlier had started to work as a class teacher in Agnes' school, Crawford Street Infants.[27] Anne had been a past member of the LTA and a member of the NUWT for some time. She suffered from ill health during her teaching career – recurrent rheumatism, malnutrition and neuralgia[28] – and in 1928 she was obliged to retire from her post due to cardiac debility.

Of her relationship with Anne, Agnes could privately write that 'Munnsie' was 'her pal and partner'.[29] Agnes seems to have drawn a distinction between her public life in the NUWT and her private life. Although Miss Munns' ill health may have prevented her taking an energetic role in NUWT events, it is surprising that there are no records in the NUWT's archive of the two of them attending functions together, nor are there photographs of them together. Agnes' regular correspondence does not mention Munnsie, and on Anne's death Agnes even felt the need to explain to Muriel Pierotti – who by then had been secretary of the NUWT for 12 years – who Anne was.[30]

Like Emily, Agnes organised her political activity around her feminist beliefs and her allegiance to the NUWT. Unlike Emily, most of her day-to-day work was undertaken outside the NUWT in the Labour Party and council chamber. It was experiences such as these which caused her to reject NUWT affiliation to the Labour Party. However, the same experiences of the labour movement and of working in mixed sex situations also affected the way she interpreted a feminist lifestyle. No doubt her friendship with Anne Munns, which lasted for 27 years – well into their respective retirements – gave her much support. Such a lifestyle, however, was no form of separatist community such as that enjoyed by Emily, nor was it seen as such by Agnes.

Ethel Froud and 'Celibacy'

Ethel Froud, no less than Emily Phipps or Agnes Dawson, seemed to fit her friendships into her particular political role, in her case the role of general secretary of the union. She had no one close friend with whom she lived, although she was particularly attached to Miss B.M. Pearson, who Nan McMillan has described as 'fixated' on Ethel.[31] Through tact and sensitivity she seemed to be able to establish friendships with women of sharply different views within the Union. To Nan McMillan she appeared as a kindly person, nice to everyone – who carried the union with her.[32]

Unlike Agnes, Ethel Froud celebrated the feminist lifestyle of unmarried women. She believed that spinsters like herself possessed energy and creativity. Ethel Froud asserted the independence of women from men in personal relationships. Women did not need physical contact with men in order to lead happy and fulfilled lives. At a time when the spinster or 'celibate' was seen as old-fashioned, warped and inadequate, she affirmed her own way of life.[33] Criticising the press she argued: 'We can't have it said that we celibates are only some fraction of a human being.'[34] For Ethel Froud, too, friendship with women was an important part of her life and political perspective, even though she seemed to have no close friendships like those of Emily, Adelaide, or Clare.[35]

Close Friends or Lesbians?

In discussing the friendships of NUWT feminists it would be tempting to suggest that these were lesbian relationships. I think this would be wrong. Nan McMillan makes some perceptive comments on the nature of the friendships:

> Their lives were together. Nearly all of them didn't have a man relationship. I'm not saying they were lesbians – the word was hardly known then, but they set up homes in twos ... Nearly all of them were with a partner. They were a group of their own very much ... It was a strange phenomenon of that time ...[36]

Today such friendships might be defined as lesbian by women involved in them, irrespective of the physical content of the relationship. Questioning fixed concepts of lesbianism Lillian Faderman has suggested that the friendships of the suffrage movement were lesbian relationships.[37] However, this was not seen as such by the feminist teachers in the NUWT. In the 1920s, and before, the term lesbian was not used with the political, social or sexual connotations of today's women's movement. The very language was derived from the medical field: scientists, sexologists, psychologists. Lesbian women were construed as objects of study and as such they were perceived as 'abnormal'. When Krafft Ebing or Havelock Ellis wrote about 'inverts' they categorised lesbians as a small group. Writing in 1901 Krafft Ebing noted that there were 'only 50 known cases of lesbianism'.[38] For women who shared their lives in the feminist movement, to define themselves as lesbian would have meant giving themselves a negative sexual identity and categorising themselves as a freak minority. Far from defining their identity as stemming from a feminist political movement, women would be defining themselves as disparate individuals outside political parameters. Even if there *were* sexual relationships between feminist teachers such as Emily Phipps and Clare Neal, in itself this adds little to what we know of their personal lives.[39] The discourse did not exist for women to identify themselves proudly as lesbians. When the 1921 Criminal Law Amendment to criminalise lesbian behaviour was discussed in Parliament, it received no opposition from the NUWT.[40] At first glance this could be read as an omission from an otherwise good record of opposition to the criminalisation of women on grounds of their sex. It may also be read as an interesting example of how the feminist teachers saw themselves. Although they realised their views were not popular they believed in them strongly and drew confidence and inspiration from them. They did not identify themselves in any way with a group of women categorised as perverts or inverts.[41]

Nor was there a discourse available to create positive sexual identities or to develop a personal 'language of sisterhood'. In their public speeches and personal correspondence alike there is a common language – the tones of the respectable schoolteacher. The letters of Emily Phipps to Ethel Froud are a case in point. Written in a colloquial style, they discussed the everyday problems of political activists: 'We do all our own housework and garden and Miss Neal has engagements 6 evenings this week: so have I but I cut them.'[42]

They also give an insight into what was regarded as decadent activity, or perhaps more appositely, the break from duty and meetings! Urging Ethel Froud to visit Swansea for a weekend to combine union business with pleasure, Emily suggested:

Friday, 14th, stay in bed in the morning – with books to read if you like. Afternoon, get up *if you want to*, write letters, also if you wish. Probably two or three people for tea ... gentle seaside walks on good roads Saturday and/or perhaps Sunday. Lovely views. (original emphasis)[43]

Clearly from the style of the letters, Emily and Ethel are friends who enjoy each other's company. But how this does explain the relationship between Emily and Clare when the latter is referred to in such correspondence by her professional 'title', Miss Neal? The polite language of the times hides from view the close nature of the women's friendships.

Feminist Leisure

The NUWT feminists were keen to find opportunities to meet together socially as an identifiable group. Feminist cultural and leisure activities outside the union did not flourish in the way they had before the war. The women (re)created for themselves a culture of leisure through the local branches and national organisation of the union. Social gatherings, fund raising and educational activities were all part of a branch's regular programme of events. In 1928 the East Ham branch, for example, numbered among its activities a 'summer garden meeting' which Miss Phipps addressed and at which the drama club performed a sketch entitled 'Balloons'. Earlier in the year Emily Phipps, Ethel Froud, Adelaide Jones and Susan Lawrence (the local MP) were amongst guests of honour at a dinner for Miss Anne Hewitt: 'The dinner was a great success and it is possible that it may become an annual event'.[44] Other activities included talks on the new prospects in education, South African education and courses in country dancing and speech training.[45]

Reading was a popular pastime, so the feminists organised a subscription library and various bookclubs through Mudies and Boots. Under the aegis of the NUWT, women organised dramatic and choral societies, and, in London, a women's orchestra. For the energetic members there were ballroom and country dancing classes and netball competitions. For the more cerebral there were whist drives, lantern lectures and talks on a range of topics. Miss Grace Coombs' drawings of birds or a talk on 'Birds of Rocky Islands, especially the Gannets of Grassholm' proved attractive to some. Others seemed content to attend talks such as that given by Miss Phipps for Harrow members with the vague but untrying title of 'matters of importance to all women teachers'.[46] In 1928 alone the London Unit organised clubs and classes on badminton, ballroom dancing, choir, cookery, country dancing, dramatics, fencing, German, hockey, netball, Mudies' circle and travel club.[47]

Parties, bring and buy, teas and bazaars provided a source of enjoyment and a means of fundraising. For Hallowe'en 1925 the London Unit held a party in a house decorated in orange and black, with witches, bats, owls and ghosts. There were 'ghostly thrills' and fortunes told by the five 'witches' present![48] For a particular American tea it was suggested that members might bring the following 'delicacies': fish or meat paste, ham, eggs, chocolate, jam, biscuits, cakes, jellies, tinned and fresh fruit and cream.[49]

Bazaars were an opportunity for members to raise funds and to dress up in theatrical costumes. The London Unit usually organised bazaars on literary themes such as the works of Shakespeare or the plays of J.M. Barrie. A photograph of the 1927 Shakespeare sale reveals a motley crowd: Agnes Dawson appears dressed as a Shakesperian bumpkin, her sister as some sort of prince. Other more obvious characters seem to be Henry VIII and Falstaff complete with cotton wool beards. Untroubled by such goings-on, a young girl views a homemade snowman for sale.[50]

For the Barrie sale the feminists secured the services of Hilda Trevelyan, the first Wendy in Peter Pan, to open the proceedings: awnings and drawings representing the sets of a wood in Barrie's play 'Dear Brutus' adorned the stalls. The day raised nearly £600 for the union's work which, the London Unit stated, endorsed J.M. Barrie's wish 'that every child shall have an equal chance'.[51]

This wide variety of leisure activies were all seen as proper and enjoyable pastimes for feminists. Yet there was sometimes friction between the women who organised leisure activities and those who were busy with political events. There were in particular disagreements about the elaborate work of the travel club. The London Unit had established a travel club in 1922 to organise trips at home and abroad. The club held lectures on the history, art and architecture of various countries, published a holiday register of accommodation recommended by colleagues and loaned out library materials, slides and a stamp collection.[52] The club could not always book rooms at NUWT headquarters because, Ethel Froud said, there were so many other activities going on.[53] There was also some controversy about some of the countries the club visited. One of the club's aims was to promote 'the great cause of international understanding and goodwill'. To this end official welcomes were often given by women's organisations and educational bodies in the countries visited. When such visits were to the USSR, or Norway or Canada the welcomes were not contentious. The projected trip to Germany in the 1930s, however, caused Ethel Froud to express much concern to Miss Coombs, the organiser.[54]

Celebrating 'the Cause'

The NUWT viewed some of their leisure activities as more than simply a way of spending time in congenial company. Many of the events publicised in the *Woman Teacher* were designed to celebrate feminist achievements and to reaffirm 'the cause'. The Union held many official dinners to celebrate women obtaining the vote at age 21, continued support for equal pay, and the individual achievement of Emily Phipps qualifying as a barrister. It organised a less formal celebration to mark Agnes Dawson's sixtieth birthday and her year of office as deputy chair of the LCC. On this occasion she was given a book of signatures from NUWT well-wishers. She appears in the photograph of the event looking somewhat embarrassed wearing a garland of flowers as she lights the candles on her four-tier birthday cake.[55] Such events were internal union functions held for members and their friends. But they also became public occasions through their recording in the *Woman Teacher* and part of the *official* life and history of the union.

Meticulous organisation went into such events. Ethel Froud ensured that the union's colours of yellow and green were used as much as possible. Flower arrangements of chrysanthemums and smilax were in the union colours and menus were printed in dark green ink on light green card. Ethel organised stewards to place people in their designated places – the elaborate seating plans are still extant – and to announce the names of people for the president to 'receive' them.[56] For the 1928 dinner Ethel organised an ad hoc choir, which included Emily Phipps, to lead community singing. The highlight was a rendition of 'The awakening', the NUWT song. This carried on the tradition 'of the suffrage fight from the early days when "The March of the Women" used to attract wondering crowds.'[57] The food served was far grander than that enjoyed at fundraising teas: oysters, Petite Marmite Henri IV, sole, roast meat, sorbets and Peach Melba. Vegetarians, too, were catered for.[58]

The guests of honour at the 1928 celebration were Miss L.E. Lane and Joseph Tate, founders of the Equal Pay League. The event took on an almost evangelical character as past presidents recounted tales of the suffrage movement. Emily Phipps told of her night in the caves on the Gower, Agnes Dawson of her 'one militant act' on census night. Toasts were drunk to feminist good causes, to 'all who dared to be free', the NUWT and its great future.[59] The event was nevertheless conducted with sobriety. As Emily Phipps wrote, 'The "wine" was in most cases merely a symbolic term, the toasts being honoured through a much less fashionable medium.'[60]

The evangelical tone of the evening extended to the concluding speech by Miss A.A. Kenyon, the vice president of 1928. She quoted

Moses' advice to Joshua, 'Be strong and of good courage:'

> She believed that the struggle became harder as we approached nearer to victory. Our goal was the summit of Mount Everest. We could have a short rest for the purpose of refreshment, but must then go on. We must think not only of women teachers, but of all the other women – those who were down-trodden, those who were driven into the streets. When complete equality of payment and of opportunity was won, these evils would no longer exist, and then indeed we should have a new heaven and a new earth.[61]

There were also celebrations of the achievements of individual women outside the NUWT. In 1924, for example, Ethel Froud organised a reception for all women MPs. The apparent chaos at this event was no doubt a factor in ensuring that future social/political events were so well organised. More than 500 women teachers turned up at the reception after school, many without informing Ethel in advance. The catering organised by the University of London was entirely inadequate. There were too few chairs and owing to the numbers attending some stood on their seats and blocked others' views. Many members wrote in to the office complaining that they had not received value for their tickets; others expressed their pride in seeing the women MPs: 'We each had about three penn'orth of food, but we consider that five women MPs (three of them perfectly new, and the oldest one far from stale) were well worth the other three and ninepence'.[62]

Although the union was a national body numbering several thousand, members did not see the organisers and secretary as part of a remote bureaucracy. The members saw the NUWT as the members' union and thus women wrote letters to Ethel Froud outlining their grievances or concerns expecting – and receiving – individual responses. It was with the union rather than with the staffroom or non-Conformist Church that the women primarily identified themselves. Martha Vicinus has suggested that in the inter-war years unmarried women teachers 'had lost the richly nurturing women's sub-culture of the past'.[63] This is not true. Both formally and informally the NUWT provided a feminist culture for thousands of women teachers. Its activities, however, reflected the suffrage lifestyle of the earlier Edwardian period. Those who entered teaching in the 1920s or 1930s had neither the same political nor social experiences. Nan McMillan did not start teaching until the late 1920s. Recalling her feelings at the time, she found the community of the NUWT old-fashioned and decidedly odd: 'It was like the suffragettes. It was their end-all and be-all with many of them. They were possessed of almost a sort of religious fervour about it ... it was their lives ...'[64]

This indeed *was* their lives; what drew women to the dinners or lantern lectures or ballroom dancing classes was their wish to be with like-minded feminists. Running through the feminists' friendships, demonstrations or dinners was their commitment to the cause. The dedication of the leaders did not dwindle in later years. Even in death, as the next chapter will show, the politics of the feminist suffrage movement remained extremely important.

8

Death of the Leaders: Birth of the 'Pioneers'

The deaths of leading feminist teachers, as much as their lives, became part of the NUWT experience. The funeral services, obituaries and private letters of condolence resounded with the same political commitments with which their lives had been conducted. Through the pages of the *Woman Teacher* the deeds and words of founder members were commemorated and celebrated. In some cases the feminists set up charitable educational funds to remember in more permanent form the lives and interests of departed colleagues.[1]

Theodora Bonwick died at the early age of 51 in 1928. The union devised a narrative for Theodora's death which incorporated it within the NUWT experience. By 1928 Theodora had been rehabilitated after her past omission in not leaving the LTA promptly enough for some members. She had been elected president of the London Unit and was about to take office. Her last public appearance, for that is how the *Woman Teacher* described it, took place at the Victory Dinner. The paper reported that news of her serious illness was given to a central council meeting. Members were despatched to the nursing home to give a NUWT message of support, but they arrived too late. She had passed away the previous night.[2]

As one of the first founder members of the NUWT to die, she was portrayed in death as one of the 'pioneers'. The obituaries and tributes make no mention of the hostility that some members had felt towards her. Not until 1951 – when an article entitled 'The NUWT Pioneers' appeared in *Woman Teacher* – was opposition officially acknowledged and publicly recorded.[3] The iconography of pioneer could then withstand mention of the opposition – without detracting from the mythology. The *Woman Teacher* attributed her death directly to her activity for the cause. She had damaged her voice almost permanently through speaking at WSPU street corner meetings[4] and she had never recovered from a nervous breakdown brought on, her friends maintained, from years of activity in the NUWT and devotion to the 'humanitarian movement'. Her present death and past service found common explanation in the feminist movement: '"Deeds not words" – was graven in her character.'[5]

The union organised the funeral service and cremation of Theodora Bonwick with the same attention to detail which characterised other 'ceremonies' of the NUWT. It stipulated that no mourning was to be worn.[6] Service cards were printed and filed in the NUWT archives. The gathering sang 'The Lord is my shepherd', and were reminded in the service card that it was 'Miss Bonwick's favourite hymn'. The service ended in the Non-Conformist and NUWT spirit with the singing of 'He who would valiant be', which ends appropriately with, 'I'll fear not what men say, I'll labour night and day, To be a Pilgrim.'[7]

Union members took flowers to Holloway prison, the site of imprisonment of so many suffragettes, and to the local infirmary and workhouse.[8] One of those to pay a written tribute was Emily Phipps. She carefully distinguished between those who had lost a worker to the cause and those who had a lost a friend. Perhaps Theodora was too closely identified with the London Unit for a warmer response to have been elicited: 'From 1905 she had been a suffrage worker, and never spared herself in the cause of women. We have lost a loyal comrade, her staff and pupils have lost a real friend.'[9]

The cause itself provided a mechanism of mourning and a discourse of martyrdom and sacrifice, as well as a hope that life was not in vain: 'The cause is always greater than they who serve it: we can each only make our contribution and pass on.'[10] The NUWT made attempts to celebrate publicly Theodora's life and mourn her death through the establishment of a holiday fund for working-class London children. Agnes Dawson broadcast an appeal on the wireless for the fund and the union produced leaflets, describing Theodora's work as a teacher, reformer and social worker. However, they received little money from the general public – or indeed from members. Instead of building a holiday home for children, funds were only available to finance visits to the countryside.[11] The reality of this memorial venture contrasts starkly with the written contributions on Theodora's life. Those writing their tributes in the two editions of the *Woman Teacher* which carried her obituaries believed that the life of Theodora Bonwick *would* be remembered – by women in the movement.

'Some People Will Forget First Principles'

By the late 1930s and 1940s the union was changing. Those who had founded it were no longer middle-aged women awaiting the imminent achievement of equal rights. They were older, nearing retirement age, very aware of the changing political climate. Their own commitment, despite their age and frequent ill health, remained undiminished. Joseph Tate, the Equal Pay League and NFWT secretary, was still active and supporting the cause. In 1944 he wrote to Mrs Churchill, urging her to give advice to the Prime Minister because 'all men needed the advice of a wise and good woman'. Although Mr Tate's advancing years brought, he said, diminishing energy, his 'desire for truth and fairness [was] by no means diminished'.[12]

A letter Ethel Froud wrote in the late 1930s expresses well her own mood at the time and her continued commitment. Ill health had prevented her from attending a meeting to say goodbye to Adelaide Jones, retiring as full-time NUWT treasurer. Her letter was written as a speech designed to be read to members as an appreciation of Miss Jones's work. It reminded members of the past:

> [the founders] were a *dynamic* force and *drove* them to organise themselves into a coherent body though they had literally nothing except their convinced belief in a great ideal to help them. They had *no* experience, *no* office, *no* money for fares (or anything else) except what came out of their own pockets ...' (original emphasis)

Miss Jones embodied, according to Ethel, the 'essential truth': 'If you want a thing done, do something about it yourself.'[13] Nowadays, she said, women teachers had a union machinery that they could use. That hadn't been the case in the past:

> Pray that women teachers use it ceaselessly to promote the fundamental aims for which it was founded i.e. to secure and establish a rightful status for women in the scheme of things, the status of equality, for without the recognition and fact of women's right to equal consideration with men in the scheme of things, there can be no permanent progress for us and our so-called 'emancipation' will be but a delusion and a snare – a shadow and not the substance.[14]

In her last year as general secretary – the first year of the Second World War – Ethel Froud expressed similar cautions about the present state of women's rights, while maintaining her own commitment to the cause. One of the biggest difficulties, she thought, was the back-sliding of members who were soft on the NUT:

> On the one hand, reactionaries will seize their present opportunities and put the clock back till it hardly works at all and, on the other, timid isolated folk ... enquire 'could there be a relaxation of the rule about dual membership?' [with the NUT] ... That is one of our great dangers in the face of present difficulties, some people who forget first principles ... Don't think I am as down-hearted as this may seem to sound: I am only serious in viewing present ruins, but I still have the faith which started us on our way and I am sure the seed which we have sown, and tended, will in due course, bring forth its harvest.[15]

In 1940 Ethel retired from her post and went to live in Saltdean near Brighton on the south coast. There she named her house after Mrs Pankhurst and Lady Rhondda and, as her obituarist records, established a fine garden despite the difficulties of the climate.[16] The ceremony to mourn her death in the following year was seen by members as an opportunity for the NUWT to have a 'time of retrospect and thankfulness for what has been'.[17] Amongst the tributes to her public work as general secretary was one from her friend, Miss Pearson, who recorded the 'many hours of happy association' within the NUWT.[18]

'You Mustn't Allow Me to Waste Your Time'

In 1934 Agnes Dawson informed the NUWT officers she wished to retire from her NUWT Legal and Tenure Committee work and would not seek re-election at the next LCC elections.[19] The last conference of the NUWT which she attended as an officer of the union was in 1938. She also relinquished her post as union trustee. At the same time Emily Phipps too resigned her post as trustee, though she was unable to be present: Clare Neal had just died.[20] Both Agnes and Emily had held these positions for 20 years since the Harrogate conference of 1918.

By 1938 Agnes had retired with Anne Munns to Newport in Essex, near her old training college town of Saffron Walden. Although she no longer took an active part in NUWT business she did not abandon political activity. She was a JP and, in 1946, a candidate for the local parish council for the Labour Party. The NUWT secretary, Miss Pierotti, wrote for news of the result: 'If you are now chairman of the Labour Group there, I should so like to have a note in The *Woman Teacher*.'[21] It was the only local council election which Agnes did not win: 'The fact that we had awakened the village as to their rights and privileges brought forth the opponents in all their strength including a team of motorcars!! It was fun and worthwhile.'[22] Contact between Agnes and the NUWT was not broken. She visited headquarters to see friends, conscious still of the importance of carrying on the struggle: 'I shall turn up again some day, only you mustn't allow me to waste your time.'[23]

In turn, the NUWT did not forget her. On her birthday headquarters telegrammed: 'Birthday greetings and love from NUWT'.[24]

Emily Phipps: Pioneer and 'Fighting Temeraire'

Emily's commitment to the NUWT remained as strong as ever although her actual involvement in the work was less than the union publicly acknowledged. She wrote a column for the *Woman Teacher* throughout the 1930s and passed to headquarters news and correspondence of past friends such as Joseph Tate.[25] However, from the early 1930s to her death in 1943 Miss Phipps was dogged by debilitating illness, which necessitated her being nursed by Miss Neal, Miss Jones, and later her brother too.[26] Although her name appeared on headed notepaper as 'standing counsel' to the union, she could not provide legal services as she wished. Emily acknowledged these circumstances and asked for her name to be removed from its public position on the union notepaper: 'It is several years since I have done anything whatever in the Legal department.'[27] The other legal adviser, Miss Colvill, should have full recognition, Emily insisted, for the work she had carried out singlehandedly. Mindful perhaps of her past differences with some members, Emily felt it necessary to explain that her request was not a weakening of commitment to the union: 'I shall still feel the same interest in the NUWT as I have always felt, and should hope to be allowed to do anything in my power to help the splendid and self-sacrificing work that is being done.'[28]

The central council did not want to agree to her request and asked her to reconsider. Increasingly aware of their political isolation the union was reluctant to acknowledge that the days which gave rise to the birth of the NUWT were no more. The failing health or retirement of older feminist teachers meant breaking a link with the union's past and its mythology of the 'pioneers'. At first Emily Phipps did what the central council requested. She endorsed a compromise and the names of the legal advisers appeared in alphabetical order, thereby giving due prominence to Miss Colvill.[29] After two years Emily again requested the removal of her name, this time even more vigorously: '... the reason I want it omitted is that it is a sham, as regards legal matters, and at present I have not even a legal book to consult.'[30]

She also challenged the presentation of her role to younger members. Emily's correspondence here makes clear that she was well aware both of the changing times and of her declining health. Neither deflected her in any way from her past and continuing commitment to the union's ideals:

> Whatever influence my name may have had in the past, it has none now. A new generation has grown up which doesn't know me ... It is for these reasons that I wish my name [to be removed] and not from any feeling of friction. I shall always do all in my power to help the union.[31]

Unusually her letter to the general secretary was accompanied by another from Adelaide Jones. Carrying news about the effects of air raids on Eastbourne and expressing relief that London friends were safe, its main purpose was to reinforce Emily's wishes:

> The fact is that, although her health has wonderfully improved, it is impossible for her to do any legal work for we are absolutely in the

backwoods here, and since I left the office, we are out of touch with things ... She does not want her name to appear merely as an 'ornament'![32]

At last the central council agreed to Miss Phipps' request. She wrote a letter of thanks in response, again stressing that there was no acrimony between her and the union. This suggests that her past disagreements and arguments had probably been sharper than archive material reveals:

> It is indeed a sad milestone to me, but the sadness is in some degree mitigated by the thought that I am still able to help the union to a small extent. Anything I can do I shall do with the greatest pleasure as long as my health permits, and the relation between the central council and myself is in no way altered. The Union still holds the first place, and will continue to do so.[33]

Her death in 1943 brought relief from a heart disease which would have prevented a normal life.[34] In death as in life she was firm in her views. At her funeral, 'by Miss Phipps' wishes, there are to be no people present and no flowers.'[35] NUWT members were therefore unable to pay their respects 'publicly' at her funeral. Instead they wrote many letters to Miss Pierotti, conveying their grief and portraying the life of Emily Phipps as a pioneer for the cause. Emily was presented, as her suffrage sisters were in the *Suffrage Annual* 30 years before, as an inspiration to individual women. The suffrage tradition of publicly portraying women's achievements, carried through in the NUWT's banners, mottoes and dinner celebrations, was found too in these personal comments of colleagues. Adelaide Jones explained to Miss Pierotti that 'never a day passed without [Miss Phipps] mentioning the Union, the chief interest in her life.'[36] The 'discourse of the pioneer' was both a public and a personal language for the NUWT:

> Miss Phipps was one of those NUWT pioneers who, above all others, inspired me to want to take responsibility for women and to develope [sic] their powers and possibilities to the full ... She had a way too, of stimulating each one of us to do more than we had ever thought possible, and I know that I personally should never have attempted the responsible task of being President of the Union if it had not been for the challenge and inspiration of her words and her life.[37]

Mrs Ferrari, who had so slated the *Woman Teacher* under Emily Phipps' editorship in the late 1920s, elaborated Emily's attributes, concentrating on her skills in acrimonious situations: 'Who can forget her platform oratory, her manner of attack, her unassailable arguments for the righteousness of her cause and her scorn for anything which in her view assigned to women an inferiority complex?'[38]

Agnes Dawson said of Emily: 'We have indeed lost a staunch friend, her works will live. One had hoped that in happier days than these a reunion might have happened, but it was not to be. One feels privileged to have known her.'[39]

In the *Woman Teacher* Miss Phipps' obituary occupied two pages, surmounted by a full face photograph of Emily dressed in legal garb. Emily is portrayed as a NUWT pioneer: 'She helped to build the road on which [members] strive to triumph.' She is also depicted as part of the *present* life of the union: on the day before her death she was still preparing material for her *Woman Teacher* 'Searchlight' column.[40] The imagery of the article well evokes the suffrage era. The tribute from Miss Pierotti uses a vivid pictoral image to depict a battler against a hostile world. It is also the same image the suffrage supporter and journalist Henry Nevinson used to describe Charlotte Despard, the Women's Freedom League leader: 'Turner's famous picture of "The fighting Temeraire" shattered and on fire, but still blazing away at the encircling ships, reminds one irresistibly of Miss Phipps.'[41]

Importantly it is used to conjure a positive image of Miss Phipps' personality – and would have been read as such by NUWT members. The tribute continued:

> Implacable enemy of the second-rate, impatient of hypocrisy and self deception, steadfast in her opposition to all injustice and to inhumanity to man or animal, Miss Phipps was essentially of the fibre of the martyrs of all ages – those who refuse to compromise with principle, but having seen the truth, pursue it ceaselessly and selflessly.[42]

Here, in the 1940s, the 'official language' of the NUWT is still that of the period which give rise to its predecessor in the first years of the century. An equally important part of this obituary is the characterisation of Emily Phipps as a 'Renaissance woman'. In the same way as their NUWT obituarists described Theodora Bonwick singing in the Philarmonic Choir, or Ethel Froud gardening, so too is Emily's life outside the public sphere described and related to her union work:

> There seemed to be nothing she could not do if she turned her attention to it. She was musical, having a lovely contralto voice, she did beautiful fine embroidery, and was an accomplished linguist. Having learned to speak Italian, German and French she characteristically turned these achievements to the service of the Union by conducting classes in these languages in the house at Gordon Square and so helped in yet another way to swell the coffers of the NUWT.[43]

The Function of the 'Story'

Such obituaries performed several functions. They helped members mourn. They celebrated the life of the departed colleague. They confirmed the individual as a part of the union's history and present existence: 'Her name will not be known to history: already it is a legend.'[44] Increasingly in the late 1940s and 1950s, the record of members' lives, through obituaries, became a recording of past achievements rather than an inspiration for future activity. The NUWT was no longer a vital part of a thriving women's movement. In 1961 – once equal pay had been formally implemented – the NUWT disbanded. To commemorate its passing Miss Pierotti, then general secretary, wrote her *Story of the NUWT*.[45] This was a record written primarily as a private document to be read by elderly, retired NUWT members as a way of recalling past times. It was not a history to inspire members to greater things in the way Emily Phipps' history had been conceived in the 1920s. Suffrage organisations had made sure that even copies of their leaflets got to the public shelves of the British Library. No copy of Pierotti's book exists in that library and no copies were sold publicly:

> I hope it will be of interest to the many who took part in the work. Since there is now no office through which this *memorial* volume might be sold, central council decided that it should be issued free to members. (my emphasis)[46]

The book conveys little of the dynamism of earlier times. The recognition that the *spirit* of the pioneers had gone was itself seen as the cause of the union's demise: 'There was, in fact, no single issue to strike the imagination, arouse deep feelings of suffering under injustice, as the Equal Pay campaign had done ...'[47]

The *Story* is a justification of the winding up of a once thriving union. Miss Pierotti thus pays great attention to the offices bought, equipped and staffed, and to motions passed and lobbies attended, in somewhat dry chronological fashion. The 'closed' nature of the text and its audience is indicated by the underhand attacks on the (unnamed) Nan McMillan, the first and only Communist president of the NUWT. Miss Pierotti makes a thinly veiled attack on the explicitly and progressively political stance which the union took throughout its existence. This is linked by sleight-of-hand to Nan McMillan's communism in the composition of the 'story'. Thus the NUWT's refusal to work with the NUT – even in the 1950s when its own membership was declining – is justified on the grounds that this joint work was advocated by such a renegade.[48] Theodora Bonwick is dealt with in similar fashion. She is virtually written out of this NUWT official history. [49]

The NUWT in Personal Memories

Miss Pierotti's *Story of the NUWT* is an unsatisfactory collective autobiography not because it omits important aspects of the life of the union but because it functions simply as a measure taken against obscurity. The *past* achievements of Ethel Froud, Emily Phipps and Agnes Dawson, all of whom play a part in the narrative, are simply that. Pierotti's book, unlike Emily Phipps' *History* of the 1920s, did not serve to play a role in any public political campaign.

Miss Pierotti's subject matter was formed in the suffrage era. Such ideas were no longer current. The notion of *public* proclamation of feminist achievement no longer existed. Rather, the work is one which evoked happy *personal* memories, which were divorced from contemporary public action.

Many surviving elderly members, however, wrote to Miss Pierotti with their memories of union life. They treasured the organisation even decades after the height of feminist activity. Helen Dedman, a former NUWT president, wrote: 'The NUWT has been for me not so much a union as a way of life. It has been a comfort and support, an opportunity for making good friends, and a focus for my faith and pride.'[50]

The members who were still able to undertake individual political activity did so. Their correspondence to Miss Pierotti recalling past experiences indicates the lifelong effect the union had had upon their philosophy and attitude to life. A letter from Elizabeth Snowden, a former NUWT secretary in Bradford and vice president of her local Constituency Labour Party, is a particularly good example. Miss Snowden was determined not to retire until she had received her first monthly salary at the rate for the job – and the local education committee granted her request. Although she was pleased that at last equal pay was a reality, Miss Snowden was only too well aware that the majority of women workers did not receive adequate pay: 'We are the privileged classes: teachers, civil servants, doctors, lawyers, and local government workers. Industrial women workers are still maintained on $1/2$ pay or $2/3$ pay for the work they do.' In order to better understand the economics of modern industry and pursue the necessary changes, Miss Snowden was registering for a B.Sc course.[51] Here in the early 1960s was evidence again that the deeds and words of the 'pioneers' were still being promoted by those who came after them.

Biography and Feminists' Lives

This biography has not tried to be a conventional narrative, chronicling birth, childhood, aspects of life noted in official state records or those of family experience. Instead it has attempted to reflect the ways in which feminist teachers themselves saw their own lives. As such it reflects the feminists' lifelong interest in the political present and their view that politics shaped their whole lives. In their biography of Emily Davison, Liz Stanley and Anne Morley have described her autobiographical entry in *The Suffrage Annual* as unusual in that it focuses almost entirely on the present and on militant events: 'There is no "before feminism" for Emily, nor even any "before militancy".'[52] But this was also the case for our protagonists. When they wrote or spoke about important events in their lives, when they recounted memories to each other these were also embodied in the present political framework of their lives – feminism. Although they were teachers we never read of them crediting their career or interest in education to the influence of a teacher upon them while they were school pupils. The rationale for their teaching experience is explained as the desire to educate future generations of young women and to provide equality of opportunity. There is no stated correspondence between their own childhood experiences and their present views. Their present feminism is sufficient explanation of their careers.

It has been possible to write this biographical narrative of the first feminist trade union because of the nature of the women's lives and the way the teachers described them. The feminists' insistence that their lives were a public, political affair makes possible in turn a public account of their lives. As Carolyn Heilbrun has commented: 'There will be a narrative of female lives only when women no longer live their lives in the houses and the stories of men.'[53]

The NUWT undertook collective autobiographical writing in Emily Phipps' *History* and in leaflets describing why the feminists left the NUT and their political views on the oppression of women. A function of such public writing of Agnes Dawson, Emily Phipps, Ethel Froud and Theodora Bonwick was to give their own explanation of their lives. The readership consisted, they hoped, of women who would be thus inspired to join their ranks. Alternatively, the readers were existing feminists in the NUWT for whom published suffrage anecdotes, or obituaries encompassing colleagues' personal and public lives, affirmed their existence and its part in a feminist political strategy.

Such 'words' developed from the 'deeds' of the teachers. The collective nature of public political activity, the social life and friendships *themselves* ensured a continuity of their identity. The work of the pioneers who had gone before – and still remained – reaffirmed women teachers' belief in themselves. Their past gained meaning in the political action of the present. When such political activity declined, when membership of the NUWT dwindled and women increasingly saw the NUT (again) as the main teachers' union for them, then the past lives of pioneers and the collective life of the NUWT became part of the past – mere memory.

Biography: A Continuum of Women's Lives?

There has been recent interest in the biographical and autobiographical mode of writing. Publishers have issued biographies of feminist
pioneers under special women's imprints; the autobiographical writings of leaders such as Sylvia Pankhurst, Hannah Mitchell and
Christabel Pankhurst have been reprinted; literary criticism has grap-
pled with the genre as a portrayal of women's lives.[54] Much of the
new biographical writing has been intended to bring to light the lives
of women 'hidden from history' and to suggest a common experience
of women across time. The 1980s, for example, saw the publication of
writing on or by politically active women in the peace movement of
the First World War. This responded to the market provided by the
public interest in CND and the work of the Greenham peace camps. It
suggested a commonality of experience between contemporary feminist peace campaigners and Edwardian women such as Catherine
Marshall.[55]

Contemporary feminists have been encouraged to 'read' the stories
of earlier generations through the politics and experience of the
modern women's movement. Thus modern readers have gained
much information about the actions of earlier feminists but not necessarily much understanding of how earlier feminists made sense of
their own lives. To have written a conventional history of the NUWT
and to have ignored the way that the members themselves wrote of
their lives and constructed their identity would have been to misun-
derstand their experiences.

The way Agnes Dawson, Emily Phipps, Ethel Froud and Theodora
Bonwick viewed their lives and took meaning from their public and
personal experiences was very different to some fashionable concepts
of feminism. They believed that women had a duty to articulate their
political case and to do it competently if they were to win the argument. They won the respect of their feminist colleagues (as well as
detractors) by their opinions and the way they were expressed. Their
achievements in the public sphere as headteachers or politicians, or
officers of a feminist union were, they believed, a validation of their
political views. It was their *politics* which influenced the way they
viewed themselves and the world.

Today, even amongst sections of the women's movement, it is the
personal circumstances of a woman's life which are seen to give
validity to her life within the public sphere. That a woman council
leader has four children, or that another can only see her children
when they are transported to the town hall by taxi, or that a woman
MP is the mother of babies is interpreted – not just by the media – as
the decisive factors in their political work.

The 'personal is political' slogan of the 1970s was initially an attempt to develop a political perspective on women's private lives: sexual relationships, attitudes to children and childcare, domestic arrangements.[56] Increasingly, however, this has been interpreted to mean that the political *is* personal. The personal circumstances of women's lives have become legitimated as the framework of their political beliefs and campaigns. The labour movement's increasing acceptance of equal opportunities policies has not meant that feminist *politics*, particularly those of the type advocated by the NUWT, have gained credence. A woman's political beliefs are ignored – it is her sex which gains her admittance to a Labour Party parliamentary shortlist or to reserved places on the executives of certain unions. To qualify for inclusion on a Labour Party shortlist a woman candidate need do nothing in the way of feminist campaigning; indeed, it may well work against her. The dominant position within such 'progressive' political life is away from an emphasis on the supremacy of political ideas. Sex and race, which are no automatic guarantors of progressive political word or deed, are often seen as more important than an individual's political views.

Such positions were anathema to the NUWT. For the feminist teachers, politics was all. From their first contacts with the ideas of the suffrage movement they realised that politics determined their whole lives. Their paid employment as teachers was governed by politics and the decision of local education authorities to employ them or not if they married was a fiercely debated political question. Their lives at every level were affected by politics. It was the feminist movement, borne of political struggle, which provided their friendships and their social and cultural lives.

The same world view, acknowledging the supremacy of politics, also dominated the socialist movement. The Clarion cycling clubs, socialist Sunday schools, Red football leagues, vegetarianism, Plebs League and National Labour College movement: a whole – social, cultural, and educational – life was determined and organised within the parameters of the socialist movement.[57]

These are ways of life that no longer exist. Although, like their earlier colleagues, progressive teachers today also teach children in classrooms and campaign against an NUT bureaucracy which refuses to see education as a political issue, it would be inaccurate to suggest a continuum of experience between these two groups.

Empathy and Understanding

The public status of teachers has changed drastically. Their function for state and media alike is to be portrayed as the cause of society's ills. The professional skills of teachers, especially politically progressive ones, count for nothing. Today, teachers' activities with children are circumscribed by a plethora of legislation and DES circulars designed to ensure that children meet no progressive political influence in school. Recent Education Acts and the Local Government Act ban political education, ban sex education not approved by governors, ban teaching about homosexuality in a positive way. Local education authorities make sure that politically active teachers are the first to lose jobs or be redeployed (sic) to other schools. As I write, the acting headmistress of a north London school has been disciplined by a Labour LEA for carrying out anti-racist policies in her school and, more specifically, informing parents through letters taken home by children of the hostile media response to the school's policies.

Politically progressive teachers campaign inside the NUT, like the NFWT before 1919. They address often unsympathetic conferences, organise demonstrations, lobbies and strike action, stand for political office (sometimes successfully) and campaign for feminist, socialist and anti-racist policies within a still reactionary union. However, unlike members of the feminist movement of the past, they do not have the same methods of bringing meaning to these experiences. There are few *positive* images of radical teachers which can serve to foster a strengthening identity. Blamed for society's ills, shunted out of long-held jobs for union activity, prevented from teaching children in an enlightening way, feminist and socialist teachers do not have the support of a sustaining alternative movement to provide the social, cultural and political support enjoyed by the NUWT.

Empathy can exist between modern feminists and Agnes Dawson, Emily Phipps, Ethel Froud and Theodora Bonwick, but this must be based upon their experiences in the 1920s and 1930s as part of an isolated movement. These women never altered their principles or their unswerving commitment to equality of opportunity despite the increasingly unfashionable nature of these demands. Those of us introduced to political campaigning in the late 1960s and early 1970s who are still socialists and feminists and who have not ditched our principles in favour of new realism, new filofaxes and old class collaboration are portrayed by media and Labour movement alike as out of touch with the times and promoting redundant ideas.

It is perhaps these circumstances which can give rise to understanding the way suffrage feminists conducted and viewed their lives rather than any ahistorical continuum of 'women's experience'. Our lives are not the same as those of Agnes, Emily, Ethel or Theodora. Our views have not been formed by the same political or social circumstances. Our attitudes to sexuality, education and leisure are very different. Their lives are so interesting to a modern researcher or reader precisely because they were rooted in the specific circumstances of the Edwardian suffrage era. The last word on them should go to Nan McMillan, still fighting for her own political beliefs

60 years after her first introduction to politics: 'They were a group of their own very much. It was a strange phenomenon of that time. It was a sort of emanation from that period which produced those people. I can't see it happening again.'[58]

Notes and References

Introduction

1. The same situation existed in Scotland. This book, however, deals only with the lives of feminist teachers in England and Wales. The NUWT, like the main teachers' union the NUT, only covered these countries of the British Isles; different union organisation existed in Scotland.
2. H. G. Wells, *Ann Veronica*, Virago, 1984, originally published 1909, p. 110.
3. Clemence Dane, *The Regiment of Women*, Heinemann, 1917, p. 248.
4. Ibid., pp. 337–8; Lillian Faderman, *Surpassing the Love of Men*, Women's Press, 1985, p. 341–3; Richard Dyer, 'Children of the night: Vampirism as homosexuality, homosexuality as vampirism', in ed. Susannah Radstone, *Sweet Dreams: Sexuality, Gender and Popular Fiction*, Lawrence and Wishart, 1988.
5. Foreword by Edith Crosby to Emily Phipps, *History of the NUWT*, NUWT, 1928.
6. Elizabeth Wilson, *Mirror Writing*, Virago, 1982, 'Utopian Identities' in *Hallucinations*, Radius, 1988; Carolyn Steedman, *Landscape for a Good Woman*, Virago, 1986; ed. Shari Benstock, *The Private Self: Theory and Practice of Women's Autobiographical Writings*, Routledge, 1988.
7. Sheila Rowbotham, Lynne Segal and Hilary Wainwright, *Beyond the Fragments*, Merlin, 1979.
8. Miss Alice Hurley to Miss Pierotti, 9.1.1962, in unnumbered brown box (NUWT archive).

Chapter 1

1. J. R. Clynes, *Memoirs*, volume 1, Hutchinson, 1937, p. 31.
2. J. S. Hurt, *Elementary Schooling and the Working Classes 1860–1918*, Routledge & Kegan Paul, 1979, pp. 160–9.
3. Phillip B. Ballard, *Things I Cannot Forget*, University of London Press, 1937, pp. 162–5.
4. A schoolmistress writing to *Manchester Guardian*, 19 April 1873, as quoted in Frances Widdowson, *Going up into the Next Class: Women and Elementary Teacher Training 1840–1914*, WRCC, 1980, p. 36.
5. Ibid.

141

6. Alternatives for women, irrespective of background, were few. Lady Constance Lytton's wish to became a journalist was thwarted by her family. Until she became politicised at 39 she saw herself as having 'neither equipment, training, nor inclination for an independent life', Constance Lytton, *Prisons and Prisoners*, Heinemann, 1914, pp. 11ff.
7. Clara E. Collet, *Educated Working Women. Essays on the Economic Position of Women Workers in the Middle Classes* , P.S. King, 1902, p. 53.
8. Amy Bulley and Margaret Whitley, *Women's Work*, Methuen, 1894, p. 7.
9. Ibid., p. 9.
10. Ibid., p. 10.
11. Ibid.
12. High school teacher interviewed in 1898 in Collet, *Educated Working Women*, p. 76.
13. Bulley and Whitley, *Women's Work*, p. 13.
14. Schools Management Committee, Swansea School Board 26.2.1895, (West Glamorgan Record Office).
15. Ibid.; Ed. 109/8299 (PRO).
16. Ed. 109/8299 1908 (PRO).
17. High school teacher interviewed in 1898 in Collet, *Educated Working Women*, p. 75.
18. Of the 21,000 unmarried women over 45, that is women unlikely to marry, engaged in professions in 1901, the largest grouping belonged to teaching: 9,668. This rose to 17,000 by 1911 when the total number of unmarried women over 45 in professions increased to 37,000. By 1911 nearly three-quarters of unmarried women had some form of paid employment, compared with only 10 per cent of married women. In the same year, over 183,000 women, married and unmarried, of all ages, were teachers, in comparison to 533 women who were doctors. (Anne Phillips, *Divided Loyalties: Dilemmas of Sex and Class*, Virago, 1987, p. 51; Martha Vicinus, *Independent Women: Work and Community for Single Women 1850–1920*, Virago, 1985, p. 29.)
19. Letter from Irene Ellis to Miss Pierotti describing her mother Mrs L. T. Ellis, formerly Miss L. T. Osborn, 14.3.1955, file 81, in box 112 (NUWT archive).
20. Collet, *Educated Working Women*, p. 13.
21. Cicely Hamilton, *Marriage as a Trade*, Women's Press, 1981, originally published 1909, p. 127.
22. Ibid.
23. Ibid.
24. Ed. A. J. R., *The Suffrage Annual and Woman's Who's Who*, Stanley Paul, 1913.
25. See Chapter 4, fn. 77.
26. *Woman Teacher*, 3.10.1911, p. 93; *Schoolmaster*, 7.10.1911, report of Class Teachers' Conference.
27. Hilda Kean and Alison Oram, 'Men must be educated and women must do it', *Gender and Education*, summer 1990.

28. Clive Griggs, *The TUC and the Struggle for Education 1868–1925*, Falmer Press, 1983, p. 13.
29. First organised as the Equal Pay League. See Chapter 2, fns. 61–3. In 1919 the NFWT left the NUT to form the National Union of Women Teachers. It maintained the same rules as the NUT about only admitting qualified teachers into membership.
30. Hilda Kean, 'Towards a Curriculum in the Interests of the Working Class', unpublished MA, University of London, 1981, pp. 56–7; Ken Jones, *Beyond Progressive Education*, Macmillan, 1983, pp. 23–5, 59–60.
31. *Swansea Municipal Secondary School Magazine*, vol. 1, no. 2, April 1910; vol. 2, no. 5, January 1911; vol. 6, no. 19, April 1915 (Swansea Public Library).
32. Ibid., vol. 22, no. 2, July 1911.
33. Education Committee: Finance and General Purposes sub-committee, 12.12.1921, no. 99 (WGRO).
34. Ed. 109/8299, 1908 (PRO).
35. Letter of Miss Phipps to Miss Froud, 'Monday 4.30'. Members' correspondence file 1918 (NUWT archive).
36. *Swansea Magazine*, vol. 5 no. 16, April 1914, p. 27.
37. Crawford Street Infants School Logbook, 23.7.1919, EO/DIV/CRA/LB/1 (GLRO).
38. Ibid., Visitors' record, 1922, 1923.
39. Ibid., September 1918.
40. St Paul's Logbook, July 1915, EO/DIV5/ST PAU 1/LB/10 (GLRO).
41. Ibid., 21.7.1913.
42. Ed. 109/8301;109/8302 (PRO); Swansea Education Committee: Special Staff sub-committee, 20.2.1925 (WGRO).
43. Swansea Education Committee: Building sub-committee, 10.1.1916, no. 32.
44. HMI report December 1913 to Swansea Education Committee, 9.2.1914 (WGRO).
45. NFWT Central Council Minutes, 3.3.1917 (NUWT archive).
46. 'From my political schoolmaster [John Maclean] I was given a sense of historical values and informed that the British ruling class was the most astute in the world ...' James Clunie, *Labour is my Faith: the Autobiography of a Housepainter*, Dunfermline, 1954, p. 62; James D. Young, *The Rousing of the Scottish Working Class*, Croom Helm, 1979, p. 192.
47. EO/DIV 7/ CRA/LB/1, logbook, 3.5.1919.
48. For example, Minutes of Swansea Education Committee, 9.2.1920, no. 268; Minutes of Finance and General Purposes sub-committee, 10.2.1913.
49. PRO: Ed. 24/422 Teacher Immorality, 29.7.1910. Teachers were employed by local education authorities and not the Board of Education. It was extremely unusual for local education authorities to allow unmarried mothers to teach. In the unlikely event of a LEA agreeing to this, then approval would have to be obtained from the Board of Education.

50. PRO: Ed. 24/455 Unemployed Teachers' Meeting 27.10.1910.
51. F. H. Spencer, *London Headteachers' Association Jubilee Volume 1888– 1938*, pp. 114–15, as quoted in Asher Tropp, *The Schoolteachers*, Heinemann, 1957, p. 121.
52. Sir George W. Kekewich, *The Education Department and After*, Constable, 1920, p. 164.
53. PRO: Ed. 109/3723, June 1921.
54. *London Teacher*, 2.5.1913, p. 339. The LTA was de facto the London branch of the NUT, although it was formally autonomous until the mid–1920s.
55. Ibid.
56. Miss Woods at the National Federation of Class Teachers' Conference, *Schoolmaster*, 7.10.1911, pp. 608–9.
57. Margaret Nevinson, *Life's Fitful Fever*, A & C Black, 1926, pp. 58–9.
58. Gertrude Colmore, 'Life of Emily Davison', 1913, as printed in Liz Stanley and Ann Morley, *The Life and Death of Emily Wilding Davison*, Women's Press, 1988, pp. 15, 19.
59. *Votes for Women*, 29.10.1909, p. 67; 22.7.1910, p. 713; 5.5.1916, p. 1025.
60. *Suffrage Annual*, p. 319.
61. *Votes for Women*, 29.10.1909, p. 67.
62. Margaret and Mary Thompson, *They Couldn't Stop Us. Experiences of Two (Usually Law-Abiding) Women in the Years 1909–1913*, W. E. Harrison, 1957, pp. 30–2 (British Library); *Votes for Women*, 2.7.1909, p. 877; Kean, *State Education*, Appendix.
63. Equal Pay League, *Report for 1904*, NUWT archive.
64. *Woman Teacher*, 16.11.1928.
65. *Woman Teacher*, 12.9.1911 editorial, p. 38.
66. Letter in *Schoolmaster*, 12.12.1903, as quoted in Pat Owen, 'Who would be free herself must strike the blow', *History of Education Review*, vol. 17, no. 1, March 1988, p. 86.
67. Ethel Smyth to Betty Balfour, 6.3.1912, in ed. Betty Balfour, *Letters of Constance Lytton*, Heinemann, p. 229.
68. M. M. Beagley to Miss Pierotti, 29.5.1964, in unnumbered brown box file, NUWT archive.

Chapter 2
1. WTFU, *Women's Suffrage and the LTA*, n.d. (1913?) (British Library).
2. After its formation as a party accepting individual members in 1918. It is not known whether they were members of the ILP before then.
3. Sandra Stanley Holton, *Feminism and Democracy:Women's Suffrage and Reform Politics in Britain 1900–1918*, Cambridge University Press, 1988, p. 15.
4. The organisation, founded by Sylvia Pankhurst, was originally part of the WSPU and called the East London Federation of Suffragettes.
5. Cicely Hamilton, *Life Errant*, M. Dent, 1935, p. 65.
6. *Women's Franchise*, 11.7.1907, p. 23, as quoted in Les Garner, *Stepping Stones to Women's Liberty: Feminist Ideas in the Suffrage Movement 1900–1918*, Heinemann, 1984, p. 13.

7. *Common Cause*, 15.4.1909, p. 3, as quoted in Garner, *Stepping Stones*, p. 13.
8. *Meaning of the Women's Movement: Service Versus Subjection*, NUWSS, 1913, p. 5 (British Library).
9. Ibid., p. 7.
10. *Teachers! Why Women's Suffrage Matters to You*, NUWSS, n.d. (1913) (British Library).
11. Ibid., and *Parliament and the Children*, October 1913, NUWSS, (British Library).
12. Leslie Parker Hume, *The NUWSS 1897–1914*, Garland Publishing Co., 1982, p. 121; Garner, *Stepping Stones*, pp. 26–7; Holton, *Feminism and Democracy*, p. 115.
13. *Woman Teacher*, 5.10.1928, p. 3.
14. Constance Rover, *Women's Suffrage and Party Politics in Britain 1866–1914*, Routledge, & Kegan Paul, 1967, p. 76; Garner, *Stepping Stones*, p. 52.
15. Garner, *Stepping Stones*, p. 53.
16. Elizabeth Robins, *Way Stations*, Hodder & Stoughton, 1913, p. 335.
17. Ibid., p. 337.
18. Christabel Pankhurst, *Unshackled*, Cresset Women's Voices, 1987, p. 118 (originally published 1959).
19. Tickner, *Spectacle*, p. 230.
20. *Vote*, 18.3.1927.
21. Two photographs of the WSPU fife and drum band are reproduced in Diane Atkinson, *Mrs Brown's Suffragette Photographs*, Nishen Photography, n.d. Ethel Froud can be seen in the back row, second from the left on p. 17.
22. *Woman Teacher*, 5.10.1928, p. 4.
23. *Woman Teacher*, 13.11.1928, p. 50; May 1951, p. 137.
24. *Suffrage Annual*, p. 119.
25. WTFU, *Annual Report*, 1917 (NUWT archive); other WSPU members in the NFWT included Miss Cutten, the secretary of the Putney and Fulham WSPU and Mrs Cocksedge, the secretary of the Balham and Tooting branch. The Townsend sisters who founded the London-based WTFU were WSPU members in Lewisham in South London (Kean, *State Education*: Appendix); see Garner, *Stepping Stones*, pp. 45–7.
26. Emmeline Pethick Lawrence, *My Part in a Changing World*, Victor Gollancz, 1938, p. 171.
27. Garner, *Stepping Stones*, p. 30. In 1913, for example, it supported the Dublin transport strikers. For particulars of the women's campaign see Dora Montefiore, *From a Victorian to a Modern*, C. Archer, 1927, p. 156.
28. *Suffrage Annual*, p. 112.
29. Andro Linklater, *An Unhusbanded Life: Charlotte Despard, Suffragette, Socialist, and Sinn Feiner*, Hutchinson, 1980, pp. 79–197.
30. L. Lind-af-Hageby, *Unbounded Gratitude! Women's Right to Work*, WFL, 1920 (British Library).
31. Ibid, pp. 7 and 9.

32. Emily Phipps to Ethel Froud, 29.12.1934, in box 410 (NUWT archive).
33. A. E. Metcalfe, *Woman's Effort*, Blackwell, 1917, pp. 124ff; Roger Fulford, *Votes for Women*, Faber & Faber, 1958, pp. 174–5.
34. NFWT member Miss John was secretary of Highbury WFL and Frances Eggett was secretary of Tottenham WFL, *Suffrage Annual*, p. 115.
35. Robins, *Way Stations*, p. 301.
36. Ibid.
37. *Votes for Women*, 18.6.1908, p. 251; 22.7.1910, p. 713.
38. Ibid., 23.7.1910, p. 795; 15.7.1910, p. 681; Lisa Tickner, *The Spectacle of Women: Imagery of the Suffrage Campaign 1907–1914*, Chatto & Windus, 1987, pp. 84,119.
39. Tickner, *Spectacle*, pp. 102,124.
40. See Tickner, *The Spectacle of Women*, for a fascinating account of the work of the Artists' Suffrage League and Suffrage Atelier, especially pp. 16–26.
41. Ibid., pp. 22, between 50 and 51,157,187,255.
42. *Woman Teacher*, 5.10.1928, p. 4.
43. *South Wales Daily Post*, 2.10.1908.
44. *Woman Teacher*, 5.10.1928, pp. 2–3.
45. Ibid., p. 4.
46. Evelyn Sharp, 'Dissension in the Home', in *Rebel Women*, 1915, pp. 126–7, originally published in *Votes for Women*.
47. Ibid., p. 130.
48. Emily Lutyens to Betty Balfour (Constance's sister and aunt) in *Letters*, p. 159.
49. Mr Jones to Home Secretary, 25.6.1911, in file 410 (NUWT archive).
50. *Suffrage Annual*, pp. 292,377,378.
51. *Woman Teacher*, 5.10.1928, p. 4.
52. *Suffrage Annual*, pp. 114–15; Metcalfe, *Woman's Effort*, p. 170.
53. *Woman Teacher*, 5.10.1928,.p. 3. Agnes mentions three male relatives, one appears to be a brother-in-law, Mrs Tidswell's husband.
54. Ibid.
55. Ibid.
56. Roger Seifert, *Teacher Militancy: A History of Teacher Strikes 1896–1987*, Falmer, 1987, p. 15.
57. Ibid., pp. 16–21.
58. Letter from 'Old stager', *Schoolmaster*, 25.5.1907, p. 1020.
59. *Woman Teacher*, 5.10.1928, p. 3.
60. Emily Phipps, *A History of the NUWT*, NUWT, 1928, pp. 1–2, (NUWT archive).
61. Equal Pay League, *Annual Report*, 1904 (NUWT archive).
62. Equal Pay League, *Leaflet* (NUWT archive).
63. Ibid.
64. *Schoolmaster*, 4.5.1907, p. 897.
65. Letter from Eleanor Mardon in *Schoolmaster*, 15.6.1907, p. 1188.
66. Letter from 'Harfat' in *Schoolmaster*, 8.6.1907, p. 1129.
67. *Schoolmaster*, 17.4.1907, p. 751.

68. *Schoolmaster*, 13.4.1907, p. 751. Minutes of Ladies Committee, NUT executive, 19.5.1906; 28.12.1906 (NUT library).
69. Minutes of the Ladies Committee, 28.6.07.
70. Ibid., 22.6.1907.
71. Ibid., 18.1.1907, 22.2.1907, 20.3.1907.
72. *Schoolmaster*, 4.1.1908, p. 11.
73. Minutes of the Ladies Committee, 20.6.1908.
74. 'Women and Education: Miss Byett's presidential address', NFWT, 1918 (NUWT archive).
75. NFWT, 'Woman's Suffrage and the NUT', NFWT n.d. (1913?) (NUWT archive). The importance the feminist teachers attached to the role of the state was shared by the Anti-Suffragists, albeit from a very different perspective: 'the interests of the state must necessarily override the interests of any class, section, sex, or community inside it. If the interests of women were opposed to the interests of the State, then I say fearlessly the interests of the state must prevail.' (Lord Curzon speaking at an anti-suffrage demonstration in Glasgow, 1.11.1912. Curzon papers F112/38, pp. 118–19 as quoted in Brian Harrison, *Separate Spheres – the Opposition to Women's Suffrage*, Croom Helm, 1978, p. 43.)
76. WTFU, 'Women's Suffrage and the LTA', n.d. (1913?) (British Library).
77. Ibid.
78. Lewisham Women's Franchise Club, 'The Woman Teacher's Own Fault', 1914 (British Library).
79. Christabel Pankhurst, *The Great Scourge and How to End it*, Emmeline Pankhurst, 1913, p. 13.
80. Charlotte Perkins Gilman, *Women and Economics*, Putnam, London, 5th edition, 1906, p. 145.
81. Hilda Kean, 'Teachers and the State', *British Journal of Sociology of Education*, vol. 10, no. 2., 1989, pp.141–54.
82. *Schoolmaster*, 21.4.1906, pp. 801–2.
83. *Schoolmaster*, 6.4.1907, p. 694.
84. H. J. Lowe, 'Socialism for School Teachers', Pass on Pamphlets no. 20, 1909, Clarion (British Library).
85. *Labour Leader*, 19.4.1907, p. 763; *Schoolmaster*, 8.4.1908, p. 766; *London Teacher*, 1.5.1909, p. 151, 1.5.1911, p. 190.
86. *Schoolmaster*, 5.10.1907, pp. 575ff.
87. Ibid.
88. Kean, 'Teachers and the State'.
89. *Standard*, 11.4.1912, in cuttings file (NUWT archive).
90. As quoted in Harrison, *Separate Spheres*, p. 215.
91. *London Teacher*, 3.10.1913, supplement v; *Schoolmaster*, 18.10.1913, p. 710.
92. NUT, *Annual Report*, 1911, aims v.
93. '... the headmistresses ... may – nay must – do the work of a citizen, but may not have a citizen's privileges ... we desire to see the whole work of the country perfected, as it can only be when the gifts of women as well as those of men can be freely given for

its service.' Mary Price and Nonita Glenday, *Reluctant Revolutionaries. A Century of Headmistresses 1874–1974*, Pitman, 1974, p. 68.

94. Notes and News, *Anti-Suffrage Review*, May 1911.
95. *London Teacher*, 8.5.1914, p. 376.
96. Miss Lane in Phipps, *History*, p. 5.
97. Nancy Lightman to Miss Pierotti, 31.5.1964, in unnumbered brown box file (NUWT archive).
98. *Woman Teacher*, 25.10.1928, p. 4.
99. Phipps, *History*, pp. 8–10; Emily Phipps, 'Why we do not work through the NUT', NUWT, 1927 (Fawcett Library).
100. Stella Newsom to Miss Pierotti, 7.6.1964, in unnumbered brown box (NUWT archive).
101. *Woman Teacher*, 19.12.1911, p. 273.
102. Printed letter from Kate Dice to Lewisham Teachers' Association, 4.1.1913, in Box 449 (NUWT archive).
103. *Woman Teacher*, 30.1.1912, p. 368.
104. *Woman Teacher*, 19.12.1911, p. 267.
105. *Schoolmaster*, 22.4.1911.
106. Phipps, *History*, p. 7.
107. Minutes of the Ladies Committee, verbatim report, 20.5.1911.
108. *Schoolmaster*, 13.4.1912, pp. 718ff.
109. *London Teacher*, 4.4.1913, p. 244.
110. *London Teacher*, 24.4.1914, p. 317.
111. Pankhurst, *Unshackled*, p. 270; NFWT Central Council passed a motion opposing the Cat and Mouse Act and calling for the release of prisoners (*Schoolmaster*, 12.7.1913, p. 73).
112. *London Teacher*, 24.4.1914, p. 318.
113. Stanley, *Life of Emily Davison*, p. 175.
114. *Votes for Women*, 21.6.1912, p. 624.
115. WTFU, *Annual Report*, 1915 (NUWT archive).
116. *London Teacher*, 28.6.1912, p. 13.
117. Ibid.
118. Minutes of the Ladies Committee, verbatim report, 20.5.1911.
119. *Schoolmaster*, 22.4.1911, p. 822; 29.4.1911, p. 876.
120. *Woman Teacher*, 21.11.11, editorial.
121. Quoted in Harrison, *Separate Spheres*, p. 59.
122. Ibid., pp. 120,149 and 190–1.
123. 'The attempt to capture the NUT by woman-suffragists' (1911); 'The fourth attempt by suffragists to capture the NUT conference' (1914), National League for Opposing Woman's Suffrage, unnumbered file, (NUWT archive).
124. 'Attempt', p. 2.
125. Ibid., p. 7.
126. 'Fourth attempt'.
127. *Woman Teacher*, 5.10.1928, p. 3.
128. *Schoolmaster*, 5.4.1913, p. 714.
129. Ibid.
130. Violence was more likely to occur at street meetings after the ASL

had held meetings, Harrison, *Separate Spheres*, pp. 190–1; Caroline Morrell, *'Black Friday', Violence against Women in the Suffrage Movement*, WRCC, 1981.
131. *Woman Teacher*, 5.10.1928, p. 3.
132. *Vote*, 24.4.1914, p. 3. The first time such prayers had been given was on 10 August 1913 when women prayed aloud for Mrs Pankhurst in Westminster Abbey. (Metcalfe, *Woman's Effort*, p. 301.)
133. Phipps, *History*, p. 12.
134. The NFWT supported the vote for all adult men and women. Minutes of the Central council, 3.3.1917 (NUWT archive); Rover, *Women's Suffrage*, pp. 70–1.
135. *Schoolmaster*, 13.4.1912, p. 719.
136. Ibid.
137. *Woman Teacher*, 5.10.1928, p. 3.
138. Photographs of feminist teachers holding display boards at NUT conference 1914 have been reproduced from the NUWT Archive in Hilda Kean and Alison Oram, '"Who would be free herself must strike the blow": Agnes Dawson', *South London Record*, no. 3, 1988, p. 52.
139. 'Why I left the NUT', n.d., NFWT (Fawcett Library).
140. *Schoolmistress*, 27.4.1911, p. 62.
141. *Woman Teacher*, 5.10.1928, p. 4.
142. *Woman Teacher*, 18.11.1932, pp. 25–6.
143. *Schoolmaster*, 30.9.1911, p. 364.
144. *Schoolmaster*, 18.1.1913, p. 129.
145. *Schoolmaster*, 6.5.1916, Letters page.
146. She also stood unsuccessfully in 1914 and 1916. On the latter occasion she only lost by 34 votes. She was elected unopposed in 1915.
147. For example, in 1912 in London NFWT/WTFU women elected included Agnes Dawson and Miss Lane in Southwark, Miss Overmark in Lambeth, Miss Titcombe in Woolwich. Unsuccessful candidates included Miss Potts in Bermondsey, Misses Fouraker and Johnson in Greenwich, Misses Nancy Lightman and S. Keen in Hackney, Florence Down and Mrs Tidswell in Hammersmith and Fulham and Miss Townsend in Lewisham. (*London Teacher*, 25.10.1912, p. 835.)
148. Robins, *Way Stations*, p. 301.
149. Pankhurst, *Unshackled*, p. 77.
150. Robins, *Way Stations*, p. 40.
151. Pankhurst, *Unshackled*, p. 77.

Chapter 3
1. EO/DIV, 7/CRA/LB/1, 1913 (GLRO); Ed. 21/11312 HMI report, 1907 (PRO).
2. EO/PS/12/E 37/1–29, 1914 (GLRO).
3. Ed. 21/57031, 1926 (PRO).
4. Glanmor Central School Logbook, 1922 and 1923 (WGRO).
5. Comments of the Swansea Director of Education at a dinner held to honour Miss Neal as president of the NUWT, *Woman Teacher*, 9.12.1927, p. 85.

6. Comment of HMI, Ed. 109/8300, 1911 (PRO).
7. These views were held by the ILP and leadership of the TUC. Marxist organisations such as the Socialist Labour Party and British Socialist Party did not believe that education per se could change society. (Hilda Kean, *Challenging the State? The Socialist and Feminist Educational Experience*, Falmer Press, 1990, chapters 1 and 2.)
8. WTFU, *Annual Report*, 1915 (NUWT archive).
9. Widdowson, *Going up into the Next Class*, pp. 47, 52, 53, 56.
10. *Woman Teacher*, 10.10.1919; *Schoolmistress*, 2.3.1911, p. 430.
11. Albert Mansbridge, *The Trodden Road*, J. M. Dent, 1940, pp. 48–71.
12. Griggs, *The Trades Union Congress and the Struggle for Education*, p. 18; TUC, *Annual Report*, 1904, p. 119, 1905, p. 142.
13. Countess of Warwick (Frances Greville), *A Nation's Youth, 1906*, Cassell, 1906 (British Library); Kean, *Challenging the State?*, pp. 24–45.
14. Kean, *Challenging the State?*, pp. 118–19
15. WTFU, *Rules*, n.d., orange file in tea chest (NUWT archive).
16. WTFU, *Annual Report*, 1915 (NUWT archive).
17. *Schoolmistress*, 11.4.1912, p. 22.
18. Kean, *Challenging the State?*, chapter 5; Kean, *State Education*, Appendix.
19. *Woman Teacher*, 26.9.1919, p. 2.
20. Ibid.
21. *Woman Teacher*, 29.8.1911, no. 1.
22. Miss Croxson speaking at 1920 NUWT conference, *Woman Teacher*, 4.6.1920.
23. The ACE was set up in 1918.
24. ACE document, 4.10.1918, box 345 (Labour Party Archive).
25. Margaret McMillan, *The Child and the State*, National Labour Press, 1911, p. 28.
26. Margaret McMillan, 'Nurseries of Tomorrow' in ed. Marion Phillips, *Women and the Labour Party*, Labour Party, 1918 (British Library); Sylvia Pankhurst, *The Home Front*, Cresset Library, 1987, originally published 1932, p. 426.
27. *Schoolmaster*, 4.1.1908, p. 13.
28. Agnes Dawson, 'Nursery Schools', NUWT, n.d., p. 4 (NUWT archive); 'Lower age limit of Compulsory Education', paper to LTA, LTA, 1917 (British Library).
29. *Woman Teacher*, 4.6.1920.
30. *Vote*, 28.4.1916, p. 1015.
31. *Schoolmaster*, 4.1.1908, p. 10. Sir Roger de Coverley is a country dance. Ironically, she suffered a breakdown and spent many years negotiating with her local education authority for proper treatment. (Correspondence with Ethel Froud in Members' file, 1917–1918, NUWT archive).
✗ 32. *Schoolmaster*, 17.4.1909, p. 721 and 24.4.1909, p. 256.
33. *Times Educational Supplement*, 5.1.1924, p. 6 (thanks to Alison Oram for the reference); Sarah King, 'Feminists in teaching: the NUWT 1920–45', in ed. Martin Lawn and Gerald Grace, *Teachers: the Culture and Politics of Work*, Falmer, 1987, p. 41.
34. *Suffrage Annual*, p. 51.

35. Founding statement, *Report of the Montessori Conference*, Conference on New Ideals in Education, 1914 (British Library).
36. *Vote*, 20.5.1927; *Woman Teacher*, 1.10.1926, 11.11.1921, 25.11.1921, annual report, 13.1.1922; C. M. A. Coombs, *Individual Teaching with Vertical Classification; Individual Teaching with the under 5s*, NUWT, n.d. ,1920s.
37. E. Sylvia Pankhurst, *The Home Front*, p. 428.
38. WTFU, *Annual Report*, 1915 (NUWT archive).
39. Pankhurst, *The Home Front*, p. 425–6; *Worker's Dreadnought*, 3.4.1918, Muriel Matters, 'The Montessori principles'; 19.1.1918, Muriel Matters, 'Dr Montessori and her education principles'; 16.3.1918, Report of lecture given on Montessori in Manchester with 800 present; 9.12.1916, Muriel Matters, 'East London Babies and Montessori'.
40. *Vote*, 6.2.1920; *Woman Teacher*, 13.7.1920.
41. Minutes of Central Council, 6.9.1919.
42. Editorial, *Schoolmaster*, 3.5.1913, p. 902.
43. Ibid.
44. LCC teachers' conference as reported in *Schoolmaster*, 11.1.1913, p. 70.
45. E0 /DIV 7/CRA/L13/1: logbook recording her teaching November 1917 and all the following entries.
46. Report of NUWT conference in *Schoolmaster*, 14.6.1919.
47. Ed. 21/57031 (PRO); *Woman Teacher*, 23.11.1928, p. 50.
48. Ed. 21/57031 1926 (PRO).
49. Ibid.
50. Emily Phipps, 'Equality of Opportunity', NUWT, n.d. (NUWT archive).
51. *Woman Teacher*, 3.10.1911, p. 84.
52. Swansea Education Committee: Finance and General Purposes sub-committee, 7.6.1915, no. 123.
53. Article by S.M. Burls in *Woman Teacher*, 9.9.1927, p. 345.
54. They were not elementary school teachers. *Suffrage Annual*, p. 40; Sheila Fletcher, *Women First: the Female Tradition in English PE 1888–1980*, Athlone Press, 1984, p. 171.
55. *Stratford Express*, 13.3.1937, in People box 8 (NUWT archive).
56. Annual reports in *Woman Teacher*, 20.5.1921, 14.1.1927.
57. *Southend Pictorial*, 2.1.1932, in Cuttings file (NUWT archive).
58. Board of Education report, PRO Ed. 12/41 minute, 3.11.1907, as quoted in Jane Lewis, *The Politics of Motherhood*, Croom Helm, 1980, p. 90–1.
59. Ibid.
60. Ada Neild Chew in *Common Cause*, 1913, quoted in Garner, *Stepping Stones*, p. 20.
61. Women's column, *Rhondda Socialist*, 26.10.1912 (South Wales Miners' Library).
62. Ibid.
63. *Schoolmaster*, 17.4.1909, p. 706.
64. Ibid., 2.4.1910, p. 626.

65. Ibid.
66. Ibid.; Schools Management and Education Committee, Swansea School Board, 17.12.1895, minute 638; Lewis, *Politics of Motherhood*, p. 94.
67. *Woman's Dreadnought*, 18.7.1914, p. 71.
68. *Schoolmaster*, 14.6.1919.
69. *Times Educational Supplement*, 10.1.1925, p. 18, 10.1.1931, p. 18 (thanks to Alison Oram for these references).
70. Judith R. Walkowitz, *Prostitution and Victorian Society: Women, Class, and the State*, Cambridge University Press, 1980; Sheila Jeffreys, *The Spinster and her Enemies: Feminism and Sexuality 1880–1930*, Pandora, 1985, pp. 6–53.
71. Frank Mort, *Dangerous Sexualities: Medico-moral Politics in England since 1830*, Routledge & Kegan Paul, 1987, p. 104.
72. Moberly Bell, *Josephine Butler*, Constable, 1962, pp. 72–164.
73. AMSH, Annual Report, 1928 (NUWT archive); *Woman Teacher*, 23.11.1928.
74. *Common Cause*, 11.10.1918, p. 294, quoted in Mort, *Dangerous Sexualities*, p. 208.
75. Lucy Bland, 'Cleansing the Portals of Life' in ed. Mary Langan and Bill Schwarz, *Crises in the British State 1880–1930*, Hutchinson, 1985, pp. 200–1; Lucy Bland, 'Guardians of the race or vampires upon the nation's health' in ed. Whitelegg, *The Changing Experience of Women*, Martin Robinson and Open University, 1982, p. 178; Mort, *Dangerous Sexualities*, p. 163.
76. Bland, 'Portals', p. 200.
77. Christabel Pankhurst, *The Great Scourge*, 1913, pp. 95, 145.
78. Mort, *Dangerous Sexualities*, p. 144.
79. Ibid. p. 145; Walkowitz, *Prostitution*.
80. *Woman's Dreadnought*, 19.12.1914, as quoted in Walkowitz, *Prostitution*, p. 256.
81. *Woman's Dreadnought*, 24.10.1914, as quoted in ibid, p. 255.
82. Pankhurst, *The Home Front*, pp. 102–3.
83. Ibid.; Bland, 'Vampires', p. 382; Mort, *Dangerous Sexualities*, p. 41.
84. *Vote*, 9.4.1915. Emily came from Plymouth, site of much activity under the Contagious Diseases Act. This may have contributed to her interest in the issue (*Prostitution*).
85. Minutes of Ladies Committee, 21.9.1918. 40d was repealed at the end of the war.
86. The AMSH also campaigned effectively against child abuse and the courts' discriminatory sentencing of women on moral issues. Jeffreys, *Spinster*, p. 74.
87. *Vote*, 17.4.1914, p. 413.
88. Irene Poulter to Miss Froud, 11.11.1917, in *Members' Correspondence* file, 1917–18.
89. Minutes of Central Council, 14.10.1916.
90. Ibid., 3.3.1917; Kean, *State Education*, pp. 194–5.
91. East Ham Annual Report, 1920, box 411; NFWT *Annual Report*, 1918, orange file in tea chest; Edith Cooper and Mary Mason, *The Teaching of Sex Hygiene*, NFWT, 1919 (NUWT archive).
92. Minutes of Central Council, 8.12.1917.

93. Letter in *Schoolmaster*, 25.3.1916.
94. Bland, 'Vampires', p. 369.
95. *Teaching of Sex Hygiene*, p. 3.
96. Ibid., p. 4.
97. Ibid., p. 11.
98. Ibid., p. 12.
99. Ibid., p. 4.
100. Letter to *Schoolmaster*, 25.3.1916.
101. Article in *Woman's Dreadnought*, 18.7.1914, p. 71.
102. Evidence of Theodora Bonwick, 'Report of the Education Committee on the Teaching of Sex Hygiene', LCC, 1914 (GLRO).
103. *Worker's Dreadnought*, 2.12.1916, p. 809.
104. EO/DIV 5/St PAU 1/LB/10: St Paul's Road Log Book, 7.12.1915.
105. LCC, 'Sex Hygiene', p. 9.
106. *Woman Teacher*, 23.11.1928.
107. Mort, *Dangerous Sexualities*, p. 197.
108. EO/PS/12/E37/1–29 (GLRO).
109. LCC, 'Sex Hygiene', p. 12.
110. NUWT, London Unit Annual Report, 1923–4, box 295 (NUWT archive).
111. Ibid.
112. LCC, 'Sex Hygiene', p. 4.
113. Ibid., p. 22.
114. Ibid., p. 15.
115. Ibid.
116. Ibid.
117. This was in response to the Royal Commission on Combating Venereal Disease which had noted that most experienced classroom teachers were opposed to class teaching on sex education. *Schoolmaster*, 25.3.1916.
118. J. Lewis in *Schoolmaster*, 8.4.1916.

Chapter 4
1. Letter in *Schoolmaster*, 3.10.1917, p. 310.
2. Emily Phipps to Ethel Froud, 8.2.1918, in Members' Correspondence file 1917–18 (NUWT archive).
3. Caroline Rowan, 'For the duration only: motherhood and nation in the First World War' in *Formations of Nation and People*, Routledge & Kegan Paul, 1984, p. 160.
4. Widdowson, *Going up into the Next Class*, p. 58.
5. Women formed 27 per cent of clerks employed in 1914; by 1918 this had risen to 57 per cent. By 1920 the figure was 40 per cent. Rowan, 'For the duration', p. 166.
6. *Vote*, 5.4.1918, p. 206.
7. *Woman Teacher*, 12.8.1911, p. 39.
8. Kean, *Challenging the State?*, p. 12.
9. CAB 24/98 CP 605. Growth of Educational Expenditure. A note by the President of the Board of Education, 10.2.1920 (PRO).
10. H. A. L. Fisher, *Unfinished Autobiography*, Oxford University Press, 1940, p. 105.

11. CAB 24/98 CP 605 (PRO); Kean, 'Teachers and the State' p. 151.
12. L. O. Ward, 'H. A. L. Fisher and the teachers', *The British Journal of Educational Studies*, vol. 22, no. 2., February 1974, pp. 191–9.
13. Helena F. Normanton, *Sex Differentiation in Salary*, NFWT, 1914 (NUWT archive).
14. Ibid., p. 21.
15. Ibid., p. 50.
16. *London Teacher*, 31.1.1913, p. 90.
17. *Eastern Daily Press*, 15.4.1914, p. 7.
18. Minutes of the Central Council, 27.4.1918 (NUWT archive).
19. *Vote*, 2.4.1920.
20. 'An appeal to the women', *London Teacher*, 19.7.1918, p. 226.
21. *Vote*, 5.5.1916.
22. Open letter to Chairman and members of the LCC Education Committee, NUWT, 1920, in box 505 (NUWT archive).
23. Normanton, 'Sex Differentiation'; Minutes of the Central Council, 5.10.1918.
24. *Schoolmaster*, 5.10.1912, p. 570; and Kean, *State Education*: Appendix.
25. Front page leaflet mock-ups, *Vote*, 12.4.1918.
26. *London Teacher*, 25.10.1912, p. 835.
27. Phipps, *History*, p. 19.
28. *London Teacher*, 20.12.1912, p. 1024.
29. *Schoolmaster*, 1.2.1913, p. 204.
30. Ibid., 8.2.1913, p. 258.
31. *London Teacher*, 20.12.1912, p. 1022.
32. Phipps, *History*, p. 18.
33. *Schoolmaster*, 18.10.1913, p. 710.
34. Ibid.
35. The campaigns against this undemocratic rule had a major impact in turning the ILTA to the left in the 1980s.
36. *London Teacher*, 21.10.1911; 24.10.1913, p. 852.
37. NUT *Annual Report*, 1916, 1917.
38. In 1988–9 of 41 executive members directly elected, including two vice-presidents, only ten were women. The post of Women's Officer was scrapped in 1988. (NUT *Annual Report*, 1915, 1989.)
39. Phipps, *History*, pp. 8–10.
40. Ibid., pp. 14–15.
41. Tickner, *Spectacle*, p. 230.
42. NUWSS circular, 6.8.1914, as quoted in Tickner, *Spectacle*, p. 229.
43. *Schoolmaster*, 13.5.1916, p. 635. She moved a motion for the LTA to organise a conference on war economies. This was carried.
44. *Schoolmaster*, 13.5.1916, p. 635.
45. Swansea Education Committee, 7.6.1915, no. 125, 12.12.1921, no. 88.
46. It is likely that Hettie Wheeldon and Winnie Mason, the daughters of Alice Wheeldon arrested and imprisoned on the fabricated charge of attempting to murder Lloyd George with a poisoned blow dart, were such unqualified teachers. Although Hettie was a WSPU

feinist and Ilkeston teacher there is no reference to membership of the NUT or NFWT in their extant annals. The correspondence of Winnie, a teacher in Southampton, and Hettie, with their mother indicates a low level of academic education. (Winnie to Alice Wheeldon 7.1.1917, in Wheeldon file PRO as quoted in Sheila Rowbotham, *The Friends of Alice Wheeldon*, Pluto Press, pp. 56 and 58.)

47. *Vote*, 28.4.1916, p. 1014.
48. *Schoolmaster*, 14.6.1919.
49. *TES*, 14.1.1920, p. 18.
50. She proposed the motion and Miss McKenzie seconded. The third supporter is not named. Minutes of Central Council, 27.4.1918 (NUWT archive).
51. Minutes of Central Council, 3.3.1917.
52. Sybil Oldfield, 'Proposal for a short collaborative research project in British Women's History', *History Workshop* 27, spring 1989, pp. 177–8.
53. Defence of the Realm Act restrictions. See page 59; *Vote*, 9.4.1915.
54. Ibid.
55. *Swansea Municipal Secondary School Magazine*, July 1917, no. 26, p. 33. On Empire Day pupils were obliged to 'celebrate' the achievement of the Empire and salute the flag.
56. *South Wales Daily Post*, 5.12.1918, quoting the *Daily Mail*.
57. See Chapter 2, fn. 60.
58. Miss Sims to Ethel Froud, 6.1.1918, in Members' Correspondence, 1917–18.
59. Such a tactic had been rejected out of hand when it had been suggested in response to the parliamentary fund of the Union, which only funded male teacher MPs (*Schoolmistress*, 11.4.1912, p. 22).
60. Undated letter Miss Sims to Ethel Froud in Members' Correspondence, 1917–18.
61. Minutes of the Central Council, 27.4.1918. Mrs Chester was accused of wasting time on 'trivial matters' by even raising this.
62. Ethel Froud to Miss Robson, 22.1.1917, Members' Correspondence file, 1917–18.
63. Emily Phipps to Ethel Froud, n.d. (November 1917), in pencil, Members' Correspondence file, 1917–18.
64. Minutes of the Central Council, 13.2.1915.
65. Emily Phipps to Ethel Froud 15.11.1917 in Members' Correspondence 1917–18
66. Fisher, *Unfinished Autobiography*, pp. 94, 106.
67. *London Teacher*, 12.4.1918, p. 130.
68. Kean, *Challenging the State?*, p. 170; and *Schoolmaster*, 17.11.1917, p. 552.
69. Emily Phipps to Ethel Froud, 2.12.1917, 27.2.1918, Members' Correspondence, 1917–18.
70. *Schoolmaster*, 6.4.1918, p. 436.
71. Editorial, *Schoolmaster*, 13.4.1918, p. 463.
72. *TES*, 8.5.1919.

73. *Daily Express*, 20.7.1919, in London 8 file, NUWT archive.
74. *London Teacher*, 22.3.1918, p. 121.
75. Ibid.
76. Phipps, *History*, p. 37; the LTA did not dispute this: *London Teacher*, 22.3.1918, p. 121.
77. Leaflet, 7.6.1918, in box 470, NUWT archive.
78. *Daily Express*, 20.7.1919, in London 8 file, NUWT archive.
79. Minutes of the Central Council, 6.9.1919.
80. Ethel Froud to Miss Grinter, 22.3.1920, in box 505, NUWT archive.
81. Kean, *Challenging the State?*, pp. 78–104.
82. Ibid., p. 100. The NUT executive drew back, however, from giving any donation from union funds, *Schoolmaster*, 11.10.1913, pp. 650ff.
83. *TES*, 25.7.1919, cutting in London 8 file, NUWT archive.
84. Various cuttings in London 8 file.
85. It only offered a war bonus payment.
86. Editorial in *London Teacher*, 22.3.1918.
87. Emily Phipps to Ethel Froud, 27.2.1918, in Members' Correspondence file, 1917–18 (NUWT archive).
88. Kean and Oram, 'Men must be educated'.
89. Kean, 'Teachers and the State', p. 151; Emily Phipps to Ethel Froud, 5.7.1921, in box 506.
90. Phipps, ibid.
91. Emily Phipps to Ethel Froud, 1.4.7.1921, in box 506.
92. Phipps, *History*, pp. 21–3.
93. Editorial in *Schoolmaster*, 6.12.1919; Phipps, *History*, p. 21.
94. London NFWT *First Annual Report*, 1918.
95. *Woman Teacher*, 26.9.1919.
96. Minutes of the Central Council, 15.11.1919.
97. *Woman Teacher*, May 1951, p. 131.
98. Irene Poulter to Emily Phipps, 21.3.1918, Members' Correspondence (NUWT archive).
99. Minutes of a general meeting, 13.7.(1921?), box 470 (NUWT archive).
100. Ibid.

Chapter 5
1. Millicent Fawcett, *What I Remember*, 1924, p.247, quoted in Garner, *Stepping Stones,* p. 104.
2. *Vote*, 3.1.1919, quoted in ibid.
3. John Saville, *The Labour Movement in Britain,* Faber and Faber, 1988, p. 42.
4. Moreton and Tate, *The British Labour Movement*, pp. 278–83; ibid., pp. 42–4.
5. Ibid., pp. 287, 296; *British Labour and the Russian Revolution: The Leeds Convention*, introduction by Ken Coates, Spokesman, n.d.
6. WTFU, *Annual Report*, 1917; Birmingham Women Teachers' Association Conference Report, 26.1.1918, box 411 (NUWT archive).
7. *Woman Teacher*, 11.6.1920, p. 303.

8. This would include Ethel Froud.
9. Minutes of the Central Council, 15.1.1921.
10. Hannah Mitchell, *The Hard Way Up*, ed. Geoffrey Mitchell, Virago, 1977; originally published 1968, p. 189.
11. Ethel Froud to Miss Grinter, 22.3.1920, box 505.
12. *Woman Teacher*, 26.9.1919.
13. Minutes of the Central Council, 15.11.1919.
14. Emily Phipps to Ethel Froud, 4.2.1920, file 48, in box 69.
15. All study could be undertaken privately; Gibson and Weldon, *How to become a Barrister*, 1921.
16. Emily Phipps to Ethel Froud, 2.5.1924, file 89, in box 123.
17. Minutes of the Central Council, 6.3.1920.
18. Editorial, 'The Rowdy Way', *Schoolmaster*, 3.4.1920, p. 647. The editorial continued by accusing the London women teachers of 'anarchy', and creating 'disorder' in the LTA in the past. It 'renounced' the 'extremists' for demanding equal pay. *Vote*, 27.3.1920, supported this action.
19. David Butler and Jennie Freeman, *British Political Facts 1990–1960*, Macmillan, 1964. Sinn Fein refused to recognise the British Parliament and took an abstentionist position. Countess Marcievicz was imprisoned in Holloway when she stood as MP. (Sean O'Faolain, *Countess Marcievicz*, Cresset Women's Voices, 1987, originally published 1934, p. 179.
20. This leaflet was addressed 'Dear Sir'. There may have been other leaflets aimed at women which are now lost. (In Parliamentary File in NUWT archive.)
21. Ibid.
22. Minutes of the Central Council, 21.5.1918.
23. Ibid., 16.11.1918,
24. Ray Strachey to Ethel Froud, 19.12.1918, Parliamentary file.
25. *Vote*, 3.1.1919.
26. *South Wales Daily Post*, 5.12.1918, quoting *Daily Mail*.
27. Emily Phipps to Ethel Froud, 8.2.1918, in Members' Correspondence, 1917–18; see also file 89 in box 123 for correspondence from Emily Phipps to Ethel Froud in response to the London Unit's criticism of her editorship of the *Woman Teacher*.
28. Circular from Ethel Froud, 25.10.1922, NUWT Parliamentary file.
29. Typed note of London Unit, 1923, in Parliamentary file. Crook defeated Susan Lawrence in 1922 by 468. She won in 1923 by 1057 votes.
30. Circular from Ethel Froud, 25.10.1922, NUWT Parliamentary file.
31. Parliamentary file, ibid.
32. Letter to members, 6.7.1922, Parliamentary file, ibid.
33. Emily Phipps to Ethel Froud, 4.2.1920, in file 48, box 69; Minutes of the Central Council, 6.3.1920.
34. Central Council, ibid.
35. It seems strange that they were not aware of Miss Bathurst's record given their predilection for self-publicity!
36. Minutes of the Central Council, 27.3.1920. Miss Hewitt's proposal was carried 9 for 2 against.

37. Letters to and from Miss Bathurst and Ethel Froud, 9.3.1920, in NUWT Parliamentary file.
38. *Vote*, 14.3.1919, p. 117.
39. Election address, file 48, in box 69.
40. Ibid. *'Cwtch'* Welsh word meaning cubby hole.
41. These included Miss Kenyon in Oldham and Ethel Stead in Bradford.
42. Transcript of taped interview with Nan McMillan, September 1988.
43. Letter to London Members from Ethel Froud, file 48, in box 69; LCC, *General Election of County Councillors*, 5.3.1925, LCC, 1925 (Official Publications Library, British Library).
44. Agnes Dawson to London Unit, 7.3.1925, file 48, in box 69.
45. Ethel Froud to Miss Turner, 5.5.1925, file 51, in box 71.
46. LCC, *Attendance of Members*, 1925–7; 1928–30; 1931–3; 1934–6, LCC (OPL:BL).
47. Special schools sub-committee, 11.7.1928, p. 338; Teaching sub-committee, 26.3.1930, p. 190; Special schools sub-committee, 12.3.1930, p. 158; Minutes of LCC 1928, 1930 (OPL:BL).
48. See Chapter 3, fn. 23.
49. Ethel Froud to Miss Turner, 7.5.1925, file 51, box 71.
50. Miss Savage to Ethel Froud, 12.3.1928, file 51, in box 71.
51. Undated handwritten note from Florence Key to Ethel Froud in file 51, in box 71.
52. Miss Savage to Ethel Froud, 6.7.1929, file 51, in box 71.
53. Ibid.
54. Labour Party Conference Reports, 1925, p. 293, 1926, p. 264; Kean, *Challenging the State?*, pp. 171–8; Jones, *Beyond Progressive Education*, pp. 95–108.
55. *Schoolmaster*, 1.1.1926, p. 20.
56. Ethel Froud to Mr Hawkins, 7.2.1929, file 51, in box 70.
57. Correspondence between David Capper and Ethel Froud, in ibid. Nan McMillan, who first knew Ethel Froud in the late 1920s, has expressed surprise that she was ever a member.
58. C. Williams to Ethel Froud, 21.6.1925, Sarah Jones to Ethel Froud, 9.2.1925, and replies, 12.2.1925 and 17.2.1925, file 51, in box 70.
59. Letter of David Capper to Ethel Froud, 16.7.1924 in ibid.
60. Ibid.
61. Letter of Ethel Froud to Miss Grimbley, 11.1.1929, and others in ibid.
62. LCC, *General Election of County Councillors*, 8.3.1934, LCC, 1934.
63. Oram, 'Serving two masters', p. 136.
64. Circular by General Secretary, May 1923, C8.49 (NUT library).
65. Oram, 'Serving two masters', p. 147.
66. Accommodation and Attendance sub-committee, 7.7.1926, p. 485, Buildings sub-committee, 10.2.1926, p. 101, LCC, *Minutes of Proceedings*, 1926 (OPL).
67. For example, 'That the employment of Mrs G. Robinson as a teacher "on supply" in contradiction of standing order no 354, from 11th to 22nd June 1926, inclusive, be condoned.' Teaching staff sub-committee, 21.7.1926, p. 570; 15.2.1928, p. 84; and 9.5.1928, p. 232, in LCC, *Minutes of Proceedings*, 1926, 1928 (OPL).

68. Teaching staff sub-committee, 15.7.1925, LCC, *Minutes of Proceedings*, 1925, p. 516.
69. Miss Byett, 'The married woman teacher, NUWT, n.d.
70. Transcript of taped interview with Nan McMillan, September 1988. Nan McMillan lived with, and, on the removal of the marriage bar, married David Capper.
71. NUWT leaflet on the lifting of the marriage bar, in file 470. It was removed by 74 votes to 37.
72. Teaching sub-committee, 20.1.1935, LCC, *Minutes of Proceedings*, 1935.
73. Cutting from *Daily Herald*, 25.11.1936. (Another says *News Chronicle*.) People box 8 (NUWT archive).
74. London circular, 1.2.1926, file 48, in box 69.
75. Ethel Froud to London members, 25.10.1926, file 48, in box 69.
76. Ibid.
77. Circular from Peter Zinkin, ward secretary, 24.10.1925, file 48, in box 69.

Chapter 6

1. Lind-af-Hageby, *Unbounded Gratitude! Women's Right to Work*, 1920, pp. 2, 9.
2. For example, Tottenham and East Ham. Alison Oram, 'Sex Antagonism in the Teaching Profession', *History of Education Review*, vol. 14, no. 2, 1985, p. 37.
3. Some LEAs were reluctant to implement even the Burnham pay levels. Kean, *Challenging the State?*, pp. 102–3; Seifert, *Teacher Militancy*, pp. 40–6.
4. *Schoolmaster*, 5.1.1923, p. 6; Seifert, *Teacher Militancy*, p. 42.
5. *Schoolmaster*, 1.2.1924, p. 169.
6. *London Teacher*, 3.4.1925, p. 113; Oram, 'Sex Antagonism'.
7. J. T. Murphy, *Preparing for Power*, Pluto, 1970, pp. 212–13, originally published 1934.
8. John MacArthur, *Shall Flappers Rule?*, Simpkin, Marshall and Hamilton Kent, 1927; Sheila Rowbotham, *Hidden from History*, Pluto, 1973, p. 124.
9. MacArthur, *Flappers*, p. 9.
10. Ibid., p. 14.
11. Charlotte Haldane, *Motherhood and its Enemies*, 1927, p. 156; quoted in Sheila Jeffreys, *The Spinster and her Enemies*, p. 175. The word spinster had been current before this time. Spinsters were often portrayed as unhappy maiden aunts, for example as portrayed in Flora Mayor's, *The Third Miss Symons*, 1913 (republished Virago, 1980).
12. Alec Craig and Walter Gallichan in Jeffreys, *Spinster*, p. 180.
13. Special Staffing sub-committee, 20.2.1925.
14. *South Wales Daily Post*, 7.4.1925.
15. Hansard, 5th series, 1921, vol. 145, 4.8.1921, p. 1804.
16. Lt. Col. Moore-Brabazan in ibid.; Jeffrey Weeks, *Sex, Politics and Society*, Longman, 1981, p. 102.
17. Hansard, 5th series, 1921, vol. 145, 4.8.1921, p. 1800, 1804–5, and Jeffreys, *Spinster*, p. 114.

18. *Schoolmasters' Review*, vol. 1, no. 1, September 1919.
19. Ibid.
20. Oram, 'Sex Antagonism', p. 42.
21. London Schoolmasters' Association, *Equal Pay and the Teaching Profession*, LSA, 1921, p. 21.
22. Ibid., p. 57.
23. Ibid., p. 65.
24. Ibid., p. 74.
25. *New Schoolmaster*, Oct. 1921, vol. 1, no. 5, p. 23.
26. *New Schoolmaster*, Jan. 1922, vol. 2, p. 5.
27. *New Schoolmaster*, June 1922, vol. 2, no. 11.
28. Ibid.
29. LSA, *Equal Pay and the Teaching Profession*, LSA, 1921, p. 49.
30. Presidential address NAS conference, *South Wales Daily Post*, 15.4.1925.
31. Editorial, *Schoolmaster*, 18.12.1921, p. 1063.
32. Cartoon in *New Schoolmaster*, vol. 2, July 1922, p. 21.
33. *Schoolmasters' Review*, Feb. 1921, vol. 2, no. 2 and 3.
34. NUWT, 'The Dr. Hayward case', n.d., in box 518.
35. *Schoolmasters' Review*, July 1924, vol. 5, no. 33, p. 7.
36. *Woman Teacher*, 25.11.1921, pp. 61–7.
37. *New Schoolmaster*, Nov. 1921, vol. 1, no. 6, p. 9.
38. Winifred Holtby to Ethel Froud, 15.5.1935, in box 410.
39. Ruth Adam, *I'm Not Complaining*, Virago, 1983, pp. 21, 343 (originally published 1938).
40. Ibid.
41. Nalbro Bartley, *A Woman's Woman*, Small, Maynard and Co., 1919, p. 170.
42. Ibid., p. 379.
43. Marjorie Hillis, *Live Alone and Like it. A Guide for the Extra Woman*, Citadel Press, 1936, pp. 18–19 (reprinted 1937, 1938, 1942, 1947).
44. Winifred Holtby, *Poor Caroline*, Virago, 1985, p. 113 (originally published 1931).
45. Eleanor Rathbone addressing annual council meeting of NUSEC, 1925. Mary Stokes, *Eleanor Rathbone, a Biography*, p. 116, as quoted in Vicinus, *Independent Women*, p. 283.
46. Suzie Fleming, intro. Eleanor Rathbone, *The Disinherited Family*, Falling Wall Press, 1984, p. 50.
47. Ibid., p. 232.
48. Ibid., p. 242.
49. Ibid.
50. Ibid.
51. Miss E. Conway, 'The Burnham Award', *London Teacher*, 8.5.1925. Miss Sarah Griffiths was appointed women's officer, *Schoolmaster*, 11.7.1924, p. 48.
52. *Vote*, 3.1.1919.
53. Ibid.
54. Undated cutting from *Schoolmistress* (1919) in Miscellaneous Cuttings file, NUWT archive.

55. Report of Central Council on 'Women's Allowances in relation to equal pay', presented at Buxton Conference 1929, file 411.
56. Ibid.
57. *Time and Tide*, 13.8.1920, in Dale Spender, *Time and Tide Wait for No Man*, Pandora, 1984, pp. 193–6; Jeffreys, *Spinster and Her Enemies*, p. 154.
58. Minutes of Central Council NUWT, 19.3.1927. Documents in box 77, NUWT archive. Kean and Oram, 'Men must be educated'.
59. Hamilton, *Life Errant*, p. 209.
60. *Woman Teacher*, 23.1.1928, p. 50.
61. Mrs Chandler and Miss Townsend from Lewisham were members of the Church League for Women's Suffrage. The Church League for Women's Suffrage, *Third Annual Report*, 1912 (British Library). A Miss Dawson made an annual subscription to the central branch during 1912.
62. Nancy Parnell, *A Venture in Faith*, St Joan's Alliance, 1961 (Fawcett Library).
63. *Catholic Citizen*, 15.23.1927, p. 11 (Fawcett Library); Northworld JM logbook, 9.9.1907 (Jewish New Year) in EO/DIV4/NOR/LB/9 (GLRO).
64. *Catholic Citizen*, 15.10.1928, back page and 15.11.1928, p. 99.
65. Eleanor Rathbone, in Jeffreys, *Spinster and Her Enemies*, p. 163.
66. Grace Cottel, 'Films for Children', *Vote*, 4.1.1929.
67. London Unit Cinema Report in box 470; *Woman Teacher*, 2.1.1927, p. 75.
68. *Vote*, 19.9.1919; 26.9.1919. Alongside such campaigns the WFL continued to press for sex instruction in schools.
69. *Time and Tide*, 6.8.1926, pp. 714–15, quoted in Spender, *Time and Tide*, p. 103.
70. Alison Oram, 'Embittered, Sexless, or Homosexual: Attacks on Spinster Teachers 1918–1939', in Lesbian History Group, *Not a Passing Phase. Reclaiming Lesbians in History*, Women's Press, 1989.
71. Emily Phipps to Ethel Froud, 22.3.1927, file 89, in box 122, NUWT archive.
72. Report of NUWT officers' meeting of 2.4.1927, reported 28.5.1927, in file 89, box 122.
73. Paper in file 89, box 123, n.d.
74. Undated handwritten note from Emily Phipps in ibid.
75. Ibid.
76. Emily Phipps to Ethel Froud, 22.3.1927, file 89, box 122.

Chapter 7
1. The professional suffrage banners were designed by the Artists' Suffrage League or the Suffrage Atelier. Tickner, *Spectacle*, p. 69.
2. Henry W. Nevinson, *More Changes, more Chances*, Nisbet, 1925, p. 313. The slogan, like other suffrage mottoes, had a literary origin, in Byron's 'Childe Harold'. ('Childe Harolde', Canto ii, stanza 76.)
3. Tickner, *Spectacle*, p. 257.

4.   'The Woman's cause is man's: they rise or sink
                  Together, dwarf'd or godlike, bond or free'.
   Tennyson, 'Princess: a medley', vii 1.259 in Tennyson, *Poems and Plays*, Oxford University Press, 1975, p. 199; Mitchell, *Hard Way Up*, p. 98.
5. *Woman Teacher*, 12.11.1920; Minute book of Joint Committee of London and Extra-Metropolitan branches 10.11.1920, in box 295.
6. East Ham NUWT *Seventh Annual Report*, 1920, box 411; Minute Book of Joint Committee of London and Extra-Metropolitan branches 8.9.20, 10.11.1920, in box 295.
7. *Woman Teacher*, 13.6.1941, p. 232.
8. London NFWT *Second Annual Report* 1919 in box 411; Will of Miss Annie Byett dated 1930, bequeathing badge to Miss Jane Dawes in unnumbered brown box (NUWT archive).
9. Tickner, *Spectacle*, pp. 94, 88, 91, 122.
10. Minutes Equal Political Rights Demonstration 1926 (NUWT archive).
11. Ibid.
12. Swansea School Board, 6.3.1895; Schools Management Committee, 14.3.1895 (WGRO).
13. *Woman Teacher*, 18.6.1943; Chapter 5, fn. 27.
14. Ethel Froud to Miss Amy Teece, 2.1.1939, in box 410.
15. 41, Christchurch Avenue.
16. Clare Neal to Ethel Froud, 7.12.1931, file 127, in box 155.
17. *Woman Teacher*, 14.1.1938, p. 109; Letter from M. M. Neal to Miss Froud, 3.1.1937 (sic) and bereavement card, file 81, in box 112.
18. Emily Phipps to Ethel Froud, 20.6.1940, file 81, in box 112.
19. Edgar Phipps to Miss Pierotti, 31.5.1943; Adelaide Jones to Miss Pierotti, 15.5.1941, file 89 (kii6), box 123.
20. Edgar Phipps to Miss Pierotti 31.5.1943 in ibid.
21. Agnes Dawson to Ethel Froud, n.d. in People Box 8.
22. Ibid.
23. *The Women's Who's Who 1934–5*, Shaw Publishing Company, 1935; Crawford Street Logbook, 30.3.1917, EO/DIV7/CRA/LB/1 (GLRO); *Time and Tide*, 24.9.1920, p. 404.
24. *Time and Tide*, ibid.; Miss Pierotti to Miss Dedman, including copy of a letter to her from Mrs Hanson (née Follett), 29.4.1953, file 81, box 112.
25. *Daily Herald*, 25.9.1926, cutting in People box 8.
26. *TES*, 20.7.1935, p .257 as quoted in Alison Oram, 'Embittered, Sexless or Homosexual'.
27. Crawford Street Infants, Logbook, EO/DIV7/CRA/LB/1 1922; *London Teacher*, 19.4.1918.
28. Crawford Street Infants, Logbook, 22.6.1923 and records of Miss Munns' absence during 1923, 1924, 1925, 1926, 1927.
29. Agnes Dawson to Miss Pierotti, 13.12.1952, file 81, box 112.
30. Ibid.
31. Nan McMillan Interview.
32. Ibid.

33. Oram, 'Embittered, Sexless or Homosexual'.
34. Correspondence in box 176, July 1935 as quoted in Oram, 'Embittered, Sexless or Homosexual'.
35. For many years Theodora Bonwick lived with her mother in Weston Park Road in Crouch End, North London. By the 1920s, however, she too had formed a close relationship with another NUWT member, Miss Newstead, which was acknowledged within the NUWT. *Woman Teacher*, 16.11.1928.
36. Nan McMillan Interview.
37. Lillian Faderman, *Surpassing the Love of Men*, Women's Press, 1985, p. 337.
38. Krafft Ebing quoted in Weeks, *Sex, Politics and Society*, p. 115; Wendy Clark, 'The Dyke, the Feminist and the Devil', *Feminist Review*, no. 11, June 1982, p. 32.
39. Sonja Ruehl, 'Sexual Theory and Practice: Another Double Standard', p. 219, and Elizabeth Wilson, 'I'll climb the stairway to Heaven: Lesbianism in the Seventies', pp. 183–7 in ed. Sue Cartledge and Joanna Ryan, *Sex and Love: New Thoughts on Old Contradictions*, Women's Press, 1983.
40. See Chapter 6, fns. 15–17.
41. Weeks, *Sex Politics and Society*, p. 117.
42. Emily Phipps to Ethel Froud, 15.11.1917, in Members' Correspondence 1917–18 (NUWT archive).
43. Emily Phipps to Ethel Froud, 18.10.1917, in ibid.
44. East Ham NUWT *Annual Report*, 1928, box 448.
45. Ibid. and box 411.
46. Leaflet of Harrow NUWT 4.3.1913 in box 448; Minute book of the Joint Committee of London and Extra-Metropolitan branches, 10.11.1920, 11.5.1921, 11.11.1925, in box 295.
47. Box 448.
48. Minute book of the Joint Committee of London and Extra-Metropolitan branches, 11.11.1925, box 295.
49. Battersea and Clapham NUWT, *Woman Teacher*, 18.3.1927.
50. Photograph in box 470; *Woman Teacher*, 7.10.1927, p. 10; 25.11.1927, p. 66.
51. London NUWT *Seventh Annual Report* 1923–4, in box 295. There was also fund raising for welfare causes. Members regularly organised events including 'clinic parties' for the Rose Lamartine Yates clinic for children in South London. (Founded by NUWT after successful lobbying of LCC as memorial to Miss Cutten and named after Mrs Lamartine Yates, Labour member and NUWT supporter on LCC, box 448.)
52. File 214, in box 174a.
53. Ethel Froud to Miss Nixon, 12.10.1929 in ibid.
54. Ethel Froud to Miss Coombs in ibid.
55. Photograph in box 470.
56. File 68 in box 94; box 432 for Equal Pay luncheon and House of Commons dinner, 1931.
57. Circular from Ethel Froud, 4.9.1928 in ibid.

58. File 68, in box 94; Equal Pay luncheon, 9.5.1931, file 432.
59. *Woman Teacher*, 5.10.1928, pp. 3–5.
60. Ibid.
61. Ibid., p. 5.
62. B. Lewis and M. Hulton to Miss Froud, 21.2.1924, box 94.
63. Vicinus, *Independent Women*, p. 292.
64. Nan McMillan Interview.

Chapter 8

1. A school clinic was established in Lambeth, in memory of Miss Cutten (box 288 in NUWT archive); a trust fund, the 'Emily Phipps gift' was established by her for girls at the Swansea Secondary School who were not scholarship holders and this continued after her death (*Woman Teacher*, July 1951, p. 165); a school journey hostel fund was established in memory of Miss Bonwick (box 470).
2. *Woman Teacher*, 16.11.1928.
3. *Woman Teacher*, May 1951, pp. 130–1.
4. *Woman Teacher*, 23.11.1928, p. 50.
5. *Woman Teacher*, 16.11.1928.
6. Ibid.
7. Filed in special documents file in tea chest (NUWT archive).
8. *Woman Teacher*, 23.11.1928, p. 50.
9. *Woman Teacher*, 16.11.1928.
10. Ibid.
11. Letter of Mrs Ferrari to Ethel Froud, 20.1.1931, in box 94.
12. Letter of Mr Tate to Miss Pierotti, 2.6.1944, in box 410.
13. Letter of Ethel Froud to Amy Teece, 2.1.1939, in box 410.
14. Ibid.
15. Letter of Ethel Froud to Miss Lewis who had written enquiring about her health, 5.12.1939, in box 410.
16. Letter of Miss Allison to Miss Hamlyn, 21.4.1961, in unnumbered brown box although the numbers 7–11 appear in faint handwriting on the box.
17. *Woman Teacher*, 13.6.1941, p. 232.
18. *Woman Teacher*, 13.6.1945, p. 233.
19. Officers' minutes, January 1934, in box 451.
20. *Woman Teacher*, 14.1.1938, p. 109.
21. Miss Pierotti to Miss Dawson, 11.4.1946, file 48, in box 69.
22. Miss Dawson to Miss Pierotti, April 1946, file 48, in box 69.
23. Miss Dawson to Miss Pierotti, 10.3.1946, file 48, in box 69.
24. NUWT headquarters to Miss Dawson, 7.3.1946, file 48, in box 69.
25. Miss Phipps to Miss Pierotti, 30.9.1942, file 89, in box 123.
26. Clare Neal to Miss Pierotti 7.12.1931, file 127 in box 158.
27. Letter from Miss Phipps to Miss Froud, 26.4.1939, in box 451.
28. Ibid.
29. Miss Phipps to Miss Froud, 20.5.1939, in box 451.
30. Miss Phipps to Miss Pierotti, 15.5.1941, in box 451.
31. Ibid.
32. Miss Jones to Miss Pierotti, 15.5.1941, in box 451.

33. Miss Phipps to Miss Pierotti, 13.12.1941, in box 451.
34. Edgar Phipps to Miss Pierotti, 2.6.1943; Miss Hewitt to Miss Pierotti, 5.5.1943; Miss Pierotti to Miss Jones, 4.5.1943, file 89, Kii6 in box 123; *South Wales Evening Post*, 6.5.1943.
35. Circular of general secretary, 4.5.1943, file 89, Kii6 in box 123.
36. Letter from Miss Jones to Miss Pierotti, 19.5.1943, file 89, in box 123.
37. Grace Cottell to Miss Pierotti, 9.5.1943, file 89, Kii6 in box 123.
38. Mrs Ferrari to Miss Pierotti, 10.5.1943, file 89, Kii6 in box 123.
39. Agnes Dawson to Miss Pierotti, 7.5.1943, file 89, Kii6 in box 123.
40. *Woman Teacher*, 18.6.1943, p. 100.
41. Ibid., p. 101; Nevinson, *More Changes, More Chances*, p. 310; Fulford, *Votes for Women*, p. 137.
42. *Woman Teacher*, 18.6.1943, p. 101.
43. Ibid., p. 100.
44. Ibid.
45. A. Pierotti, *The Story of the NUWT*, NUWT, 1963.
46. Letter dated April 1964, appended to back page of *The Story of the NUWT*.
47. Pierotti, *Story*, p. 76.
48. Ibid., p. 38.
49. Ibid., p. 21, and *Woman Teacher*, May 1951, for background to the hostility.
50. Helen Dedman to Miss Pierotti, 7.3.1960, in unnumbered brown box.
51. Miss Snowden to Miss Pierotti, 23.8.1961, in box 572.
52. Stanley and Morley, *The Life of Emily Davison*, p. 74.
53. Carolyn Heilbrun, *Writing a Woman's Life*, Women's Press, 1989, p. 47.
54. Ed. Sheri Benstock, *The Private Self. Theory and Practice of Women's Autobiographical Writings*, Routledge, 1988; Elizabeth Wilson, 'Tell it like it is: women and confessional writing', in ed. Susannah Radstone, *Sweet Dreams. Sexuality, Gender and Popular Fiction*, Lawrence and Wishart, 1988.
55. Eds. Margaret Kamester and Jo Vellacott, *Militarism versus Feminism: Writings on Women and War*, Virago, 1987.
56. Sheila Rowbotham, Lynne Segal, Hilary Wainwright, *Beyond the Fragments*, Merlin Press, 1979.
57. Raphael Samuel, 'The lost World of British Communism', *New Left Review*, no. 154, Nov./Dec. 1985; 'Staying Power', *New Left Review*, no. 156, March/April 1986; Kean, *Challenging the State?*, pp. 54–67.
58. Nan McMillan Interview.

Bibliography

Contemporary Books, Pamphlets and Articles

As many of these publications are difficult to locate I have noted where I found them as follows: Fawcett Library (F), British Library (BL), NUWT archive (A).

Ruth Adam, *I'm Not Complaining,* Virago, 1983, originally published 1938.
Anon, *The Women's Who's Who 1934–5,* Shaw Publishing Co., 1935 (BL).
Ed. Betty Balfour, *Letters of Constance Lytton,* Heinemann, 1925 (BL).
Nalbro Bartley, *A Woman's Woman,* Small, Maynard & Co., 1919 (BL).
M. Mostyn Bird, *Woman at Work,* Chapman and Hall, 1911 (BL).
Amy Bulley and Margaret Whitley, *Women's Work,* Methuen, 1894 (BL).
A. S. Byett LLA, *Women and Education,* Presidential Address NFWT, 1918 (A).
——. *The Married Woman Teacher,* NUWT, n.d. (A).
Clare E. Collet, *Educated Working Women,* P. S. King, 1902 (BL).
Gertrude Colmore, *Suffragettes: A Story of Three Women,* Pandora, 1984 (originally published 1911).
——. *Mr Jones and the Governess,* WFL, 1913 (BL).
Edith Cooper LLA and Mary Mason LLA, *Teaching of Sex Hygiene,* NFWT, n.d. (A).
Clemence Dane, *Regiment of Women,* Heinemann, 1917, first published 1915 (BL).
Agnes Dawson, 'The Lower Age Limit of Compulsory Attendance' in *Conference Papers,* LTA, 1917 (BL).
——. *Nursery Schools,* NUWT, n.d. (F).
——. *Nursery Classes,* NUWT, n.d. (F).
Charlotte Perkins Gilman, *Women and Economics,* Putnam's, Fifth Edition, 1906 (BL).
Arthur Gronno, *The Attempt to Capture the NUT by Woman Suffragists,* n.d. (A).
Cicely Hamilton, *Marriage as a Trade,* Pandora, 1981, originally published 1909.
——. 'Women in the Great State' in ed. H. G. Wells, *The Great State,* Harper, 1912.
——. *Life Errant,* M. Dent, 1935 (BL).
Marjorie Hillis, *Live Alone and Like It. A Guide for the Extra Woman,* Citadel Press, 1936.

Winifred Holtby, *A New Voter's Guide to Party Politics*, Kegan Paul, 1929 (BL).
——. *Poor Caroline*, Virago, 1985, originally published 1931.
Lewisham Women's Franchise Club, *The Woman Teacher's Own Fault*, 1914 (BL).
L. Lind-af-Hageby, *Unbounded Gratitude! Women's Right to Work*, WFL, 1920 (BL).
London Schoolmasters' Association, *Equal Pay and the Teaching Profession*, LSA, 1921 (BL).
Constance Lytton, *Prisons and Prisoners*, Heinemann, 1914.
John MacArthur, *Shall Flappers Rule?* Simpkin, Marshall and Hamilton Kent, 1927 (BL).
F. M. Mayor, *The Third Miss Symons*, Virago, 1980, originally published 1913.
A. E. Metcalfe, *Woman's Effort*, Blackwell, 1917 (BL).
Dora Montefiore, *From a Victorian to a Modern*, E. Archer, 1927 (BL).
Edith J. Morley, *Women Workers in Seven Professions*, George Routledge & Sons, 1914 (BL).
Henry W. Nevinson, *More Changes, More Chances*, Nisbet, 1925.
Margaret W. Nevinson, *The Legal Wrongs of Married Women*, WFL, 1923 (BL).
——. *Life's Fitful Fever*, A & C Black, 1926 (BL).
Helena F. Normanton, *Sex Differentiation in Salary*, NFWT, 1914 (F).
NUWSS: 'Broken Windows and After', 1912.
——. '14 Reasons for Supporting Women's Suffrage', 1913.
——. 'The Meaning of the Women's Movement: Service versus Subjection', 1913.
——. 'Parliament and the Children', 1913.
——. 'Protest against Violence', 1913.
——. 'Teachers! Why Women's Suffrage Matters to You', 1913.
——. 'The House of Lords & Women's Suffrage': speech by the Earl of Lytton, 1914.
——. 'Our Common Humanity' – a speech by Maude Royden 1914.
——. 'Teachers and Politics' (Eastern Counties Federation), 1914.
——. 'The Programme of the NUWSS', 1919. (All BL.)
NUWT, *Papers on Individual Teaching Apparatus & Schemes of Work*, NUWT, 1923 (F).
Christabel Pankhurst, *The Great Scourge and How to End It*, E. Pankhurst, 1913 (F).
Marion Phillips, *Women and the Labour Party*, Headley Bros., 1918 (BL).
Emily Phipps, BA, *Equality of Opportunity*, NUWT, n.d. (F).
——. *History of the NUWT*, NUWT, 1928 (A).
Ed. A. J. R., *The Suffrage Annual and Women's Who's Who*, Stanley Paul & Co., 1913 (F).
M. Radclyffe Hall, *The Unlit Lamp*, Virago, 1981 (originally published 1926).
Elizabeth Robins, *Way Stations*, Hodder & Stoughton, 1913 (BL).
——. *The Convert*, Women's Press, 1980 (originally published 1907).
Evelyn Sharp, *Rebel Women*, 1915 (BL).

——. *Unfinished Adventure,* John Lane, 1933.
Rebecca West, *The Judge,* Virago, 1980 (originally published 1922).
WTFU, Pamphlet 1: 'The Referendum', n.d.
——. 'Why the Women's Suffrage Resolution is Legitimate', NUT Business, n.d.
——. 'Women's Suffrage and the LTA' (1913).
——. 'The Spirit of Citizenship', 1913. (All BL.)

Secondary Books, Pamphlets and Articles

Diane Atkinson, *Mrs Broom's Suffragette Photographs,* Photo-Library 10, Nishen Photography, n.d.
E. Moberly Bell, *Josephine Butler,* Constable, 1962.
Ed. Shari Benstock, *The Private Self. Theory and Practice of Women's Autobiographical Writings,* Routledge, 1988.
Lucy Bland, 'Guardians of the Race or Vampires upon the Nation's Health? Female sexuality and its regulation in early twentieth century Britain' in ed. Elizabeth Whitelegg, *The Changing Experience of Women,* Martin Robinson and Open University, 1982.
Eds. Sue Cartledge and Joanna Ryan, *Sex and Love. New Thoughts on Old Contradictions,* Women's Press, 1983.
Wendy Clark, 'The Dyke, the Feminist and the Devil', *Feminist Review* 11, summer 1982.
Lillian Faderman, *Surpassing the Love of Men,* Women's Press, 1985.
H. A. L. Fisher, *An Unfinished Autobiography,* Oxford University Press, 1940.
Suzie Fleming, *Eleanor Rathbone: The Disinherited Family,* Falling Wall Press, 1984.
Sheila Fletcher, *Women First. The Female Traditional Role in English Physical Education 1888–1980,* Athlone Press, 1984.
Ed. Estelle Freedman, *The Lesbian Issue: Essays from Signs,* University of Chicago Press, 1985.
Roger Fulford, *Votes for Women,* Faber and Faber, 1958.
Les Garner, *Stepping Stones to Women's Liberty,* Heinemann, 1984.
Nonita Glenday and Mary Price, *Reluctant Revolutionaries. A Century of Headmistresses 1874–1974,* Pitman, 1974.
Clive Griggs, *The Trades Union Congress and the Struggle for Education 1868–1925,* Falmer, 1983.
Brian Harrison, *Separate Spheres. The Opposition to Women's Suffrage,* Croom Helm, 1978.
Carolyn G. Heilbrun, *Writing a Woman's Life,* Women's Press, 1989.
James Hinton, *Labour and Socialism. A History of the Labour Movement 1867-1974,* Wheatsheaf, 1983.
Sandra Stanley Holton, *Feminism and Democracy in Women's Suffrage and Reform Politics in Britain 1906–1918,* Cambridge University Press, 1986.
Leslie P. Hume, *The NUWSS 1897–1914,* Garland, 1982.
Allen Hutt, *British Trade Unionism,* Lawrence and Wishart, 1975.
Sheila Jeffreys, *The Spinster and Her Enemies. Feminism and Sexuality 1880–1930,* Pandora, 1985.

Ken Jones, *Beyond Progressive Education*, Macmillan, 1983.

Hilda Kean, 'Teachers and the State', *British Journal of Sociology of Education*, vol. 10, no. 2, 1989.

——. *Challenging the State? The Socialist and Feminist Educational Experience 1900–1930*, Falmer Press, 1990.

Hilda Kean and Alison Oram, '"Who would be free herself must strike the Blow": Agnes Dawson and the NUWT', *South London Record 3*, South London History Workshop, 1988.

——. '"Men must be educated and women must do it". NFWT and contemporary feminism 1910–1930', *Gender and Education*, summer 1990.

Eds. Mary Langan and Bill Schwarz, *Crises in the British State 1880–1930*, Hutchinson, 1985.

Emmeline Pethick-Lawrence, *My Part in a Changing World*, Victor Gollancz, 1938.

Jane Lewis, *The Politics of Motherhood*, Croom Helm, 1980.

Andro Linklater, *An Unhusbanded Life: Charlotte Despard, Suffragette, Socialist, and Sinn Feiner*, Hutchinson, 1980.

Stuart Macintyre, *A Proletarian Science. Marxism in Britain 1917–1933*, Cambridge University Press, 1980.

Ed. Geoffrey Mitchell, *The Hard Way Up: the Autobiography of Hannah Mitchell, Suffragette and Rebel*, Virago, 1977 (originally published 1968).

A. L. Moreton and George Tate, *The British Labour Movement 1770–1970*, Lawrence and Wishart, 1956, revised 1973.

Ann Morley with Liz Stanley, *The Life and Death of Emily Wilding Davison*, Women's Press, 1988.

Caroline Morrell, *'Black Friday'. Violence against Women in the Suffrage Movement*, WRCC, 1981.

Frank Mort, *Dangerous Sexualities. Medico-Moral Politics in England Since 1830*, Routledge & Kegan Paul, 1987.

Stella Newsome, *The Women's Freedom League*, WFL, 1960.

Alison Oram, 'Sex Antagonism in the Teaching Profession: the Equal Pay Issue 1914–1939', *History of Education Review*, vol. 14, no. 2, 1985.

——. 'Serving Two Masters. The Introduction of a Marriage Bar in Teaching in the 1920s' in *Sexual Dynamics of History*, London Feminist History Group, Pluto, 1983.

——. '"Embittered, Sexless, or Homosexual": Attacks on Spinster Teachers 1918–1939' in Lesbian History Group, *Not a Passing Phase. Reclaiming Lesbians in History*, Women's Press, 1989.

Christabel Pankhurst, *Unshackled*, Cresset Library, 1987 (first published 1959).

E. Sylvia Pankhurst, *The Home Front*, Cresset Library, 1987 (first published 1932).

Nancy Parnell, *A Venture in Faith*, St Joan's Alliance, 1961.

Geoffrey Partington, *Women Teachers in the Twentieth Century in England and Wales*, NFER, 1976.

Anne Phillips, *Divided Loyalties: Dilemmas of Sex and Class*, Virago, 1987.

A. M. Pierotti, *The Story of the NUWT*, NUWT, 1963 (NUT Library).

Ed. Susannah Radstone, *Sweet Dreams. Sexuality, Gender, and Popular Fiction*, Lawrence and Wishart, 1988.

Constance Rover, *Women's Suffrage and Party Politics in Britain 1866–1914*,

Routledge & Kegan Paul, 1967.
Caroline Rowan, 'For the Duration Only: Motherhood and Nation in the First World War' in *Formations of Nation and People,* Routledge & Kegan Paul, 1984.
Sheila Rowbotham, *Hidden from History,* Pluto, 1973.
———. *Friends of Alice Wheeldon,* Pluto, 1986.
Raphael Samuel, 'The Lost World of British Communism', *New Left Review* 154, Nov./Dec. 1985.
———. 'Staying Power: the Lost World of British Communism: Part 2, *New Left Review* 156, March/April 1986.
———. 'Class Politics: The Lost World of British Communism' in *New Left Review* 165, Sept./Oct. 1987.
John Saville, *The Labour Movement in Britain,* Faber and Faber, 1988.
Roger Seifert, *Teacher Militancy,* Falmer, 1987.
R. J. W. Selleck, *New Primary Education and the Progressives 1914–1939,* Routledge & Kegan Paul, 1972.
Dale Spender, *Time and Tide Wait for No Man,* Pandora, 1984.
Brian Simon, *Education and the Labour Movement 1870–1920,* Lawrence and Wishart, 1974.
———. *The Politics of Educational Reform 1920–1940,* Lawrence and Wishart, 1974.
Carolyn Steedman, *Landscape for a Good Woman,* Virago, 1986.
Mary and Margaret Thompson, *They Couldn't Stop Us! Experiences of Two (Usually Law-Abiding) Women in the Years 1909–1913,* W. E. Harrison, 1957 (BL).
Lisa Tickner, *The Spectacle of Women. Imagery of the Suffrage Campaign 1907–1914,* Chatto and Windus, 1987.
Asher Tropp, *The Schoolteachers,* Heinemann, 1957.
Betty D. Vernon, *Ellen Wilkinson,* Croom Helm, 1982.
Martha Vicinus, *Independent Women. Work and Community for Single Women 1850–1920,* Virago, 1985.
Judith R. Walkowitz, *Prostitution and Victorian Society. Women, Class and the State,* Cambridge University Press, 1982.
Jeffrey Weeks, *Sex, Politics and Society: The Regulation of Sexuality Since 1800,* Longman, 1981.
Frances Widdowson, *Going up into the Next Class: Women and Elementary Teacher Training 1840–1914,* WRCC, 1980.

Periodicals

Anti-Suffrage Review
Catholic Citizen
Class Teacher
Educational Worker
London Class Teacher
London Teacher
New Schoolmaster
Schoolmaster
Schoolmaster's Review

Schoolmistress
South Wales Daily Post
Swansea Municipal Secondary School Magazine
Vote
Votes for Women
Woman's Dreadnought
Woman Teacher 1911–1912 (an independent journal)
Woman Teacher 1919 ff
Worker's Dreadnought

Conference/Annual Reports

Association for Moral and Social Hygiene
Church League for Women's Suffrage
Labour Party
London Teachers' Association
National Federation of Women Teachers (London Unit)
National Union for Social and Equal Citizenship
National Union of Teachers
National Union of Women Teachers
Women's Social and Political Union
Women Teachers' Franchise Union (London Unit)

Archive and Unpublished Material

Fawcett Library, City & East London Polytechnic: Various leaflets of NFWT and NUWT, leaflets and papers of suffrage organisations.
Greater London Record Office: Log Books and Inspectors' reports for Crawford Street Infants, Enfield Road, Northwold JM, St Paul's Road and York Way Schools; LCC Report of the Education Committee on the Teaching of Sex Hygiene, 1914.
Labour Party Archive: Memoranda and Minutes of the Advisory Committee on Education.
NUT Library, Mabledon Place: Minute Books, Conference Reports and Circulars of the NUT Executive and its Sub-Committees and London Members' Committee.
NUWT Archive, Institute of Education Library: Minute Books, Correspondence, Photographs, Leaflets of EPL, NFWT and NUWT and Leaflets of Teachers' Labour League.
Official Publications Library, British Library: LCC Attendance of Members 1925–7, 1928–30, 1931–3, 1934–6; General Election of County Councillors LCC 1925, 1928, 1931, 1934; Education Committee Minutes of Proceedings LCC 1925–35; Hansard.
Public Record Office, Kew: Ed. 24, CAB 24, Inspectors' reports in Ed. 21 and Ed. 109.
West Glamorgan Record Office, Swansea: Swansea School Board Education Committee Minutes 1895; Swansea Education Committee Minutes 1908–1925; Log Books of Dyfatty Girls and Glanmor Central Schools.
Taped interviews and correspondence with Nan McMillan 1988–9.

Theses

R.H.C. Billington, 'The Women's Education and Suffrage Movement 1850–1914: Innovation and Institutionalisation', PhD, Hull University, 1976.

Hilda Kean, 'Towards a Curriculum in the Interests of the Working Class', MA, Institute of Education, University of London, 1981.

——. 'State Education Policy 1900–1930: the Nature of the Socialist and Teacher Trade Unionist Response', PhD, King's College, University of London, 1988.

Index

173

P103,

men's brains = boys, Q.
↑

If you believe this then the
present staffing patterns in prim
schools are acceptable; if not
then they are not.

+ graph re: male/female
EY—PR.

P27 → Promotion → boys/discipline! ☺ +t P140. Q

P117 → s. work + teach; nursing → 'mother' work.

P11 → movement out of elementary teaching (class)
+ t Spencer!
– social superiority!.

P9 → status

P2 → Q. up the social ladder (wc)

Q P1 → add t Spencer = keep control !!.!

P138 – the "public status" of teachers in the
Q 1990's has changed !!!.